PLATE VIII.

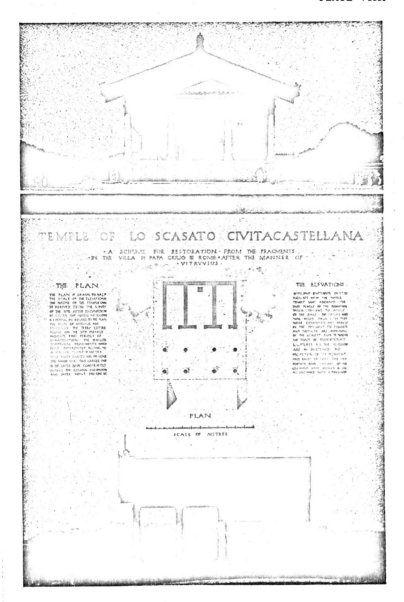

ETRUSCAN TEMPLE, LO SCASATO, CIVITA CASTELLANA.
RESTORATION BY H. CHALTON BRADSHAW.

TERRA-COTTA DECORATION, VILLA GIULIA.

TERRA-COTTA DECORATION, VILLA GIULIA.

TERRA-COTTA DECORATION FROM CIVITA LAVINIA.
(BRITISH MUSEUM.)

PLATE IX.

CHAPTER II.

ARCHITECTURE IN ROME FROM THE BEGINNING OF THE THIRD CENTURY B.C. TO THE MIDDLE OF THE FIRST CENTURY B.C.

We have already seen that the architectural forms and decorations of the earliest temples known to us in Rome itself are Etruscan, or rather Italic: and though we have no remains of architectural decoration of the fourth and third centuries B.C. in Rome, we are bound to infer that the same was the case there as in the rest of Italy.

But as Rome gradually conquered the world, she was, naturally, influenced by the civilizations with which she came into contact. The commonplace, that Greece led her captor captive, is true in architecture as in art: and the work by Delbrück, already cited, contains a long and detailed examination of Roman constructions and architectural forms in Rome and its neighbourhood from the beginning of the second century B.C. to the time of Sulla, tracing their origins from the Hellenized East, and especially from Syria[1] and Egypt, and from Sicily—which according to his account, was sometimes merely the channel by which they were transmitted, sometimes the place in which they originated. This account of the origin of the arch is, however, vitiated by the fact of his omission of the examples in the city of Rome itself which have been mentioned above (p. 3).

After these, as we have said, there are no others known until we come to the city gates of the third and second centuries, and to the road bridges of the same period[2]; and it is this omission that led

---

[1] The influence exercised on Pompeii during the first half of the second century B.C. through the medium of Puteoli has been further demonstrated by Spano: cf. Van Buren in *Classical Journal*, XV (1920), 416.

[2] The first Roman highroad, the Via Appia, was built in 312 B.C., but it is doubtful whether any of the original bridges are preserved.

Delbrück to maintain that the arch, too, came into Italy from the same source and in the same period.

The only fortified enceinte in Etruria that can be accurately dated is that of the Roman Falerii, which was rebuilt on a new site after the destruction of the original Etruscan city (which occupied the site of the present town of Civita Castellana) in 241 B.C. (See Plate IV.)

An important innovation which we find in some of these enceintes[1] and in others where no gates are preserved may be traced to the same or an earlier period,[2] the introduction, in districts where the stone was comparatively easy to quarry, of rectangular blocks 2 feet in height and thickness, which could be used either as headers or as stretchers. This method of construction seems to be traceable in Sicily as early as the sixth century B.C., but it is a question whether it is necessary to suppose, as Delbrück does, that it was derived anew from Southern Asia Minor or Northern Syria in the third century B.C., and it would seem safer to appeal once more to Choisy's dictum. Nevertheless, there is little doubt that Delbrück is right in maintaining that the Roman technique of the later Republic has very little to do with that of the sixth and fifth and fourth centuries B.C. in Italy, and that it is largely Hellenistic. The absence of evidence in Magna Graecia (and in some cases in Sicily) is noteworthy ; but these were only the stepping stones from the eastern and south-eastern Mediterranean.

In judging of the architectural forms, it must never be forgotten that the stone of which these buildings were constructed was (as in earlier days) covered with a more or less heavy coating of stucco, either plain white, in order to give the appearance of marble, or intended to serve as a medium for the colour with which many of the members were decorated, as well as to preserve the stone itself. Where this is not preserved, archæologists (among them Delbrück himself) have sometimes treated as a primitive form what is really only the skeleton of a later one.

An interesting building of the first half of the third century B.C. is the Corinthian-Doric or Æolian-Doric temple at Pæstum, a tetrastyle prostyle structure with a capital of peculiar form. We may

---

[1] At Volterra and Perugia, for example, the walls are probably older, and certainly constructed with far less care, than the gates.

[2] It depends upon the dating assigned to the later version of the so-called Servian city wall of Rome, which probably belongs to the rebuilding of 379 B.C. after the capture of Rome by the Gauls : though Delbrück wishes to assign it to the third century B.C.

also attribute to the same period the façade of the tomb of the Scipios, of which but little is preserved, but which is dated by the existence within it of the sarcophagus of L.Cornelius Scipio Barbatus, now in the Vatican Museum, which has a Doric frieze and Ionic volutes on the lid ; unless, as some believe, this sarcophagus dates from a considerably later period.

One of the earliest temples in the neighbourhood of Rome is certainly that of Gabii. It was hexastyle prostyle with a line of columns on each side, but none at the back, and may be attributed to about 250-200 B.C. from the character of the cornice and plinth mouldings of the podium[1] and of a Doric capital which was seen there at the end of the 18th century, belonging to the surrounding portico ; while the order of the temple itself may have been Ionic, Corinthian or Æolian.

The cella is built of blocks of the local volcanic stone (tufa) 2 feet in height, with deep anathyrosis. It is very doubtful whether any other temple in Rome or its neighbourhood can be with any safety assigned to a date before the time of Sulla, i.e. the first 20 years of the first century B.C. : for although the group of three temples in the Forum Holitorium (into which the church of S. Nicolo in Carcere was built) date in origin from about 200 B.C., they have all of them been restored subsequently. Indeed, the transformation which the city underwent in the time of Julius Cæsar and Augustus has obliterated a great number of the buildings of the later Republic. As a fact, under the influence of Greece, M. Porcius Cato Censorinus, enemy of Greek culture though he was, erected the first basilica in the Forum in 184 B.C. (see below) : while the censors of 179-174 B.C., M. Æmilius Lepidus and M. Fulvius Nobilior, were responsible for an important programme of building activity, including the construction of another basilica in the Forum (the Basilica Fulvia et Æmilia) a new fishmarket surrounded by shops, some temples,[2] a theatre,[3] a market or emporium[4] (in imitation of that at Athens)

---

[1] This feature, which is generally present in Roman podia, is due to Greek influence. We find a Lesbian moulding in the temple of Gabii and in the rectangular temple at Tivoli; an Ionic profile in the Tabularium and in the circular Temple at Tivoli; and Doric mouldings in the apsidal hall at Palestrina and on the altar which stands in front of the temple of Zeus Meilichios at Pompeii.

[2] Among these we may note that the walls and columns of the temple of Jupiter Capitolinus were newly stuccoed.

[3] This was in all probability only a wooden one, erected on the site later occupied by the theatre of Marcellus.

[4] This was further improved by their successors, who paved it with stone, and constructed steps leading from it to the river. (Livy, XLI, 27, but the reading is uncertain.)

below the Aventine near the Tiber, together with stone quays along the river, a line of porticos leading from the Emporium to the foot of the Capitol, and the pillars of a bridge, which was finished in 142 B.C., and rebuilt by Augustus (the Pons Æmilius or Ponte Rotto) and a harbour at Terracina. The only pre-Sullan buildings in Rome which present any definite architectural characteristics are the Aqua Marcia (144 B.C.) and the Pons Mulvius (109 B.C.),[1] and even here we have only to deal with plain pillars and arches without decoration[2]; while for the rest of Italy we have nothing but the buildings of the tufa period in Pompeii.[3] This period, which coincides more or less with the second century B.C., reveals the climax of Pompeian architecture prior to the Roman domination. To it belong a number of important public buildings and private houses, with simple Greek architectural forms expressed in stucco ; and the style of decoration is the first or incrustation style.

The period of Sulla marks a considerable increase of activity in building, and we have a number of edifices belonging to it both in Rome and elsewhere, which it will be well to examine more closely. The chief examples of the Doric order are the Tabularium, one of the three temples in the Forum Holitorium, the arcades of the temple of Heracles at Tivoli, and the Temple at Cori.

The first of these buildings is the earliest secular building still existing of the Republican period,[4] inasmuch as it was built by Catulus in the year 78 B.C. It was built in the interval between the two summits of the Capitoline Hill, its lower portion resting upon a mass of earth, supported by a retaining wall. The substructure consisted of an immense wall built with a batter on its outer face, each course of the speronè stone, with which it was faced (though it, too, was probably stuccoed over), receding one inch behind the face of the course below. The stones were respectively 2 feet high

---

[1] The remains of about half of the Pons Æmilius which existed until recent years (now there is only one arch in mid-stream) belonged in the main to the time of Augustus.

[2] Whether the circular Corinthian temple of white marble near the Tiber (perhaps the temple of Portunus) can be attributed to this comparatively early period is very doubtful. It has indeed been placed as late as the time of Septimus Severus.

[3] The much discussed early column belongs to a previous period, that of the houses with limestone atriums (before 200 B.C.). Mau in *Röm. Mitt.* XXIII (1908), 78. Patroni and Cozzi in *Memorie dell'Accademia di Napoli*, Nuova serie I (1911), 211.

[4] Delbrück, *Hellenistische Bauten*, I, 23 *sqq.*

PLATE X.

TILE RIBS IN CONCRETE OF CRYPTO
PORTICOES OF THE VILLA OF

BLIND ARCADES IN A ROMAN VILLA

DOORWAY IN THE SO-CALLED

PLATE XI.

COLONNADE ROUND COURTYARD CONNECTED WITH
TEMPLE OF HERCULES, TIVOLI.

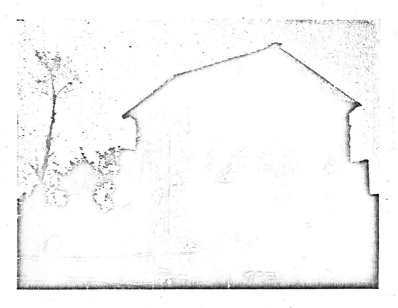

BRICK-FACED TOMB
(SO-CALLED TEMPLE OF DEUS REDICULUS).

and 2 feet deep, laid in alternate courses of headers and stretchers with a thin layer of mortar in all the joints. Through it ran a passage lighted by rectangular windows. The internal vaulting is partly in stone, partly in concrete. At a height of over 50 feet from the ground was an arcade running from one end to the other, and forming a public passage from one summit of the Capitol to the other. This passage was lighted by a series of arches opening towards the forum, with intermediate engaged Doric columns, carrying an entablature (of which only the architrave exists), the earliest example of this use of the orders which in later times became universal. There was a Corinthian colonnade with travertine columns above this. A row of rooms opened into this public arcade. A staircase led up from the Forum through a doorway, which was blocked up when Domitian built the Temple of Vespasian. The doorway was square-headed, with an almost flat arch of travertine, and a semicircular relieving arch above, and there is an even wider flat arch in sperone in a niche in the south-west façade, now converted into a doorway (5.10 metres span). Of the north-west façade nothing remains but a small portion of the dado, which is built in under the modern facade. A fragment of the Forum Julium, built in 47 B.C., on the north side of the Tabularium, still exists, in which the same disposition of flat arch and semicircular relieving arch is found, the courses of masonry varying somewhat in height and the face of each stone being bossed or rusticated.

A similar example (Plate X) may be seen in a building not later than the time of Vespasian and perhaps earlier (generally known as the Templum sacræ urbis),[1] which was incorporated by him in the Forum of Peace, and served to carry the marble plan of Rome which Agrippa was the first to make, while it was renewed by Vespasian and by Septimius Severus.

[1] The marble plan referred to was made during the reign of Severus (193-212 A.D.), being engraved on slabs of marble. A large portion of it was found in the sixteenth century and placed in the Capitoline Museum. In 1867-8 other fragments were found in the courtyard of the church of SS. Cosmas and Damianus at the foot of a lofty wall of the third century (the most recent investigators consider it to be even later), in which, at regular intervals, were small bronze holdfasts by which the marble slabs were held; and many other fragments came to light in 1901. The city was first surveyed in the time of Augustus, and a plan in colour on plaster was drawn on the walls of the Porticus Vipsania in the Campus Martius. After its destruction by fire a second plan was made by Vespasian and placed on the walls of the so-called Templum "Sacræ Urbis." This was also destroyed by fire in 191 A.D., and Severus's *marble plan* was affixed on the outer wall of the same temple, being protected either by a projecting cornice or a portico. Since 1903 all the fragments of the plan have been removed to the Conservatori Palace, in the garden of which a restored facsimile has been set up.

Apart from the temples and porticoes, the public monuments of Rome, prior to the Augustan era, depended more for architectural effect on their superb masonry than on any decorative treatment, and the arcade of the Tabularium is the first example in which the purely decorative application of the orders was resorted to in order to enrich the wall surface.

The hexastyle peristyle Doric temple in the Forum Holitorium has by some authorities been attributed to the beginning of the second century B.C., but the fact that the stucco coating of the architectural members is lacking has led to misconception as to its date. The arcades which surrounded the lower courtyard of the temple of Hercules at Tivoli (generally, but wrongly, known as the Villa of Mæcenas) are Doric, and very similar to those of the Tabularium, except that they were built in concrete faced with stucco ; they are, probably, slightly later in date (Plate XI). The temple of Hercules at Cori[1] (see Plate XII) is tetrastyle, with a high podium and deep colonnade.   Concrete is only used in the supporting walls and in the pediment. The shaft is facetted for one-third of its height and then fluted.

Both the capital and the entablature are small,. the latter being only one-sixth of the height of the column, instead of one-third as in archaic Greek work. The bases of the columns are abnormal. There is a concave curvature in the front architrave, which is considerably greater than that observed in any of the classical Greek temples.

No examples of the Ionic order can be with safety assigned to the period of Sulla. The rectangular Ionic temple in the Forum Boarium is probably to be placed a few years later, and attributed to the time of Julius Cæsar, being in a new style which is due to influence from the East, after the abandonment of the " tufa style " which we find in the Tabularium. It provides the first example of a cornice supported by consoles (see below). This temple is variously called the Temple of Fortuna Virilis or of Mater Matuta.[2] It is tetrastyle-pseudoperipteral, with a portico two columns deep and raised on a podium. The employment of the engaged columns to decorate the walls of the cella of this temple (Fig. 5) is not a Roman invention, for we can cite several examples in Greece,

---

[1] The dating is approximately fixed by the inscription on the architrave of the cella door, and by the character of the architectural forms.

[2] Fiechter in *Röm. Mitt.* XXI (1906), 220 : the latter attribution is the more probable. It is to be noticed that Delbrück omits it altogether.

the two most notable ones being the great Temple of Jupiter at Agrigentum, and the Choragic monument of Lysicrates. In

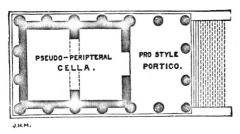

the first case, however, the immense size of the temple and the width of the space between the columns required it ; and in the second case, as already noted, the shafts of the columns are complete, with screen-walls worked in between.

FIG. 5.—PLAN OF THE TEMPLE FORTUNA VIRILIS OR MATER MATUTA.

There are, moreover, three other examples already referred to, viz., the Temple of Æsculapius at Agrigentum, probably inspired by the first-named, the Temple of Serapis at Taormina, and the Propylæa at Priene. The two Ionic temples in the Forum Holitorium probably belong to the period of Augustus, having been restored in the older style, in stone coated with stucco.

The Corinthian examples of the time of Sulla are, on the other hand, comparatively numerous and important. They include the upper order of the Tabularium (the remains of which, in travertine, lie in the Forum below), the two temples near the waterfalls at Tivoli (Plate XIII), the greater part of the buildings connected with the Temple of Fortune at Præneste (Plate XV) and the Temple of Castor and Pollux at Cori.[1] The round temple at Tivoli, known to generations of artists and tourists as the Temple of Vesta, cannot with certainty be attributed to any definite deity. (Plate XIII, Fig. 6.) The core of the podium and the cella walls are built of concrete (the latter being faced with *opus incertum*), while the rest is travertine. The cella is 21 feet in diameter, and is surrounded by a peristyle of 18 Corinthian columns 18 feet 5 inches high, the whole resting on a podium 6 feet high. The roof was probably in one pitch, rising to the centre, and covered with tiles. The cella still retains one of its windows and the doorway, with a flight of steps in front. The columns are only about nine and a quarter diameters high and the capitals one diameter, this sturdy proportion being adopted probably on account of its

[1] Delbrück, *Hellenistische Bauten*, II, 43, makes the temple of Hercules at Tivoli, that of Castor and Pollux at Cori, and the upper terraces at Præneste slightly later in date than the rest.

FIG. 6.—CAPITAL AND BASE OF THE TEMPLE OF VESTA AT TIVOLI.

PLATE XII.

TEMPLE OF HERCULES AT CORI.

PLATE XIII.

THE TEMPLE OF VESTA AT TIVOLI.

position on a cliff. The foliage of the capitals seems to have been derived from the acanthus mollis, and their carving, as well as that of the festoons of fruit and heads of oxen on the frieze, is of an extremely vigorous type.

The rectangular temple at Tivoli is less well preserved than the circular temple which stands close by. In plan it closely resembles the temple of Fortuna Virilis, but to judge from its forms is slightly earlier in date : and it is built entirely of hewn stone. The temple of Fortuna at Palestrina is described below (p. 32). The Corinthian temple of Castor and Pollux at Cori is less well preserved than the Doric temple, having only two columns left, but the lettering of the dedicatory inscription shows that it belongs approximately to the same period. The capital is of the classical Corinthian type (see Plate XXII).

It may be well to add here one or two examples of Corinthian temples of the succeeding period—that of Julius Cæsar and Augustus in which the traditional style of construction in stone faced with stucco is retained. We may mention the temple of Cybele on the Palatine, where we still find under Augustus the use of peperino coated with stucco, as in the temples of the Forum Holitorium, but where the similarity of the cornice to that of the Ionic temple in the Forum Holitorium on the one hand, and those of the temples of Saturn and Julius Cæsar and of the Regia on the other, indicate pretty clearly the date of the building.

Its podium is faced with *opus incertum*, while the cella wall is of quasi reticulatum : and the podium appears to have been faced only with stucco, not with ashlar masonry, which is exceptional.[1]

To the same style and period belongs the arcade of the Horrea Agrippiana recently discovered below the Palatine, to the south-west of the so-called temple of Augustus.

Our knowledge of the private houses of the last half-century of the Republic and the beginning of the Empire has of late years been considerably increased, both by the general acceptance of the theory that what was known as the house of Livia on the Palatine is in reality the house of the family of the Hortensii purchased by Augustus and by the discovery of the remains of various other private houses, belonging probably to the end of the Republican period, under the imperial palaces. The whole plan

---

[1] A survey and reconstruction of the temple will be found in Hülsen's article in *Römische Mitteilungen*, X (1905), 3.

cannot, however, as a rule be recovered ; and that of the house of Augustus, owing to various alterations and additions, cannot be treated as normal.

If the period of Sulla may be taken as the first in which we begin to form a definite conception of the characteristics of Roman architecture (which, if we accept the view of Delbrück, owes a very great deal to the architecture of Hellenistic Greece) the succeeding generation, that of Julius Cæsar, is the first in which there seems to be any attempt to deal with the planning of the city as a whole. Up till his time the lines of the streets were in the main dictated by the natural features of the site, and by the position of the gates in the Servian wall, from which issued the military roads by means of which Rome maintained her supremacy over Italy and, later on, the whole of the known world. But the city as a whole had grown up quite unsystematically, with narrow and ill-built streets, and the central portion, between the hills and the river was cramped and overcrowded, though it had already overflowed into the Campus Martius—an area which had originally served for military purposes and for recreation, but which had already begun to be occupied by public buildings.

Julius Cæsar was the first to grapple with the problem. He realised the necessity of improving the communications between the Forum Romanum and the northern portion of the city, and the changes which he made in the Forum and the building of the new Forum Julium were directed to this end. These changes were difficult and costly. In a letter written in the summer of 54 B.C., Cicero says : " Cæsar's friends (I refer to myself and Oppius) have felt no hesitation in spending £600,000 in extending the Forum. The owners of the property would not consider any smaller proposition. We are hoping besides to accomplish another large undertaking. We are building in the Campus Martius a covered voting hall, which will be about a mile in circumference " (this is the Porticus Sæptorum, shown in the plan on the south-west side of the Via Lata). It was in his time also that the bed of the Tiber was for the first time regulated and stone cippi erected along its banks (54 B.C.). He formed, indeed, a project of diverting its course just above the city, with a view to a considerable enlargement of the Campus Martius, a project which has several times since come to the fore, once in the latter part of the sixteenth century, and again in 1879. Pompey, at the same time, erected the first important

group of public buildings in the Campus Martius—his theatre and the porticoes connected with it.[1] Of these but little is left (see below *Theatres*) but it is possible to form a far better idea of Julius Cæsar's work, bearing in mind that as in the political, so also in the architectural sphere, he left much to be completed by his successor Augustus. The Forum Romanum owes to them the planning which it retained throughout the rest of the classical period (see below *Forums*); and this may be said indeed of the entire city. Thenceforth, therefore, it would seem advisable to abandon the chronological order which we have hitherto followed, and deal with buildings in the classes into which they fall : but before doing so, it would seem to be an appropriate moment to take a brief survey of the materials and methods of construction adopted by Roman architects during both the Republican and the Imperial period.

---

[1] This passage is taken almost verbatim from my paper on Rome in the *Transactions of the Town Planning Conference* (Oct. 1910), pp. 133 sqq., itself largely repeated in the *Town Planning Review*, X (1923), pp. 431 sqq., cf., also *Companion to Latin Studies* (Cambridge, 1921), 351 sqq., Haverfield *Ancient Town Planning*, 82 sqq.

CHAPTER III.

MATERIALS AND MODES OF CONSTRUCTION: THE ORDERS.

We may take as a definite break between the *spirit* of the Republic and the Empire in Rome the abandonment of tufa coated with stucco in favour of marble facings, and still more, the use of brick-faced concrete, which begins only in the time of Augustus (see Miss Van Deman's articles cited *infra* pp. 31 and 34).

The author to whom we are the most indebted for our knowledge of the architecture of Rome, prior to the Augustan era, is Marcus Vitruvius Pollio, an architect[1] and engineer who wrote a work entitled *de Architectura*. In this work among other subjects, he describes in detail the different materials employed in building, and suggests the rules of proportion which should guide architects in their employment of the orders. His work would seem to have been written in the latter part of his career, and it was dedicated to his patron, Augustus, about 25 B.C. As no mention of any of the important monuments erected by Augustus is made, we may assume that he died shortly after his patron's accession. The information he gives about Greek temples was obtained from various Greek authors, with whose writings he seems to have been acquainted, such as those of Ictinus, the architect of the Parthenon; Hermogenes, the architect of the temples of Diana at Magnesia and Bacchus at Teos, and others. Vitruvius never visited Greece, but in architecture he represents, as Choisy points out,[2] the Greek point of view of two hundred years before the Christian era. He used more than one source, and it was from Hermogenes, Arcesius and Pytheos that he quoted the dictum of " some ancient architects that sacred buildings ought not to be constructed of the Doric order " (IV. 3). The objection is based

---

[1] Rivoira's view (*Roman Architecture*, p. 84, sqq.) is that most of the Roman architects of Vitruvius' own day were taken from the ranks of the military engineers, and were Italians, not Greeks.

[2] *Vitruve*, I, p. vi.

PLATE XIV.

ROMAN TOMB (THE SO-CALLED
SEDIA DEL DIAVOLO).

OPUS RETICULATUM FACING,
HADRIAN'S VILLA.

ARCH IN THE TEMPLE OF FORTUNE AT PRAENESTE.

PLATE XV.

TEMPLE OF FORTUNE AT PRAENESTE—INTERIOR OF A HALL.

on the difficulty of the arrangement of the triglyphs : but his remark
that " the ancients appear to have avoided the scheme of the
Doric order in their temples " is a strange one, though it would
hardly be possible to suppose that he had never heard of the existence
of the Doric temples in Magna Græcia and Sicily.   The accounts
of various materials which he gives, however, in Book II and VII
are of great value.

The three classes of walls described by Vitruvius are :—
1. Walls of unburnt brick (lateres).
2. Stone walls in coursed masonry.
3. Concrete walls, with or without facing.

I.—WALLS OF UNBURNT BRICK.

The city wall of Arezzo, a portion of which has recently come to
light, was constructed in the Lydian mode, which he describes as
that in habitual use, of bricks measuring 1½ by 1 Roman foot :
they are ½-foot in thickness, lightly baked, and of a bright red colour.
It may be attributed to the fourth or third century before Christ.
On the other hand, from the lengthy description given of unburnt
brick, the precautions taken to preserve the walls, the rules relating
to the thickness of walls, the manufacture of the bricks, the length
of time they should be kept before being used, and the numerous
references made to unburnt brick structures in Greece which the
discoveries in the last few years have confirmed, we may assume
that it constituted a very important element in the construction of
the walls of private residences, and was in fact the material referred
to in the boast of Augustus, that he found Rome of brick and left
it in marble.   Kiln-burnt bricks or tiles were employed in Vitruvius'
time for floors and hypocausts, for the protection of the upper
part of crude-built walls, and for the covering of roofs.   The
bricks used were 2 feet square, virtually the same size, therefore,
as those which were universally employed in the time of Augustus.
Vitruvius (V. 10) describes also a method of building ceilings over
the *sudatorium*, or hot room in the public baths, in which similar
burnt bricks rest on iron rods or arcs 2 feet apart, the under-side
first plastered with pounded tiles and lime, and then finished with
stucco or fine plastering.   " If this vaulting (*concamerationes*)
be made double," he says, it will be better, because " the moisture
of the steam cannot then affect the timber in the framework, but
will be condensed between the two vaults."   The only other

references to vaults concern those covering granaries and store-rooms, probably of small span. To the further development of the vault reference will be made later on.

2.—STONE WALLS.

Vitruvius' references to stone walls in coursed masonry are not very complete. The Romans at first naturally employed the materials they had at hand, and although they were obliged to build their walls with soft tufa stone, these walls, some of which date from the earliest period, still exist up to our day. Where the soft cappellaccio is used as in the sixth and fifth centuries B.C. in Rome itself, the blocks are about a foot high, and almost like slabs in shape : where the harder varieties of tufa are employed, the stones run about 1 foot 8 inches (50 centimetres) in height, as at Veii and Cære ; but there is much variation in different localities, according to the material used.   In Rome from the fourth century B.C. onwards the blocks vary from 3 to 4 feet in length, 22 to 24 inches in height, and 21 inches thick.   As tufa is a bad weather stone, the walls were often protected externally by a coat of stucco. In the Tabularium tufa is used internally only, the facing being of sperone stone quarried near Gabii, which has the further advantage of being unaffected by fire.   Travertine stone, quarried near Tivoli, is a compact, hard limestone, and was used by the Romans when great strength or resistance to crushing was required, as in the voussoirs of arches.   The flat-arches of the doorways, referred to when describing the Forum Julium, are of travertine, as in one case also in the Tabularium, and in the so-called Templum Sacræ Urbis (S. Cosma e Damiano) (Plate X).   It is also used immediately under the columns of the temple of Castor and Pollux, and as a skeleton in the interior of the Colosseum.

Its employment in Rome cannot be traced before the late third century B.C. and its free use and combination with tufa is to be dated early in the second century B.C. ; and its use at points of strain is believed by Delbruck to be derived from Asia Minor, inasmuch as a similar procedure is adopted at Pergamon and Miletus.   Owing to its great hardness it was worked in blocks of varying height. Vitruvius, noting that ashlar masonry was proper to Greek rather than to Roman architecture, distinguishes ἰσόδομον, in which all the courses were of equal height, from ψευδισόδομον, in which they were irregular.   False joints, however, were sometimes

used to give an appearance of regularity. The first case in which marble was used as a building material in Rome was in the temples of Jupiter and Juno erected in 146 B.C., by Hermodorus of Salamis. Delbrück is inclined to attribute the round temple near the Tiber to the same period, recognising in it a temple of Hercules erected about 130 B.C., by Aemilius Paullus. From the beginning of the first century B.C. marble was frequently imported from abroad for columns and thresholds in private houses, while marble incrustation, which is well known to have been a Hellenistic method of decoration, cannot be traced before 48 B.C.[1] Curiously enough, the only reference in Vitruvius to marble as a building material is in Bk. VII, where he speaks of its value when converted into lime for plastering. The temple of Julius, however, built 42-29 B.C., and referred to by Vitruvius (III, 2) as an example of pycnostyle (i.e., with narrow intercolumniations), was built in white marble on a podium of concrete, set within walls of tufa and peperino, and faced with blocks of marble and travertine.

3.—CONCRETE WALLS, WITH OR WITHOUT FACING.

Delbrück (op. cit. II, p. 85) traces the development of Roman concrete from :—

(a) Walls of irregular pieces of stone with clay jointing (often, especially in Phœnician constructions,[2] there are pillars of large squared blocks of stone at frequent intervals, to give greater strength).

(b) Walls of pisé, i.e., of rammed earth made in frames . . . Pliny the Elder (N.H. XXXV, 48) mentions watchtowers of this material erected by Hannibal in Spain as still existing in his day, and speaks of them as untouched by rain, wind and fire, and stronger than any cement. They also existed in North Africa and in the neighbourhood of Tarentum, but no specimens have come down to us.

(c) Actual concrete (in the East often made with gypsum mortar, in Greece and Italy with lime mortar) from about 500 B.C. onwards. The earliest examples are to be found in Cyprus, but most are a

---

[1] The marble facing of the hemicycle behind the Rostra in the Forum should not be cited as an early example, as the hemicycle probably belongs to the third century A.D.

[2] e.g., Motya (before 397 B.C.). This method of construction continued even in Roman times in lands which had once been under Phœnician influence—compare the temple of the Capitol at Dougga in N. Africa.

good deal later (fourth century onwards) : we may take as examples the walls of Megara Hyblæa (perhaps before 482 B.C.) and the
massive substructions of the theatre of Segesta (third or second
century B.C.).

In Italy itself he points to the repairs to the fortification walls
of Alba Fucens, effected after 310 B.C., as presenting the earliest
example of the use of concrete, which is faced with small, closely
fitted polygonal limestone blocks.   In the first half of the second
century we find Cato[1] speaking of the use of concrete as something
quite usual : a farmhouse might have walls of small stones set in
mortar with rectangular stone quoins ; or the walls might have a
foundation of squared stones set with mortar to the height of a foot
above ground, the upper part of the walls being of (unbaked) brick.

The conclusion Delbrück draws is that it was from Phœnicia
and the neighbouring lands that concrete construction spread
to the Western Mediterranean, especially in the Hellenistic period :
but that there was little or no progress in technique between the
work of the second millennium B.C. in Egypt and that of the middle
of the second century B.C., except that fine mortar with sand added
was substituted for gypsum.   " The architects who were obliged
by the sudden transformation of Rome in the second century B.C.
into an important Hellenistic capital to look round for a solid and
economical method of construction, decided to make greater use
of concrete, which had up till that time been little used in the west,
though long known in connection with fortification."[2]   They then,
under the influence of the pisé technique, either abandoned stone
facing altogether, or made it far thinner and employed smaller
stones than before.   The Roman *opus incertum* facing (composed of
small irregular blocks of stone 3 or 4 inches across, with the outer
face worked more or less smooth) (see Plate XIV) is thus a direct
descendant of the early " polygonal " facing, and it can be traced
through successive stages, including the pseudoreticulatum of the
time of Sulla, down to the *opus reticulatum* of the first century B.C.
(Plates XIV, XVI).

Polygonal facing, as we have already said, does survive in central
Italy as the facing of villa platforms, whether to give greater
strength, or from intentional archaism, or both[3] ; while *opus
quadratum* was used as the facing of podia of temples and other

---

[1] *R.R.*   14, 1, 4.
[2] *Op. cit.*   II. 91.
[3] See *Papers of the British School at Rome.*   III. *passim.*

PLATE XVI.

NERO'S GOLDEN HOUSE: BRICK FACING OF NERO, WITH LATER
BRICK AND OPUS RETICULATUM FACING OF TRAJAN.

OPUS RETICULATUM AT HADRIAN'S VILLA
(WITH NAILS FOR FIXING MARBLE).

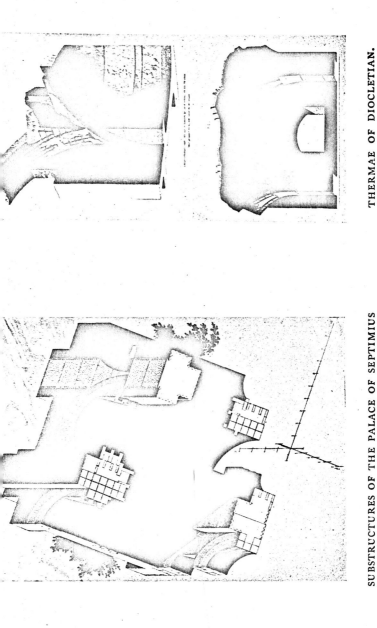

SUBSTRUCTURES OF THE PALACE OF SEPTIMIUS
SEVERUS ON THE PALATINE.

THERMAE OF DIOCLETIAN.

CONSTRUCTIONAL DETAILS FROM CHOISY.

massive constructions. Further, the forms of vaulting which had previously been employed in construction in stone were all transformed into concrete and, in that form, used far more extensively than before : and an important new form, the intersecting barrel vault, was developed in the East (*infra*, Fig. 31) but soon transferred to the West.

When we come to study the use of the stone arch in Rome and Italy in detail, we find that while it had become less frequent in Greece and Asia, a large number occur from the middle of the second century B.C. onwards, most of them city gates, bridges and aqueducts. Segmental and flat arches are less common, concrete being preferred for use in the solution of the more difficult problems of construction. The earliest stages of this development are to be found in the Oscan buildings of Pompeii, while the earliest dated monuments in concrete to be found in Rome, the podia of the temples of Concord and of Castor and Pollux, belong to a slightly later stage (late second and early first century B.C.).[1] The first of these had no proper facing, while that of the second has disappeared : but we find facing in *opus incertum* on the arches behind the *fons Juturnae*, which are probably pre-Sullan.[2] Remains of this style of construction of the time of Sulla may be found in the arches behind the Rostra of Augustus in the Forum,[3] and, in far greater abundance, in the neighbourhood of Rome, at Palestrina (Plate XIV), Tivoli and Cori.

Precedents for the development of series of vaults in Rome in the last two centuries of the Republic, first in stone (as in bridges, in which larger spans were used than had ever before been attained, city gates and aqueducts) may also be traced in the east in Mesopotamia, Egypt,[4] Pergamon, and Athens. The use of concrete for the purpose enormously facilitated the construction ; and in the last century of the Republic we get complicated series of barrel vaulted substructions, as in the Tabularium and the substructions of the temple of Hercules at Tivoli (where the space of the vault

---

[1] Van Deman in *American Journal of Archæology* XVI (1912), 244, 417.

[2] Delbrück notes that the intrados of these, as of the Emporium, are faced entirely (and not as later merely at the edges) with small voussoirs.

[3] The exact date of the substructions on the N.E. side of the Palatine (the so-called Porticus Catuli) and of the so-called Emporium is doubtful. Delbrück wishes to make the former pre Sullan (so also Lanciani). See also Van Deman *cit.* p. 247, n.1.

[4] Baldwin Brown. *The Origin of Roman Imperial Architecture.* J.R.I.B.A. 1889.

over the ancient Via Tiburtina is about 25 feet) and at Præneste ; and the stress already begins to be distributed from one vault to another. The progress made in vaulting under the Empire was enormous, and it was Rome that in its turn influenced the East (Asia Minor and Syria) in the third and fourth centuries after Christ. In Syria the scarcity of wood led to the use of the native basalt for almost all purposes (even for shutters) and we have remains of basilicas with stone vaulting carried on transverse arches.[1]

The wide diffusion of the use of Roman concrete and the great strength and durability which it possesses are due to the excellence of the materials available—the lime, which can easily be got from the local limestone, the absorbent volcanic stones, which, as well as travertine and brick fragments, are used for the core ; but above all to the pozzolana or volcanic ash, which takes its name from Puteoli, but is not found merely within the sphere of activity of Vesuvius and the other Neapolitan craters (Vitruvius II, 6), but quite as much in the extinct volcanic areas of the neighbourhood of Rome. The discovery of the red variety (far superior to the gray in use previous to the time of Augustus) was an important factor in the development of brick-faced concrete. The breaking up of wall surfaces by means of doors, windows, and niches can also be traced in Hellenistic architecture, but is believed by Delbrück to be a still older, non-Greek (i.e., Oriental) tradition. It naturally necessitated, in its earlier stages, a corresponding strengthening of the walls, e.g., by the use of a stone beam framework (as in the limestone atria of Pompeii) of relieving arches, and of buttresses or pilasters.

We also find, in Pompeii and near Rome, the imitation of architecture with openings—above the incrustation of the first style in the former we find galleries of small half columns, these imitating architecture with openings in stone by means of relief : and we also get imitations of a whole order, as in the Casa del Centauro. Near Rome, from the second century B.C. onwards, we get similar features—thus, the interior of the apsidal hall at Palestrina, if reconstructed in space, would become a pseudobasilica ; the architectural decoration is, however, in this case raised on a podium (Plate XV) : and in other cases we get endless arcades represented in relief. This hollowing out and breaking through of the wall surfaces is a new and important feature of Sulla's work, though

---

[1] Stuart Jones, *Companion*, 59.

it is only the development of a tendency already present. We may also observe the variety in the supports and the centralization of the composition, both of them Roman characteristics : while there are late Hellenistic analogies in the East for both false doors and false windows. After Sulla's time we get arches inserted into the sham orders, *i.e.*, if reconstructed spatially, we should have a row of columns in front of, and on the same axis as, a row of barrel vaults : while at the end of the Republic and under the Empire we get vaults, and then arches, actually resting on columns. In later Roman architecture these sham orders and niches lose their original significance, and become forms of decoration with an independent existence of their own (Plates LIX and LXXXI). The forms then become more plastic and less fixed, and we get a kind of Baroque tendency, especially in the second and third centuries after Christ. Later on the use of brick-faced concrete, which began in Rome under Augustus, facilitated the growth of this tendency and in the buildings of Domitian and Hadrian the wall surfaces almost entirely disappear. These tendencies spread to the East under the Empire, and we find them exemplified in the thermæ of Miletus and Ephesus, the round temple at Baalbek, and the domed churches of the time of Constantine. In fact, the most important improvement which concrete received after the Republican period was the adoption of facing with baked brick. There is no brickwork to be found in Rome which can be attributed to the end of the second and the beginning of the first century B.C. Use is generally made of *opus reticulatum*, formed of small wedge-shaped blocks of stone set lozenge-wise, with close joints running in diagonal lines, about 2½-4 inches square on the face, and 4-6 inches deep, the point tailing into the concrete (Plate XVI) : the quoins are also of stone.[1] In fact, Van Deman definitely assigns the first kiln-dried bricks in Rome to the Augustan period ; and this is probably correct. Even the Mausoleum of Augustus (14 A.D.) is built entirely of concrete faced with *opus reticulatum*.

---

[1] Vitruvius (II., 8) speaks of *opus reticulatum* as in general use in his day, but prefers *opus incertum* as being less liable to crack, though less beautiful in appearance. He recommends that the pieces of stone should be as small as possible, so that they should not suck too much moisture out of the mortar. He complains that the Roman workmen devote themselves only to the facings of the wall, and then fill the space between with a lot of broken stone and mortar thrown in anyhow : whereas the Greeks lay their courses of stones bonded together right through the thickness of the wall, so there is no danger of its cracking. We may note the subsequent adoption of bonding courses in brick facing as a proof that his remarks are not unjustified.

E

The city walls of Arezzo have already been mentioned. At Pompeii, brickwork is employed in the columns of the Basilica and other buildings, and broken roof tiles are used as quoins in the small theatre and the baths near the Forum; and at Reggio Calabria tombs of the third century B.C. have been found, with walls and vaults built of bricks.[1] In Mesopotamia, on the other hand, brickwork is to be found on a large scale before the middle of this century: and Delbrück considers that at a time when intercourse was so easy the coincidence cannot be due to chance. If this is true, however, it is somewhat surprising, perhaps, that the Romans took so long to perceive the advantages of this method of construction; and, indeed, we may well wonder that, considering the excellence of the firing of the terracottas employed in the architectural decoration of temples in Greece and Italy, the making of baked bricks had not become common several centuries earlier. It is probable that the Romans had not come to appreciate the excellence of the brickearth in the immediate neighbourhood of their city. The hills behind the Vatican, which are of marine formation, provide specially good material, which is in use at the present day.

Opus reticulatum was retained at least as late as the time of Hadrian (Plates XIV, XVI), in whose villa, as in other buildings of the same date, we also find small rectangular blocks of tufa used as facing to concrete. In that period in both cases, however, we get brick quoins and sometimes bands of three or four courses of brickwork running through the walls at intervals while the " bricks " used in the facing of concrete walls in the time of Augustus were really broken pieces of flanged roof tiles, the flanges being broken off and a new face given by sawing.[2] Triangular bricks were used from the time of Claudius to that of Domitian,[3] while under Trajan and the Antonine emperors the earlier method was revived. Bonding courses of flat tiles 2 feet square running right through the wall are found from the time of Domitian onwards. As will be seen from Miss Van Deman's elaborate study of the brickfacing of the first three centuries of the Empire, the earlier the period *as a rule* (though not always) the thicker are the bricks and the thinner and more

---

[1] The bricks are about 3½ inches thick, and the intervening mortar courses only from 2 to 5 mm.

[2] Vitruvius (II, 8, 19) tells us that the strongest burnt brick walls are those which are constructed out of old roofing tiles.

[3] See Van Deman. *cit.* From Septimus Severus to Diocletian fragments of unflanged square tiles are used.

F

regular are the mortar joints. An exception to the rule is presented by the brickwork of the reign of Nero (Plate XVI) (on the left of the illustration), which, as seen in the Golden House, is far more irregular than the very fine facing of the substruction walls which Trajan built to carry his thermæ. It may be interesting to mention a case in which a concrete wall faced with brick, has been substituted by Domitian for the back wall of the *tabernae*, or shops, on one side of the Horrea Agrippiana, below the Palatine, which was originally constructed in *opus quadratum*. The brick facing is lacking where the ends of the side walls, and the roof of the upper floor of the shops, served as a sufficient support for the concrete.

In the building of these walls there was an alternation of two processes. First, one or two courses of facing bricks were laid on each side ; then a semi-fluid mixture of lime and pozzolana was poured in, in which the *caementa* (fragments of stone or brick) were set by hand.

In many cases this elaborate facing was not left exposed to view even on the outside of a building, and never on the inside. In this connexion, however, we must notice the use of ornamental brick facing, which is especially frequent in tombs, two colours of brick, yellow and red, often being employed, as in the graceful tomb (perhaps that of Annia Regilla, and if so, belonging to the latter half of the second century A.D.) known as the temple of the Deus Rediculus, not far from the Via Appia (Plate XI). There the mortar joints are kept as thin as possible, and are often only 3 or 4 millimetres thick. The exterior is decorated with pilasters, except on one side, where polygonal columns are used. At Ostia the arches of large flat tiles were picked out in red. The use of semi-circular relieving arches over an opening (especially over a doorway, which is generally formed of a flat or flattened arch, hardly ever of a semi-circular arch) should also be noticed. The earliest case known seems to be at the northeast angle of the Prætorian Camp (Rivoira, *Roman Architecture* 44, and Fig. 50).

We have not yet noticed the method generally adopted for building concrete foundations. They were cast in frames formed by vertical posts with wooden boards nailed on inside.

A characteristic of the architecture of the period of Julius Cæsar and Augustus is the concrete vault springing from a narrow projection formed by a stone capital or corbel. This is seen in the Horrea

Agrippiana, in the Basilica Aemilia, the Basilica Iulia, and in the temple of Castor and Pollux, to name only a few instances.

A method of construction similar to that described in the case of walls would seem to have been employed from the time of Augustus in building vaults; but in those of great dimensions, such as the intersecting barrel vaults covering the great halls, ribs and ties of brick were employed first, to economise the centering.[1] The principle is already seen in the aqueduct which Nero constructed across the Cælian to the Palatine; but the first dateable instances belong to the time of Vespasian, and are to be found in the vaulting of the lower arcades of the Colosseum.[2] Others, of the time of Domitian, may be seen in the so-called temple of Augustus (*infra*) and else-where in his palace on the Palatine, and in the crypto-porticus of his Villa at Albano (Plate X); while intersecting ribs are first found in the villa known as Sette Bassi, half-way between Rome and Frascati (about 140 A.D.).[3] Hadrian's villa provides an interesting example of the passage from an octagon to a circular vault in the domed hall of the Piazza d'Oro (Fig. 7), and the flat dome with triangular

FIG. 7.—DOMED ROOM IN PIAZZA D'ORO, HADRIAN'S VILLA.

---

[1] The various methods employed are clearly set forth in M. Choisy's *l'Art de batir chez les Romains*, and in Viollet-le-Duc's *Dictionnaire Raisonne* under the article "Voute."

[2] Rivoira, *Roman Architecture*, 92.

[3] *Papers of the British School at Rome*, IV, 102, 111 : Rivoira *op. cit.*, 140 sqq.

pendentives may be studied in the tomb known as the Sedia del Diavolo (Plate XIV).[1]

The first use of amphoræ and empty pipes at the haunches of a vault that is known in Italy is to be found in the Stabian baths at Pompeii,[2] while the earliest example in Rome is to be found in the substructions of the palace of Septimus Severus on the Palatine though there is an example in a villa of the time of Hadrian (not, however, at the haunches), about three miles from the city.

Vitruvius' meagre references to vaults suggest that they were recognised traditional methods of covering over cellars, and therefore required no detailed account. His description of the ceilings over hot baths (already referred to) is given in Book V, Chapter 10, and reads " iron rods or arcs, placed 2 feet apart and suspended by . iron hooks from an upper framing of timber, carry tiles side by side, the upper parts of the joints being stopped with clay and hair, and the underside first plastered with pounded tiles and lime and then finished with stucco and lime plastering." In the erection of vaults the Egyptians dispensed altogether with centering, and the tradition exists to the present day, whereas (as will be seen later on) the Roman architect employed centres, on which the skeleton of the vault was first built with arches in burnt brick. The filling-in of the same and of the haunches was carried out by the two same processes already described when speaking of the walls, i.e., the alternation of layers of a semi-fluid mixture of lime and pozzolana and of small stones ; and these layers are always horizontal.

There is, however, one invention of great importance which may have an oriental origin, viz., the intersecting barrel vault, to which attention has been already drawn. M. Choisy instances a tomb in Pergamum, belonging to the beginning of the second century B.C.,[3] which is covered by the intersecting barrel vaults regularly constructed with stone voussoirs. It is a problem the solution of which is more likely to have taken place in stone construction than in brick or concrete, and its earliest examples would have a comparatively small span ; but it must have been

---

[1] Rivoira, op. cit., 183-185.

[2] Rivoira: op. cit, 38.

[3] The date is doubted by Rivoira, who prefers to seek an Etruscan origin for this type of vault (op. cit., 77). But the tomb which he mentions on the Via Salaria is a purely Roman structure, and I know of no reason for assigning it to a date earlier than Sulla. In fact, excavations in 1838 brought to light remains of marble decorations which were assigned to the Imperial period (Bull. Inst. 1838, 73).

carried out by masons long accustomed to the erection of stone vaults, and the perfection of its execution in this tomb in Pergamum suggests that it was by no means the first attempt.

In the late republican vault, *e.g.*, that of the Tabularium, which is of small span, there would be no difficulty in providing centres, and the same applies to the portico surrounding the temple of Hercules at Tibur (Plate XI) which Rivoira attributes to the same period.[1]

The Roman vaults always consisted of regular geometrical forms, such as the continuous semi-circular barrel vault, the intersecting barrel vault (the groins of which were formed by the intersection of two barrel vaults at right angles to one another), the segmental vault, and the hemispherical dome.[2]

The researches of M. Choisy have shown that in their inner construction the Roman vaults show the articulated forms of the Gothic vault, with transverse and diagonal ribs, all built in brick with horizontal ties, the web being a subsequent filling-in (Plates XVII, XVIII). This method of construction was adopted not only to economise the centering, but because it could be carried out by large gangs of labourers working under a few skilled overseers and the direction of the architect or engineer. The centering was economised in two ways : firstly, the transverse and diagonal ribs, being built first, formed when completed a permanent centering by themselves, so that the scantlings of the timbers employed in the temporary centering were comparatively slight ; and secondly, the latter could be employed again for other portions of the vault. The framework of that of the so-called temple of Minerva Medica (a ten-sided room of the latter half of the third century A.D. Plate XLIII) consists of a number of vertical ribs meeting in a ring, which provides the opening for light and air at the top of the dome. Rivoira considers the earliest instance of the use of such ribs to belong to the time of Alexander Severus (*op. cit.* 128). There remained, however, another problem to be worked out, the solution of which as set forth by M. Choisy constitutes the most valuable part of his discoveries. Taking the central bay of the Baths of Caracalla as an example : the transverse, diagonal (Plate XVII) and inter-

---

[1] *loc. cit.*.

[2] The hemispherical dome as a feature by itself, and not the covering of a semi-circular apse of a hall, is first found in the Baths of Trajan.

mediate[1] centerings having been placed and planks laid across from one to the other, the Romans commenced the formation of the vault with a double layer of bricks[2] laid flat-wise and breaking joint. This formed a shell-vault which relieved the planks from the superincumbent weight. Then over the principal centerings they built rings of similar bricks on edge, connecting these with horizontal brick ties.

(This procedure is, however, by no means universal, and was omitted especially when coffering was used (Cf. Durm, *op. cit.* pp. 256-8). This method of decoration, originally suggested by the intersection of the wooden beams which form at once the ceiling of one room and the floor of the room above, is a characteristic Roman development. When the skeleton construction by means of ribs came in, it was natural to set back the filling behind it, and coffering was the result (Fig. 8)).

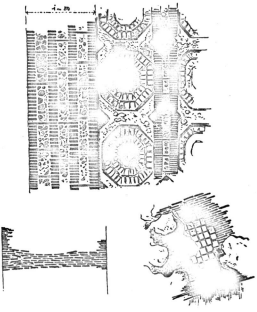

FIG. 8.—CONSTRUCTION OF BARREL VAULT IN THERMÆ OF CARACALLA.

The skeleton thus formed seems to have been regarded by the Romans as equivalent to the vertical posts already described, which they employed in building their walls ; for the two processes (*i.e.*, the semi-fluid mixture of lime, pozzolona and small stones, and the layers of large stones) were followed in the formation of their filling-in not only of the haunches but of the whole vault, and, according

---

[1] About 8 to 9 feet would seem to have been the average distance between the timber centres, so that three or four intermediate centerings would have been required in the central hall of the Baths of Caracalla.

[2] See Rivoira, *op. cit.*, Fig. 101.

to M. Choisy, laid horizontally as in their walls. In other words, the brick ribs only constituted the arched construction and have the same function as the metal girders or ties in reinforced concrete. *The shell-vault laid on the planks enabled the web to be thus filled in, and probably accounts for its invention.* In the case of large vaults, such as those of the Palaces of the Cæsars on the Palatine Hill, and in the Basilica of Constantine, a second superincumbent ring was added above the tranverse and diagonal ribs, but the vault was probably already self-supporting, so that the centerings could be removed to another bay. In theory at all events, if not in practice, the resistance to thrust of such immense vaults required buttresses of great projection, and these, as we shall see later on, were provided. Middleton points out that " it would have been impossible to vault their enormous spans if they had used vaulting of brick or masonry such as were built in mediæval times. The Roman concrete vault was quite devoid of any lateral thrust, and covered its space with the rigidity of a metal lid." This quality was given to it partly by the nature of its construction, but mainly from the peculiar quality of the pozzolana, which, when mixed with lime, forms a very strong hydraulic cement ; " this pozzolana more than any other material, contributed to make Rome the pro- verbially ' eternal city.'[1] Without it, a great domed building like the Pantheon would have been impossible, as would also the immense vaulted Thermæ and a wide-spanned Basilica such as that of Con- stantine." The Romans did not seem to have realised at first how very strong and substantial their concrete was, and in the planning of the Thermæ not only took every precaution to supply a counter- thrust, but having, by their intersecting vaults, concentrated this thrust on piers at a distance one from the other, and having connected the foundation of their piers by tie walls (as in the palæstræ of the Thermæ of Caracalla), they utilised the spaces between so that the buttresses became an integral part of the building. There are also examples of simple barrel vaults (Plate XVIII : the vault illustrated is interesting as showing the layer of square tiles which carried the plaster). The problem once solved how to vault over large spans with a permanent covering indestructible by fire, not only gave an impetus to the development which constitutes the real Imperial Roman style of architecture, but it also led to a new type of plan, and this spread to all parts of

---

[1] *Remains of Ancient Rome*, Vol. I, p. 9.

PLATE XVIII.

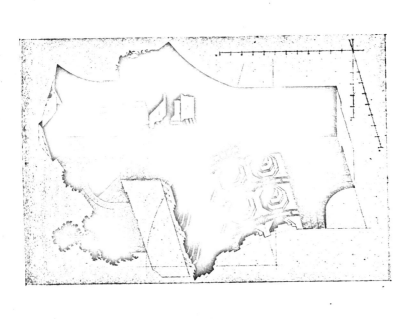

Construction des voûtes.

ÉCHELLE DES DÉTAILS
5 MÈTRES

Construction des murs et des hypocaustes.

CONSTRUCTION OF VAULTS AND
OF HYPOCAUSTS.

BASILICA OF CONSTANTINE.

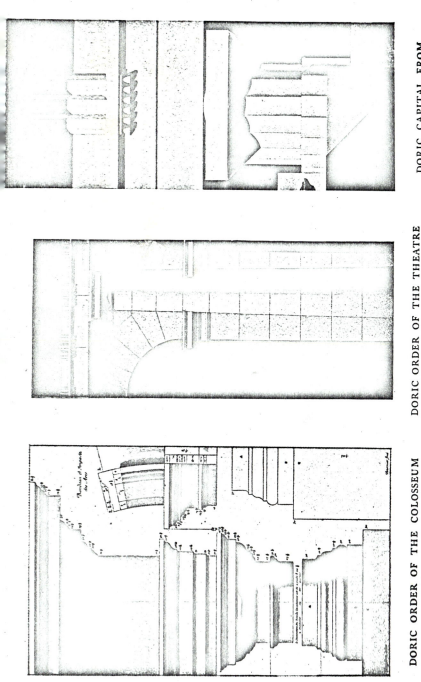

DORIC ORDER OF THE COLOSSEUM AT ROME.

DORIC ORDER OF THE THEATRE OF MARCELLUS AT ROME.

DORIC CAPITAL FROM POMPEII.

the Empire, with only such variations as were necessitated by the materials at hand. Throughout Syria, for instance, excellent stone abounded everywhere, but no pozzolana; consequently the spaces vaulted over were comparatively smaller than those in Rome, and all the vaults have long since fallen in. The qualities of the Roman mortar are always conspicuous, however, and the ruins of the temple of Jupiter at Baalbek (Plate I) amongst others, prove that its tenacity was greater than that of the stone itself. The lines of fracture lie in the stone and not in the mortar, which in the cores of their walls and vaults seems to have been employed very much in the same way as in Rome.

Stucco, Cements and Marble Facing.

The various facings to concrete which we have described were, in Rome itself at any rate, generally concealed by an external facing of marble or stucco, and this was universal in the interior of buildings.

We are indebted to Vitruvius[1] for the description given of the marble cement (*caementum marmoreum*, or *opus albarium*) used by the Romans, the care which had to be taken in its preparation, and the materials of which it should be composed. Its qualities were such that, when set, it had the colour and texture of real marble, and was not much inferior to it in durability. It was owing to the coating of this kind of stucco given to the crude brick walls of the houses built prior to the time of Augustus in Rome, that they were able to resist the weather. It was used also to preserve stone, especially when tufa was the material employed. In Sicily and at Pæstum, and generally throughout Greece, the whole of the stonework was covered with a fine coat of stucco to fill up the crevices of the aqueous limestones, and to obtain a greater refinement of detail in the profiles of the mouldings, with a view to the ultimate decoration with painting. In Greek buildings the coating was very thin; in Roman work it was usually about an inch thick, and sometimes extended to 3 inches when it was intended to panel-out the surface, to sink grooves in imitation of stone joints, or to imbed mosaics.

Another kind of cement was the hydraulic cement (*opus signinum*) in which a large proportion of pounded tiles was added to the lime and pozzolana. In the first chapter of Book VII, Vitruvius describes the formation of floors, preparatory to the laying of the marble

---

[1] Book VII, 2, 3, and 6.

G

slabs or tesseræ, and their subsequent grouting and polishing.   For the decoration of the upper portion of walls internally, and of the vault, glass mosaics were employed, worked sometimes into large and elaborate pictures.[1]   We have already described the facing of burnt brick given to walls built in concrete.   This served to enclose the semi-fluid mixture which was poured in, while the introduction of bonding courses of tiles running through the wall facilitated rapid construction.   The illustration (Plate XVIII) taken from a drawing by Choisy shows the brick facing of a concrete wall (shown in section with its bonding courses at intervals), which was covered with a cement bed for the marble.   The clamps or nails which hold the slabs of marble in position are always driven in alongside of a small piece of marble set in the brick facing, no doubt in order to give the nail a better grip.   Slabs of marble, slate or tile, were bedded in the concrete, against which the marble panels of large size were fixed.   This system was employed in facing the interior walls of the temples, palaces and thermæ.   Below is the hypocaust by which the room was heated, supported on pillars formed of square tiles.

THE ORDERS.

The description of the Greek orders must be given in chronological sequence, as one has first to search for the earliest forms known, then to trace their development till they reached their perfected types, and lastly to follow their decadence during the Alexandrian period. Even in this last stage they preserved their rational basis, and formed still, not only the decorative, but the leading constructive features of the monuments of which they were part.   When, however, we come to deal with the Roman orders, our position is changed.   With the exception of the Corinthian order, no further development was possible, and the employment of the modified forms of the Doric and Ionic orders by the Romans seems to have been dictated by the extreme simplicity of the former, and by the variety of the latter.   There are few examples in Rome of the Doric order as a detached column, but it was employed in Pompeii, in Asia Minor, and in various cities in Syria and North Africa.   There are not many examples either of the Ionic order still existing, but to judge by the great variety and number of Ionic capitals used up in the early Christian basilicas of Rome it must at one time have been

[1] See Plates L, LII, LIII, from M. Paulin's Restoration of the Baths of Diocletian.

H

PLATE XX

DORIC ORDER OF THE BASILICA AEMILIA.

From a drawing in the Soane Museum.

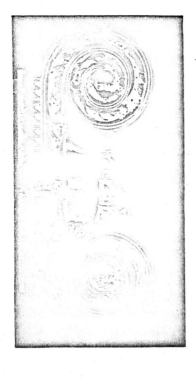

LATE ROMAN IONIC CAPITAL, NOW IN
STA. MARIA MAGGIORE.

IONIC CAPITAL FOUND IN FORUM OF TRAJAN.

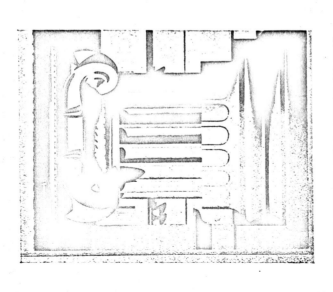

IONIC CAPITAL OF A HOUSE IN THE
STREET OF THE THEATRES
AT POMPEII.

largely employed. In our description of Etruscan architecture we have referred to three or four types of capitals, but in no case do we find that which constitutes an Order, viz., a combination of column and entablature designed in relation one to the other. The Etruscan support was either square or circular. In the former case it probably carried a stone beam or architrave, but except in tombs cut in the rock no examples exist.[1] In the Tuscan order[2] described by Vitruvius the proportions of the column, with its base, shaft, and capital, are given. The superstructure, however, being in timber only, protected by terra-cotta slabs, never acquired any definite proportions. Already in the third century B.C. some of the elements of the Greek Doric order, viz., the triglyphs and metopes, had been imported, and the only important influence which the Etruscan column seems to have had was the addition of a base to the Doric column.

THE ROMAN DORIC ORDER.

The Roman Doric order is Hellenistic in origin, but has one or two peculiarities which distinguish it from its prototype—the conical (not cylindrical) guttae, the plain moulding below the echinus (the old Achæan form) and the smooth necking at the top of the shaft, and also the pedestals on which the columns rest. The shaft, too, is more slender than in its Greek prototype.

The principal examples of the Doric order in Rome are those which are found in the Tabularium, the Theatre of Marcellus, and the Colosseum. In all these cases, however, they were only engaged columns, used in a decorative sense, and, so employed, the difficulty raised by Vitruvius as to the triglyph at the angles never arose. In the only Roman Doric temple known, at Cori[3] (Plate XII), the

---

[1] The earliest document for the Tuscan column (a simplified form of the Doric with a base, unfluted, and with a more developed capital) is in the rock cut tomb called the Cucumella at Vulci, and a primitive form has also been accidentally preserved at Pompeii.

[2] The only examples now existing of the Tuscan order are the three-quarter detached columns on the lower storey of the Colosseum, but their proportions do not agree with those laid down by Vitruvius, which are given for the isolated columns of a portico ; he assigns to the order seven diameters with a diminution at the top of one-fourth of the lower diameter. Their capitals should be half a diameter high, one-third of which is given to the abacus, one-third to the echinus, and one-third to the hypotrachelium with its apophyge. The base was also half a diameter equally divided between the die or plinth and the torus with fillet.

[3] The Doric temple in the Forum Holitorium and the so-called temple of Hercules at Tivoli are not sufficiently well preserved for the determination of this point to be possible.

triglyph is placed at the corner and not in the axis of the angle column, as suggested by Vitruvius, and it is difficult to understand why he should have objected, in a hexastyle temple, to the slight contraction of the intercolumniation of the two angle columns, especially as he recommends a wider intercolumniation of the two central columns to give a freer passage to those who approach the statues of the gods. In both the tombs at Norchia the triglyph is placed at the extreme angle, and the same arrangement is found in many of the sarcophagi, so that it is possible Vitruvius's recommendation was never followed. The Doric order of the Theatre of Marcellus (Plate XIX) (the favourite example selected for publication) is always represented as an isolated column taken from the angle of a building or temple, instead of being a semi-detached shaft and part of the decorative treatment of a circular building. The echinus moulding of the capital still preserves its conic section, if it is not really a quarter round. Another fine example is the Doric entablature of the Basilica Aemilia, which belongs to the Augustan period (Plate XX). In the Colosseum even this refinement is lost, and henceforth it becomes always a quarter round, with a few exceptions where an ogee moulding replaces the echinus (Plate XIX). In the Theatre of Pompey a circular die of slight projection exists under the shaft.[1] In the Colosseum and in later examples a base is generally found, the principal exceptions, which are of much earlier date being in Pompeii (Plate XIX).

THE ROMAN IONIC ORDER.

In the Republican period the Ionic capital with anted volute is the commonest, as also in Sicily and in Corinth. Plate XXI shows an example from Pompeii : and a similar one has recently been found in a Republican house under the Lararium of the Flavian palace. The projection of the volutes is much less than that found in Greek examples. The principle examples in Rome of the Roman Ionic capital are those of the temple of Fortuna Virilis, the Theatre of Marcellus (Plate XIX) and of the temple of Saturn, the latter of a very debased type. In Syria the order was occasionally employed. At Gerasa a portion of one of the colonnaded streets and the great circular piazza have columns and capitals of the Ionic order. From Sulla's time onwards, however, the classical Ionic capital of

---

[1] The American architect, Percy Ash, ascertained by excavation in 1896 that there was no base in the Theatre of Marcellus, where the order rested on a single step.

Hermogenes was adopted from the East, and became thenceforth the definite type. A later development of it, found in the Forum of Trajan, is illustrated here (Plate XXI).

A number of Ionic capitals are to be found in the Christian basilicas of Rome, many (though not all) of which have been taken from classical buildings (compare Plate XXI). The shaft is often unfluted; its height was from 8 to 9 diameters.

The Corinthian Order.[1]

In Republican Rome the Ionic and Corinthian orders are distinguished only by their capitals. The type of cornice in use at the end of the Republic and down to the time of Augustus was that of the temple of Fortune Virilis, so-called and it has recently been pointed out by Fiechter that the cornices of the temples of Saturn and Julius Cæsar, of the Regia (Plate XXII), and, we may add, of the Horrea Agrippiana all belong to this period.

If the Doric and Ionic orders found but little favour with the Roman architects in the designs for their temples, it was far otherwise with the Corinthian. Not only did the richness of its decoration appeal much more to the Roman instinct, but it had the special advantage of presenting the same design in all four faces, and could be employed equally well for the peristyle of a rectangular or circular building, or in the decoration of the hemicycles which played so important a factor in the setting out of the plan. The Greek Corinthian capital, though varied in design, and in many cases of great beauty, was never completely developed, and it remained to the Roman to systematise the double range of leaves which surround the lower part of the bell, and to give a greater sense of

---

[1] Vitruvius informs us that the capital was invented by Callimachus at Corinth. Now Callimachus was the craftsman who is said by Pausanias to have *made a golden lamp for the goddess* Minerva Polias in the Erechtheum, and probably also *the bronze palm tree reaching to the roof* which drew off the smoke. As the earliest Greek Corinthian capitals all suggest a metallic origin, and as Callimachus is known to have worked also in marble, it is conjectured that he reproduced in marble a type of capital which was copied from one in bronze. Pausanias (ii, 3) refers also to Corinthian bronze, which he says " got its colour by being plunged red-hot into this water," referring to some particular spring. Corinthian bronze, for various reasons, was celebrated in ancient times, and Pliny (*Nt. H.,* XXXIV, 13) speaking of the Porticus built by Cæus Octavius in 168 B.C., says it was *called Corinthian from its brazen Corinthian capitals.* The title, therefore, may have been given because it was invented by Callimachus of Corinth, or on account of the material in which the first prototype was wrought. Pliny's statement, however, goes still further, as it suggests that the leaves and tendrils of the Corinthian capital were occasionally wrought in bronze, instead of being carved in stone or marble.

support to the abacus by the accentuation of the spiral tendrils at the four angles. Another Roman characteristic is the presence of two spiral tendrils facing each other in the centre of each of the four sides. The type of capital was probably already known in Rome, and, in fact, there is a reference in Pliny to the Porticus built by Cæus Octavius in 168 B.C.. The model, however, on which the Roman Corinthian capital, as developed under the Empire, was based was probably that of the temple of Jupiter Olympius at Athens, the columns of which Sulla exported, to enrich the temple of Jupiter Capitolinus at Rome. Penrose was of opinion that the monolith columns taken away at that time were probably those destined for the cella of the Greek temple, and if utilised in Rome were probably placed inside the cella of the Roman temple, being much too small for the portico.

In the development of the capital the Romans not only systematised the double range of leaves and strengthened the angle spirals, but they also marked the bell more effectually than in the Greek examples. In the carving of the acanthus leaf, based on the plant of the *Acanthus spinosus*, they made the section flat in the place of the V section which characterises all Greek work. In Syria, where Greek artists would seem to have been invariably employed, the V section was still retained, and even in the works carried out by the Roman Emperors in Athens and elsewhere in Greece we find the same distinction. Even in Rome itself there are one or two examples in which this characteristic may be noted, as in the circular temple in the Forum Boarium. The assumption, therefore, which has been made as to the employment of Greek artists in Rome is not borne out by the best-known examples of capitals, such as those of the Portico of the Pantheon of Hadrian (Plate XXIII), or of the temple of Mars Ultor. There is, however, a peculiar refinement in the leaves of the capital of the temple of Castor at Rome (Plate XXII), which seems to follow the olive leaf rather than the acanthus, and suggests the Greek chisel. A second type of capital, found at Pompeii and in the temple of Vesta at Tivoli (Plate XIII) is decorated with foliage which is based on another variety of the plant—the Acanthus mollis. A third type is found in the capitals of the temple of Castor and Pollux at Cora (Plate XXII), which might be termed Graeco-Roman ; it is also found in Olympia, where many extensive works were carried out under the patronage of the Roman Emperors.

PLATE XXII.

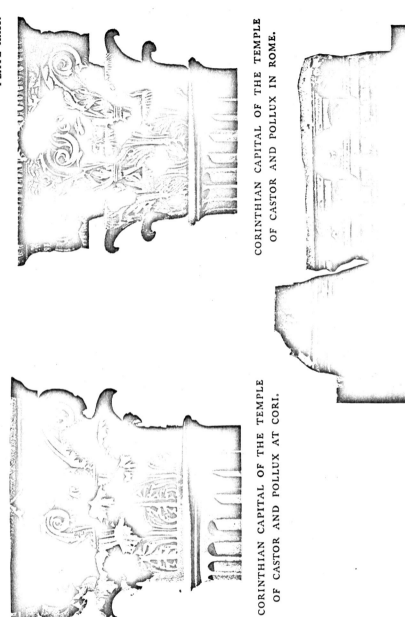

CORINTHIAN CAPITAL OF THE TEMPLE
OF CASTOR AND POLLUX IN ROME.

CORINTHIAN CAPITAL OF THE TEMPLE
OF CASTOR AND POLLUX AT CORI.

PLATE XXIII.

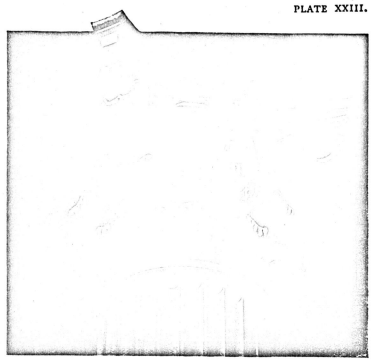

TEMPLE OF MARS ULTOR AT ROME.
RESTORATION BY H. D'ESPOUY.

CORNICE OF TEMPLE OF VESPASIAN AT ROME.

Later on, under the Empire, the lobes of the Acanthus spinosus disappear, and the Romans return to the type of foliage carved in the capitals of the temple of Vesta at Tivoli, without, however, its vigorous character. The leaves of the Composite capital of the Baths of Diocletian show the ultimate phase of Roman work, not only in Rome, but throughout Italy and the South of France (Plate XXIV).

The most beautiful example of the Roman Corinthian capital is that which is found in the temple of Castor already referred to, and in this capital a new element is found which does not exist in any other example. Between the angle and centre volutes rises a tendril from which foliage is carried along the cavetto moulding of the abacus.

The desire for novelty led the Romans to many vagaries, among which the capitals of the decorative order inside the temple of Concord (Plate XXV), where the volutes consist of rams' heads, and in the temple of Mars Ultor of winged horses (Plate XXV). In the church of S. Lorenzo at Rome are capitals with figures of Victory at the angles, and trophies of armour on each face, and in the Composite capitals of the Thermæ of Caracalla a figure of Hercules forms the central feature on each face (Plate XXIV).

The entablature of the Greek Corinthian order was not evolved from the earlier constructional forms in timber in the same way as those of the Doric and Ionic orders, and in the earliest example, viz., that of the monument of Lysicrates the subdivisions of the architrave, the figure decoration of the frieze, and the mouldings of the cornice, would seem to have been borrowed from Asiatic types of the Ionic order, the dentils, however, being much reduced in projection. The Romans followed the same course, except that in the portico of the Pantheon, the dentils are left uncarved. The Romans, however, introduced at the end of the Republic a new feature (possibly from Syria) (*i.e.*, the modillion), a corbel giving support to the projecting corona. The spaces between the corbels were, as a rule, made square, the soffit being sunk as a coffer and decorated with a central flower. The over-elaboration in the decoration of the temple of Castor (Plate XXVI) and even more in that of Vespasian (Plate XXIII) is probably the result of carving the ornaments which in the Greek entablature were only painted ; but the relative proportions of the mouldings, the greater inportance given to the dentil course, and the depth

of the corona, place this temple far above any other examples,
with the exception, perhaps, of the Pantheon and the temples of
Antoninus and Faustina, in which latter example there are no
modillions.   Already in the order of the Forum of Nerva the decadence of the style would seem to have set in, and this may be
observed in the cornices of the composite order of the Arches of
Titus and of Septimius Severus, in the Forum of Trajan (Plate
XXVII) the Thermæ of Diocletian, and of the Corinthian order
of the Arch of Constantine.   The remains of the temple of Serapis
on the Quirinal Hill[1] (Plate XXVIII) are of so refined a character,
not only in the proportions of the order, but in the profile and decoration of the mouldings of the entablature that it is easier to recognise
in it the temple of Serapis built by Caracalla than that of the Sun
constructed by Aurelian[2] on his return from Palmyra in 273 A.D.
The modillions are set back behind the corona, take the same position, and are of the same proportions as the widely-projecting
dentil mouldings of the Ionic temples of Asia Minor.

THE COMPOSITE ORDER.

The earliest examples of this order in Rome are found in the
Colosseum and in the Arch of Titus, but, as we have already stated,
earlier examples exist in Asia Minor.   It is usually assumed that the
Romans, conscious of the weakness of the tendril volutes of the
Corinthian order, replaced them by the volutes of the Ionic order.
This, however, is not borne out by the facts.   In one of the earliest
examples of the Greek Ionic order, viz., that of the temple of Apollo
at Naucratis, the necking is already decorated with the anthemion.
Its more perfect evolution is found in the capitals of the Erechtheum,
the Roman version of which may be seen in an Ionic capital
found in the Forum of Trajan (Plate XXV).   The selection of the
acanthus foliage in preference to the anthemion[3] is found in the
capitals of the pronaos of the Temple of Jupiter at Aizani, where
a single row of leaves only is carved, and marks the next
development ; and the adoption of the two rows of leaves in the
capitals of the proscenium of the theatres of Asia Minor suggests

[1] Du Pérac calls it the Frontispiece of Nero, and gives an engraving of the
rear wall of the temple as it existed in 1575.
[2] The columns of this temple were 58 feet high, and the entablature nearly
16 feet.   The fragment of the entablature now in the Colonna gardens weighs
about 90 tons.
[3] Prof. Meurer is of opinion that the anthemion is derived from the flower
of the acanthus and its sheathing leaves, while the leaves on the lower part
of the stem form the prototype of those employed in the Corinthian capital.

PLATE XXIV.

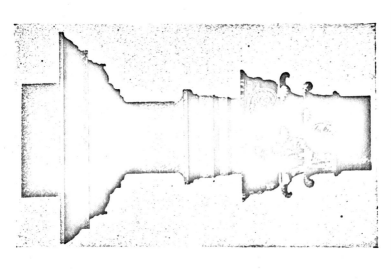

COMPOSITE CAPITAL AND ENTABLATURE
IN THE THERMAE OF DIOCLETIAN.

COMPOSITE CAPITAL
IN THE THERMAE OF CARACALLA.

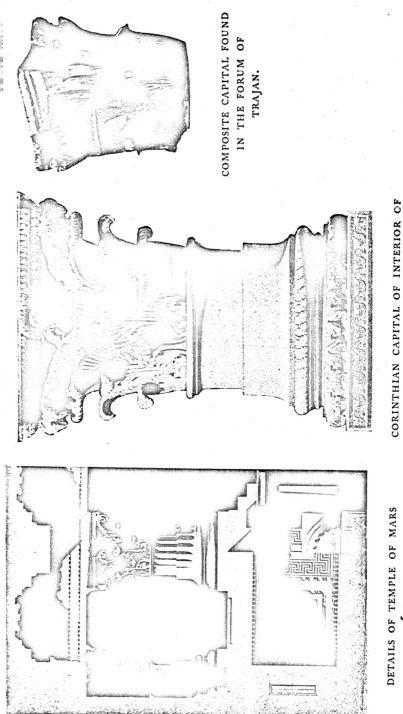

COMPOSITE CAPITAL FOUND IN THE FORUM OF TRAJAN.

CORINTHIAN CAPITAL OF INTERIOR OF TEMPLE OF CONCORD AT ROME.

DETAILS OF TEMPLE OF MARS [ULTOR.

PLATE XXVI.

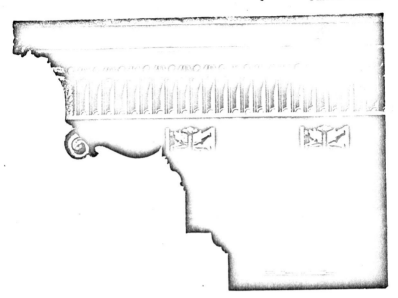

CORNICE OF TEMPLE OF CASTOR IN ROME.

SOFFIT OF TEMPLE OF CASTOR IN ROME.

PLATE XXVII.

ENTABLATURE FROM THE FORUM OF TRAJAN.

DETAIL OF FRIEZE FROM THE FORUM OF TRAJAN.

that the composite capital originated in the desire to give a richer effect to the capitals of the Ionic order. The composite capitals of the Colosseum are plain, and the leaves are left quite smooth. In those of the Arches of Titus, Septimius Severus, of a capital from the Forum of Trajan (Plate XXV), and of the Thermæ of Diocletian, the upper fillet of the volute is raised into the cavetto moulding of the abacus, and is carried through horizontally[1]; a similar treatment exists in every Roman composite capital, of which there are many examples still existing in the museums and churches of Rome.[2]

THE SUPERPOSED ORDERS.

The combination of the arcade as a constructive feature with the orders employed as a wall decoration, and the superposition of the orders, may be taken to constitute that which virtually became a new Roman order, inasmuch as in the earlier examples there seems to have been a definite proportion both in the intercolumniation of the shafts and the relative proportion of the orders superposed. Thus in the Tabularium the distance from centre to centre of column is five diameters, and five and a quarter in the Theatre of Marcellus and in that of Pompey. In the Basilica Julia it was five and a half. In the lower or Doric order of the Theatre of Marcellus (Plate XIX) the columns are eight diameters high, and taper by one-seventh of the lower diameter at the top, and this becomes the lower diameter of the Ionic column above, of which the height is nine diameters.

The upper storey has gone, so that it is not possible to trace the principle further. In the Colosseum, where there are three super-posed orders, the proportions are defective ; and the mouldings which, in the Theatre of Marcellus and the Tabularium, still preserved some Greek character, in the Colosseum become portions of circles, and of a very commonplace type. This suggests that the architect confined his attention to the general design of the plan, and left the details to his subordinates. The distance from centre

---

[1] In many of the published drawings the volutes are represented as dying into the echinus, and in the interpretation of the capital by the Italian masters and as executed at the present day the origin and meaning of the upper fillet as the junction of the volutes is entirely lost, as each volute is made a separate feature tucked in on the top of the echinus.

[2] For the Byzantine composite capital, see Rivoira, *Lombardic Architecture*, i, 16. We may also notice the spread of the use of figured capitals which is found at Pompeii and doubtless goes back to the Hellenistic period.

to centre of the columns in the Colosseum is seven and a half diameters, the Doric column is *nine and one-third diameters high*, and
the Ionic and Corinthian *eight and three-quarters only*, all having
the same diameter at the base.

The Romans failed to grasp the true principle of decoration,
that it should emphasise and not obscure structural function.
Their artistic handling of space is unsurpassed, but they always
tended in the direction of more extravagant enrichment. Thus
free columns were often employed (as in the Forums of Nerva and
Trajan) and in triumphal arches to support a projecting block
round which the mouldings of the entablature were returned.

In the interpretation of the orders by the Italian Revivalists,
they would seem to have assumed that no order, in conjunction
with an arcade, was complete without a pedestal.   There is no
example of this feature in the Doric order in Rome, and that of
the Ionic order in the Theatre of Marcellus and in the Colosseum
is part of a plinth which was required to give height for the
vaulting of the lower storey; but they were not detached
features as shown in Vignola and Palladio.   There is, however,
one well-known example in the temple of Minerva at Assisi
(Plate XXIX) where, to give additional width to the road
passing in front, the steps are set back between pedestals carrying
the columns of the main front.   In North Africa, the columns
decorating the front of the Prætorium at Lambaesis are raised on
pedestals, and in Syria are other examples, as in the Prætorium at
Mousmieh (now destroyed), the so-called temple at Sunamein,
south of Damascus (Plate XXX), the temple of Kanawat in
Hauran, the temple of Neptune at Palmyra and the Propylæa at
Baalbek.

In the Roman triumphal arches pedestals were required on
account of the height of the central archway, but they vary so
much in relation of their height to those of the columns they carry,
that no rules could be applied to them as part of the order. Thus,
in the Arches of Titus, Septimius Severus and Constantine, the relation is as 2 : 5 ; at Beneventum 2 : 4 ; at Tebessa 2 : 4¾ ; at Orange
2 : 8 ; and at Ancont 2 : 9¾.

PLATE XXVIII.

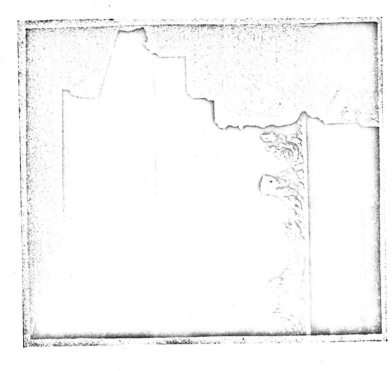

ENTABLATURE OF THE TEMPLE OF SERAPIS, ROME

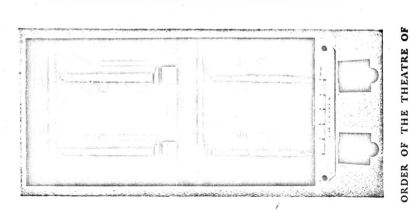

ORDER OF THE THEATRE OF
MARCELLUS AT ROME.

THE TEMPLE OF MINERVA
AT ASSISI.

DOORWAY OF THE PANTHEON,
ROME.

CHAPTER IV.

THE FORUMS OF ROME.

THE COLONNADED STREETS AND ENCLOSURES OF TEMPLES IN THE EAST.

The forum in Roman architecture corresponded to the Greek agora, of which there were two types—the public forum, and the market place. Under the Republic the Forum Romanum (and the same applies to the Fora of other cities) seems to have served both purposes, as some of the chief temples and important public buildings occupied sites round it, and up to the time of Julius Cæsar there were shops on both sides. Besides this, like the Agora at Elis, it sometimes served for combats and various other displays. Under the Empire these latter were relegated to the amphitheatre, the circus, and the theatre ; markets were provided elsewhere, the Forum was cleared of its shops, and became the great centre for the law courts, exchange, and other buildings of public importance.

In the course of time the Forum Romanum no longer sufficed for the increased demands made upon its space, and a number of Forums were subsequently built by succeeding Emperors, those of Julius Cæsar, Augustus, Vespasian, Nerva, and Trajan. All these additional Forums were planned symmetrically ; and from their size and magnificence, both in design and material, they give a far more complete idea of the Roman architectural style than can be obtained by the study of the temples, basilicas, and other monuments apart from their surroundings. (Plates XCIII and XCIV (at the end of the volume) should be constantly referred to.)

In Rome no importance would seem to have been attached to the orientation of the temples, which were regarded more from the monumental than from the religious point of view ; they occupied the most important positions facing the Forum, so as to leave as much space in front of them as possible, only in a few instances being isolated in a court surrounded by porticoes, in imitation of those in Greece. As a result of its gradual growth, the Forum Romanum

(Plate XXXI) was not symmetrically planned, until the alterations made by Julius Cæsar, to whom it owes its present form. He placed the Rostra, the platform for the orators, at one of the narrow ends of the trapezoidal open space in the centre ; the two long sides were flanked by the Basilica Aemilia, which in its original form dated from 179 B.C., but was frequently rebuilt, and the Basilica Julia, which he himself erected. After his death, a temple in his honour was erected at the opposite end of the open space to the Rostra, across the line of the street which flanked the south-east long side of the temple of Castor and Pollux. The temples on either side or at the ends, varying as they did in plan, in dimensions and orientation, and being interspersed with other monuments, presented a much more magnificent effect than when enclosed in a court, and so resembled more the accidental and picturesque arrangement of the Greek shrines. The Greek not only selected beautiful sites, but utilised their varying levels, and planned their buildings in harmony therewith, thus wedding art to nature. This was not always the case with the Romans, who, possessed of greater means, invariably levelled their sites, and then set out plans of symmetrical design in which a central axis formed the chief characteristic. While the planning of open spaces is regular as far as possible, and the rectangular form is preferred, other forms, which in Republican times are only found in smaller rooms, make their appearance in Imperial times—polygons (as at Baalbek), circles, and mixed plans as in the Imperial Fora, where rectangles are combined with hemicycles. When founding new cities, or in cases where the ground was occupied by unimportant buildings only, which could be cleared away, no great difficulties presented themselves ; but in Rome, where the ground in the vicinity of the Forum Romanum had already in the first years of the Empire acquired an immense value, the sites were frequently curtailed in size, and sometimes abutted on other buildings or streets running at various angles, and as it was considered to be of importance that the new Forums should be contiguous to the Forum Romanum, the only site available was that under the cliffs of the Quirinal Hill; consequently, at all events on the north-east side, they had to be enclosed with lofty walls in order to mask the slopes of the hill behind and the buildings surmounting them. The walls were, however, continued all round the Fora, and their object was probably partly decorative and partly that of protection from fire. The height of the walls round the Forum of

Augustus was over 100 feet (Plate XXXI), and such an enclosure
would have had a dreary effect if the Romans had not known how
to give interest to these walls by their decoration, and by the
variety of their outline and form. This will be better followed on
reference to the restoration of the Forum of Augustus, where it will
be noted that the temple of Mars Ultor is built at the farther end
of the site, thus giving an ample space to the Forum (Fig. 9). As
the temple was erected against a portion of the Quirinal Hill
it was visible only from the front and sides, which may account
for the wide difference between its plan and that of a Greek temple.
Externally, far greater importance was given to the portico of the
front ; internally, a finer effect to the statue of the god by the apse

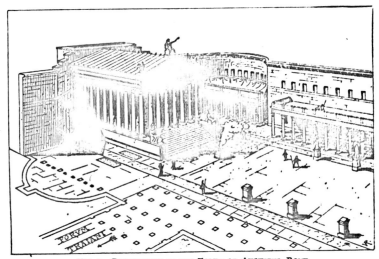

FIG. 9.—RESTORATION OF THE FORUM OF AUGUSTUS, ROME.

in which it stood. The irregularity of the site at the back, on the
right, has been balanced on the left, so that, as seen from the
Forum, the two sides would appear to be symmetrical. In this
Forum is one of the earliest examples known of that feature which
seems to have had a special attraction for the Roman architect,
viz., the hemicycle, and we can thus appreciate, on examination of
the remains, the magnificent effect of the expansion of the farther
end of the court by those semi-circular walls on each side, decorated
as they were with ranges of niches flanked by monoliths of coloured
marbles and filled with statues, the whole of the rest of the surface
of the wall being covered with slabs of coloured marbles.

The first of the new Forums in chronological order was that of Julius Cæsar, built on the north side of the principal Forum. It was rectangular in plan, and was surrounded on three sides by a porticus giving access to a series of vaulted chambers. In the centre of the Forum was the temple of Venus, which is instanced by Vitruvius as an example of pycnostyle, or close intercolumniation. The temple was erected 46 B.C., and was peripteral hexastyle, of the Corinthian order, and built or cased entirely in white marble.[1]

Reference has already been made to the next Forum built, i.e., that of Augustus. To the temple of Mars Ultor, which formed its chief architectural feature, we shall return again.

The Forum built by Vespasian, which is better known as the Forum Pacis, was begun in 71 A.D. It was situated 100 feet east of the walls of the Forum of Augustus, and was rectangular, with a porticus round it, and it enclosed the temple of Peace, of which no remains have ever been found.

The Forum Transitorium, erected by Domitian, but finished by Nerva after his death, and often, therefore, called after that emperor, is the next in date, 88-98 A.D. It occupied a site between the Forums of Augustus and Vespasian, and the lofty walls on either side were decorated with a series of detached Corinthian columns of Greek marble, twenty-one on each side, with respond capitals only; two of these columns still exist, and show that above the entablature was an attic with plinth and cornice, the latter being returned round the corner, and probably carried statues to break the skyline. In the centre of the portion which remains is a relief of Minerva about life size. At the farther end of the Forum was a temple dedicated to Minerva, hexastyle and prostyle, with an apsidal termination to the cella similar to that of Mars Ultor. The Forum is about 100 feet wide, and it must have had a magnificent effect with the side ranges of Corinthian columns. The details of its entablature correspond so absolutely with those of the peristyle of Domitian's palace on the Palatine, that both must be due to his architect Rabirius.

The last Imperial Forum built, and by far the most magnificent, was that of Trajan, which was designed by Apollodorus of Damascus, and covered an area equal to all the other Forums put together. The Forum consisted of three parts, viz., the Forum proper, the Ulpian basilica and the temple of Trajan ; the first was an open

---

[1] A fragment of the frieze exists in the Villa Medici.

PLATE XXX.

PLATE XXXI.

FORUM ROMANUM LOOKING SOUTH EAST.

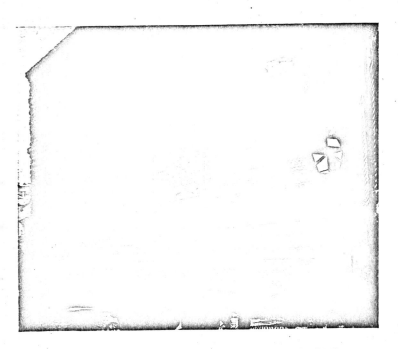

ENCLOSURE WALL OF THE FORUM OF AUGUSTUS.

area decorated internally like the Forum of Nerva,[1] and flanked on the right and left by two immense hemicycles ; as the northern hemicycle has a series of shops and offices several storeys high, the upper rooms in which were entered from the top of the adjoining hill, it is evident that this feature was designed to mask the over-hanging cliff of the Quirinal Hill, and (for the sake of symmetry) a similar hemicycle with shops and offices was built on the south side. Some of the architectural peculiarities of the northern hemicycle have led Boni and Rivoira to the supposition that it was begun by Domitian. The Forum was entered through a magnificent archway, the design of which is known from coins. The farther side of the open area of the Forum was occupied by the Ulpian basilica, inaugurated 113 A.D., consisting of a vast central nave surrounded by a double range of columns in two storyes. At its north and south ends were semi-circular apses, possibly covered with hemi-spherical vaults. These apses were the law courts, and they may have been shut off from the basilica by curtains or screens, so as to mask the incongruity of the arcuated and trabeated styles in the great circular arch opening of the hemicycle and the double range of columns of the aisles carrying their entablatures.[2]

In a central court beyond the basilica, which was surrounded by a peristyle two or more storeys high, stood the famous Column of Trajan (114 A.D.) ; this was of the Roman Doric order, raised on a pedestal richly carved with reliefs of armour and trophies taken from the Dacians (Fig. 10). Winding round the shaft is a spiral band of twenty-three revolutions, carved with relief sculpture representing the history of Trajan's campaigns against the Dacians. The shaft, built in 18 huge blocks of Greek marble, has a lower diameter of 12 feet, diminishing to 10 feet under the capital. The whole column is 100 Roman feet (97.6 feet) high, the pedestal 18 feet high. Boni's researches have shown that the column cannot mark the height of a ridge which was by many supposed to have connected the capitol with the Quirinal before the construction of Trajan's Forum, inasmuch as remains of structures of an earlier date have been discovered, and it probably marks the maximum

---

[1] This has recently been ascertained by Dr. A. Bartoli from a Renaissance drawing (*Mem. Acc. Pont. Arch.* I, ii). Palladio indicates the same thing in exediæ of the thermæ (Rivoira, *Roman Architecture,* 117).

[2] Whether *these* apses were roofed is very doubtful. Bigot's restoration indicates them as unroofed. The smaller apses at the extremities of the immense hemicycles at the north end of the Forum were, on the other hand, roofed ; and their vaults are still preserved.

FIG. 10.—COLUMN OF TRAJAN AT ROME.

PLATE XXXII.

PLATFORM OF TEMPLE OF JUPITER ANXUR, TERRACINA.

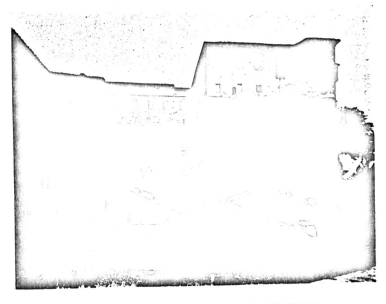

SUBSTRUCTURES OF THE FORUM FERENTINO.

PLATE XXXIII.

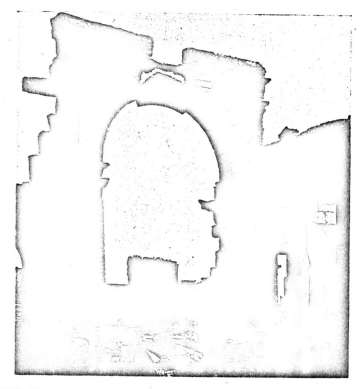

THE GREAT ARCHWAY AT PALMYRA, SHOWING ON THE RIGHT
THE COLUMNS OF THE PERISTYLE: IN THE DISTANCE
IS THE TEMPLE OF THE SUN.

THE CIRCULAR TEMPLE AT BAALBEK.

height of the vertical cutting which was made on the side of the Quirinal in order to provide a sufficiently large site. On the top of the capital was a colossal bronze statue of the Emperor, 13 feet high. On either side of this central court were libraries, one for Greek, the other for Latin manuscripts. The third part of the Forum was occupied by the temple of Trajan, which was of the Corinthian order,[1] octastyle and peristylar, mounted on a podium and approached by a flight of steps. The temple stood in a court surrounded on three sides by a peristyle in two storeys, and was an addition made to Trajan's Forum by Hadrian, who dedicated the temple to the deified Trajan. The construction of the Forum of Trajan finally solved the question of communication between the Forum Romanum and the Campus Martius, which, it is interesting to note, is one of the most pressing traffic problems in modern Rome.

The plans of the several forums we have been describing were governed to a certain extent by the sites selected, and the lofty walls by which some of them were enclosed would seem to have been deemed necessary to mask adjoining heights of cliffs, other buildings, and existing streets. In the provincial towns, as in Pompeii, throughout Europe and in North Africa (see, as an example, Fig. 11) the forum was enclosed by the principal temples and shrines, government buildings, as the Basilica, Senate House, etc., and Municipal Buildings, serving as markets. The forum itself consisted of an open rectangular area enclosed by a porticus or peristyle. On the

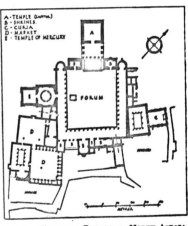

FIG. 11.—FORUM OF PHUBURBO, NORTH AFRICA.

foundation of a new town the first consideration would appear to have been the two chief thoroughfares, and these were laid out at right angles to one another, running as a rule north to south and east to west. In order to be as central as possible

---

[1] A monolithic shaft of granite, 6 feet in diameter and 55 feet high, was discovered on the site in 1887, and probably belonged to this temple.

the forum occupied an angle of two of the streets, but there were always buildings between the street and the forum ; the entrance to the central area of the latter being at one of the narrow ends, sometimes in the centre, sometimes near one of the angles, so as to interfere as little as possible with the covered porticus round it.   The Forum of Pompeii, which may be taken as a typical example, was about 500 feet long, north to south, and 150 feet wide, in both cases including the peristyle.   At the north end, projecting about 100 feet into the forum, was the temple of Jupiter, and an entrance gateway, the Arch of Tiberius, at the north-east corner.[1] On the east side were in succession the provision market, the sanctuary of the city Lares, a small temple of Vespasian, the building of Eumachia (which was probably a cloth market) and the Comitium, or voting place.   On the south side were three municipal buildings, and on the west side the Basilica, to the north of which was the temple of Apollo in a court surrounded by a peristyle in two storeys ; and, farther north, another market and latrines.   Excepting the temple of Jupiter the only other monumental features in the forum itself were statues raised on pedestals to various Emperors and distinguished citizens.   In the hill towns of Central Italy enormous substructions were employed to obtain the level space required for the forum (Plate XXXII) or for a temple as also for the villas of the wealthy, where it was necessary to obtain a level site.   As an example of the former, we may cite the arcaded platform of the temple of Jupiter Anxur at Terracina, which rose on the promontory above the town (Plate XXXII), while the villas round Frascati and Tivoli provide plenty of examples of the latter.

The Romans, as a rule, employed their own style of architecture, as developed during the first century of the Empire in Rome, throughout all their dominions.   The construction of their buildings, however, was varied sometimes on account of the materials at hand (which were occasionally of an entirely different nature to those in use in the capital), and at other times in order to avail themselves of the special labour of the country.   In Syria,[2] for instance, and more particularly at Baalbek, they employed immense masses of stone, not only for the substructures of the citadel, but in the temples themselves, which in dimensions are far in excess of those employed elsewhere.

---

[1] Such a building was more frequently placed on one side of the forum rather than in the centre, so as to leave more free space in front.
[2] For Roman Africa see Gsell, *Les Monuments Antiques de l'Algérie.*

M. Ernest Renan [1] and his coadjutors in fact arrived at the conclusion that the famous trilithon, the well-known group of three stones which forms part of the substructure of the great Temple of the Sun at Baalbek was the work of the Romans, who had employed the traditional Phœnician labour of the country. This is confirmed by other characteristics. Phœnician architecture was very massive ; when unable to find rocks of sufficient height wherein to excavate their dwellings, they employed stones of immense size, and aimed at obtaining joints of such fineness that the ultimate work appeared to be in one stone. When working for the Romans (and employing the classic orders), both capitals and bases are carved in the same stone with portions of the shaft. This tradition was carried on in later times under the Christians, when the arch of an arcade was either cut out of a single block or divided into only three voussoirs. This special characteristic is found throughout Roman work in Syria, but for the moment our attention must be directed to the laying out of their towns, which in the eastern portion of Asia Minor and in Syria seems to have followed the traditional requirements of the country in the erection of what are known as " colonnaded streets." In consequence of the great size of the stones, and of the difficulty of utilising cylindrical blocks in the erection of more modern dwellings, a large number of columns still stand erect, like bleached skeletons, on the sites of the ancient cities. The folio volumes of Wood [2] and of Cassas [3] give us the plans of the streets and of the principal temples of Palmyra, but of the buildings which flanked those streets there is no record. Many of the columns of the colonnaded streets remain *in situ*, and the bases of others allow of a complete conjectural restoration of their extent being made ; but the buildings outside the covered peristyle on each side (being built in coursed masonry, or only in rubble bedded in clay) have long since been removed and utilised to construct the walls of the town or houses for the numerous tribes which have since occupied the site.

From the writings of a Spanish Arab geographer who visited Damascus in 1184, and described what he thought was a great hall, but which is known from other sources to have been one of the colonnaded streets leading to the Great Mosque built on the site of the ancient temple, it may be gathered that the central space

---

[1] *Mission de Phénicie*, Paris, 1864.
[2] *Ruins of Palmyra*, London, 1753.
[3] *Voyage pittoresque de la Syrie et de la Phœnicie*, Paris, 1799.

between the rows of columns was open to the sky, and that the side avenues were covered over with a terrace roof which extended over the shops and offices on each side, and that on this roof the occupiers of the chambers and shops passed the nights in the summer. The shops and residential chambers were in two storeys.[1] This description applies to the great street at Palmyra, where a projecting cornice still exists on the side of the central avenue, and the trace of the terrace roof which covered the side avenue may be seen against the great archway which terminated a portion colonnade.[2]

The earliest records of these colonnaded streets are those describing the city of Antioch, where the Seleucidae (300-167 B.C.) constructed a street with double colonnades extending about two miles in length, with other streets crossing it at right angles. Herod the Great also constructed a new street there with colonnades similar to those which he had erected at Samaria, and many of the columns are still standing erect at the present day. With the exception of the latter, all the colonnaded streets in Syria belong to the Roman occupation; but the two bends in the main street at Palmyra suggest that it occupied the line of a more ancient thoroughfare. The central avenue of the principal portion of its main street (which runs from west to east), is 37 feet wide, and is flanked by a row of columns 31 feet high on each side. There were originally four hundred and fifty-four columns in this street, of which one hundred and sixteen still stood erect in Cassas' time. The side avenues were 16 feet wide, and at about 600 feet from the eastern end was the centre of an important cross street. In some cases, as at Antioch, Bosra, Gerasa, and other towns, the intersection of two cross streets is marked by a four-arched gateway vaulted over. At Palmyra there were four immense pedestals only, each carrying a group of four columns, with their entablature. With this exception the entablature of the colonnade, measuring 7 feet 2 inches high, and crowned with a blocking course or low attic, was carried straight through from end to end. In four other

---

[1] Damascus has recently been described in detail, and a street plan of the ancient city drawn out (*Damaskus*, by Watzinger and Wulzinger, being Heft 4 of the *Scientific publications of the Germano-Turkish authority for the preservation of ancient monuments*), cf. p. 16, for the propylæa of the market and temple enclosures, and p. 43 for the colonnaded streets. Cf. also *Palestine Exploration Fund, Quarterly Statement*, 1897, 268; 1911, 42; 1924, 68.

[2] See F. Haverfield, *Ancient Town Planning* (Oxford, 1913). Owing to the irregularity of the site, town planning, except in the Campius Martius, may be said to be conspicuously absent in Rome itself.

cases where there were cross streets the columns were replaced by archways. At the eastern end of this street was an immense triple gateway (Plate XXIII), with a central archway 23 feet 6 inches wide and 45 feet high, and two side archways for pedestrians, 11 feet 6 inches wide and 23 feet high. The gateway was apparently planned to mask the junction of the street just described with another street, 700 feet long, leading to the entrance propylaea of the great temple. It is triangular on plan, and seems to have been misunderstood by Wood, but is correctly shown in Cassas' work. The angle of the two streets (one to the other) is about 131°, and we assume that, after the temple with its immense enclosure was built, it was thought right to connect its entrance with the main street, and the great archway was designed for the purpose above mentioned.

In Damascus, the longest street, known as the " Via recta," ran from one gateway of the town to the other, and was 1,550 feet long. The main street of Gerasa was 1,880 feet long, of which one portion, about 1,300 feet, had a range of columns of the Corinthian order 25 feet high on each side, and the remaining portion, columns of the Ionic order, 20 feet high. This latter terminated in an immense circular piazza, apparently to change the line of axis to an important temple beyond. The remains of other colonnaded streets are found at Amman, Bosra, Gadara, Pella, Apamea, Kanawat, etc. They seem to have existed in every town, and are shown on early maps as existing in Jerusalem, and at Pompeiopolis, in the south of Asia Minor, a large number of columns still stand erect.

At Bosra, where the town was regularly planned within walls forming a rectangle, the main street ran from east to west, joining the two gateways of the city. This street was intersected by two other important streets running north and south, and at their junction were tetrapylons which were vaulted over.

The existence of these colonnaded streets did not obviate the erection of other public buildings, such as the forum, senate house, etc., but with the exception of the temples, only the colonnaded streets have been traced in the surveys made.

Tablets with dedicatory inscriptions existed throughout Syria, but the Romans did more than this, they erected statues as well. The shafts of the columns at Palmyra are in three drums of stone, the central one about 2 feet high only, with a corbel bracket (see Plate XXXIII) projecting inwards towards the central avenue to carry a statue.   It was the custom of the citizens to raise statues to those benefactors who had contributed to the magnificence of the town by erecting buildings of public importance ; but whether these corbels were all occupied is not known.   All the columns standing erect in the great street have these brackets, and also those of the peristyle or porticus round the peribolus of the great temple.

The principal temples in Syria would appear generally to have been enclosed in a great court, with lofty walls and porticus round, similar to those of the Forums of Rome.   The great court of the Temple of the Sun at Palmyra is about 750 feet square, the whole area being raised some 16 feet above the general level of the town, and enclosed by a wall 50 feet high, which was entered through a magnificent propylæa with a broad flight of steps in front.   The twelve columns of the Propylæa are arranged in pairs, and the wider central intercolumniation suggests that an arch was employed to span them instead of carrying through the architrave.   The height of the front wall (west) was 83 feet, the peristyle on the inner side being 61 feet high (including column and entablature), and the width between wall and columns 45 feet.   The other three sides of the court had a double peristyle, with two rows of columns 34 feet high.   At Damascus, the walled enclosure would appear to have measured 1,100 by 1,000 feet, with a double portico round, and two propylæa to the east and west respectively.   The inner part of the western propylæa is still more or less perfect (Fig. 12).   The extreme purity of its detail points to its execution within the second century of our era, and possibly in the first half.[1]   In comparison with the two great temples at Baalbek, built in the second half of the century, it exhibits little of that decadence of style which we find in the latter end of it, and, if it were possible to ascribe a still earlier date, it might be the work of the celebrated Apollodorus of Damascus, of whose services Trajan availed himself when laying out his Forum at Rome.   There is one feature in it, however (i.e., the arch spanning the central intercolumniation), which seems to be too startling a novelty for this early date.   But a little later there is an example in the Temple of Atil (Plate XXXIV) in the Hauran, which was built by Antoninus Pius, and is dated by an inscription to A.D. 151.   Another example may be found in a temple at Termessus in Pisidia ;

---

[1] The German authorities quoted above are inclined to put it with the other propylæa and assign it to the end of the century (op. cit., 35).

while it may be found in the form of wall decoration as early as the arch at Orange where its presence on the short sides shows that the idea was already familiar. Compare also the Trajanic reliefs published in *Papers of the British School at Rome,* IV. p. 230, and Plates XXI., XXII. The Greek fret decoration of the architrave at Atil is so similar to that of this gateway at Damascus that the same date might be fairly claimed for it, and

FIG. 12.—THE WEST FRONT OF THE PROPYLÆA AT DAMASCUS.

they both precede the well-known example at Spalato by one hundred and fifty-three years. In the great peribolus of Damascus the double portico appears to have been raised above the level of the city, and a flight of steps led down into the enclosed court, the temple itself being raised on a separate platform.

The most important of the Syrian enclosures is that found at Baalbek, where the principal temples were raised on an immense platform, which constituted an acropolis or citadel. Although at one time it was thought that the substructure of the north and west walls might have been, according to Renan, the work of the Seleucidae erected on the site of a much earlier temple (that of the Temple of Baal, built by the Phœnicians), there is no doubt now that the buildings constituting the whole acropolis formed part of one great scheme commenced by Antoninus Pius (138-161 A.D.). The foundations were carried down to the solid rock, in some cases 25 feet below the ground, above which the height of the platform is 25 feet at the east end and 30 feet at the west owing to the slope of the ground. If one may judge by the massive masonry[1] employed, Antoninus Pius's work would seem to have been stopped when the structure was about 30 feet from the ground, possibly on account of his death 161 A.D., and it was not resumed till many years later, probably by Septimius Severus (193-211 A.D.), the superstructure above that level being in masonry of far smaller dimensions.[2]

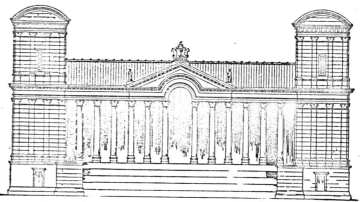

FIG. 13.—CONJECTURAL RESTORATION OF THE PROPYLÆA AT BAALBEK.

The entrance to the citadel was on the east side. A flight of fifty-one steps, 150 feet wide, led to the Propylæa[3] (Fig. 13, 14 ; Plate XXXV), a block measuring 238 feet wide by 45 feet deep, and consisting of a portico, 164 feet wide, of twelve Corinthian columns (on pedestals) in-antis, between two wings of 37 feet frontage and 45 deep.

---

[1] The wall carrying the Propylæa is 25 feet high, and consists of four courses only of masonry ; these dimensions are exceeded by others described on p. 65.

[2] Coins seem to prove that the Propylæa were finished as late as 244-249 A.D. under Philip the Arabian.

[3] The illustration here given (Fig. 13) is based on the dimensions of plan made by Joyau, Grand-Prix de Rome, who spent six months there in 1865, but died before he was able to work out his conjectural restoration. It is a different version from that put forward by Donaldson in his work *Architectura Numismatica*, both being based on a well-known coin. Rivoira (*Lombardic Archit.*, i, 48), maintains that we have here an example of the prototype of a church façade flanked by towers.

The Corinthian order with its entablature was carried across the wings, with four pilasters on the front and a similar number on the returns. Wood conceived that there was an attic storey above the cornice ; and in his conjectural restoration he carried one along the front above the portico, but there is no authority for it, and Prof. Donaldson, in his *Architectura Numismatica*, basing his conclusions on a medal representing the Propylæa, assumed the square dies which rise above the entablature of the wings to be the bases of an upper range of Corinthian pilasters. The same medal shows that over the six central columns there was a pediment, and that the two central columns carried an arch similar to that in the Propylæa at Damascus. This portion of the temple was built by Caracalla, about 212 A.D. The portico was probably covered with a tiled roof rising from the cornice in front to the rear wall of the block, and intersected by the pediment roof in the centre. We find, therefore, in the Propylæa at Baalbek a type of design based on the Temple at Jerusalem, *i.e.*, a central columnar portico flanked by two towers. The same type existed in the Temple of Sia in the Hauran, built by Herod the Great.

Three doorways led from the Propylæa to an hexagonal court, surrounded by a peristyle[1] resting on a stylobate of three steps. On four of the sides of this peristyle, and separated from it by columns and piers, were four rectangular halls of irregular plan. Three other doorways led to the great court, with a peristyle on stylobate of three steps on three sides. In the rear of this peristyle were eight rectangular and other halls, those on the north and south sides alternating with semi-circular exedræ, these latter being vaulted in stone, and the halls and peristyles having roofs in timber. Underneath the whole ranges of these halls and peristyles in both courts, are vaulted corridors 16 feet wide, showing that the outer portion of the great platform was artificial.

The temple of the Sun was axially placed at the further end of the square court ; it was of the Corinthian order, decastyle and pseudodipteral with nineteen columns on the flanks. The temple measured 160 feet in front by 289 feet deep, and was raised in a lofty podium with an immense flight of steps leading up to it, of which the

---

[1] The discovery of this peristyle and the stylobate on which it rested, is due to the Germans, who excavated there in 1899-1900. In the centre of the court they found an immense altar with steps leading up to it, and marble enclosures of what were apparently *piscinæ* for ceremonial ablution, one on each side. See *Jahrbuch des Instituts*, XVI (1901), 134 ; XVII (1902), 87.

J

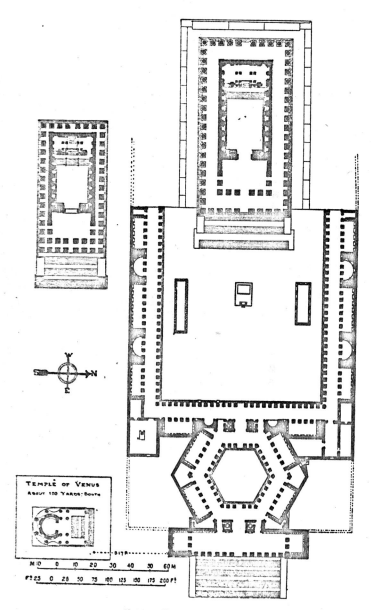

FIG. 14.—PLAN OF BAALBEK.

K

PLATE XXXI

CAPITAL OF THE TEMPLE AT A?
SHOWING THE SPRINGING OF T
ARCH BETWEEN THE TWO CENTR
COLUMNS.

DOOR OF THE SYNAGOGUE,
KEFR BIRM.

A FRIEZE FROM THE PANTHEON.

PLATE XXXV.

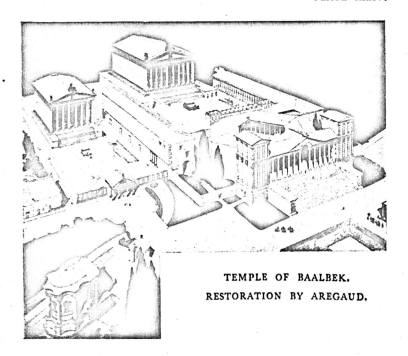

TEMPLE OF BAALBEK.
RESTORATION BY AREGAUD.

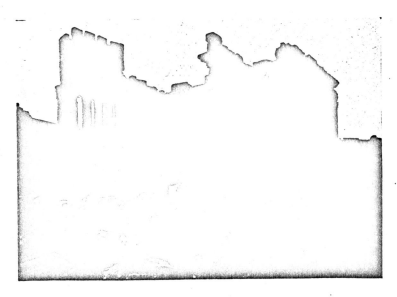

TEMPLE OF BACCHUS AT BAALBEK.

lower portion has been discovered by the Germans *in situ*. Of the temple itself there remains part of the great stereobate walls which carried the columns of the peristyle, one side of which was utilised by the Moslems as the north enclosure of their fortress. Only six columns of the peristyle remain standing on the south side, but portions of others are embedded in the north wall. These columns, which are 65 feet in height, carry still their entablature, which is 13 feet high. The German archæologists cleared out the interior, showing that the whole of the masonry of the substructure of the cella had been removed, part by the Christians when they erected their basilica, probably in the sixth century A.D., and the remainder by the Moslems to complete the enclosure walls of the citadel and of the town of Baalbek. The excavators, however, laid bare the lower foundations of the substructure of the cella, and the conjectural restoration of the plan in Fig. 14, is based on these and on the design of the temple of Bacchus, in which the cella wall with its architectural decoration (see Frontispiece, Plate I) and the Sanctuary are in good preservation.

In the substructure of the west wall of this temple, and about 25 feet west of it, is the well-known "trilithon" (the name is incorrectly applied), consisting of three large stones,[1] each of them being about 63 feet long, 12 feet high, and 11 feet thick, which are raised some 20 feet above the ground outside, on a plinth course of stones averaging 30 feet long each, and a substructure of smaller stones. The joints between these immense stones are so fine that it is impossible to insert the small blade of a knife into them. These great blocks of stone have been already alluded to (p. 59), and reasons given for attributing them to the Roman period. On this point Fergusson[2] states: "There seems no reason for doubting their being of the same age as the temples they support, though their use is certainly exceptional in Roman temples of this class."

In a court to the south of this temple, at a slightly lower level, was the temple of Bacchus, and about 317 feet to the south and in the town is a small circular temple, to both of which reference will be made later on.

---

[1] For further description see the *Builder*, February 11th, 1905.
[2] *History of Architecture*, Vol. I, p. 326.

CHAPTER V.

TEMPLES, BASILICAS, THEATRES AND AMPHITHEATRES.

THE Greek temples, whether peripteral or otherwise, were always isolated and intended to be seen on all sides, though the most important were invariably placed in a sacred enclosure or temenos. Except in a few instances they were raised on a simple stylobate of three steps, and if built on the slope of a hill as at Delphi, or on an irregular or low site, they were raised on a terrace or platform. The Romans, following probably Etruscan customs, erected their temples on a podium, with a flight of steps to the main front, flanked by projecting walls or spurs of masonry, along which were carved the mouldings of the podium. This, of course, gave a special importance to the main front—an importance which the Romans emphasized by an increased depth in the portico or pronaos. To have repeated this at the rear for the sake of symmetry would have had no value, unless the approach by the flight of steps were added. So little importance, in fact, did the Romans attach to the rear of their temples that even when the peristyle was carried on both sides of the cella it was generally stopped at the rear wall, which was carried through. This also was an ancient Etruscan custom ; there may also have been other reasons. The Greek temple was always orientated, the principal front, with rare exceptions, facing the east. The Romans, on the other hand, attached no value to this principal, and as their temples were regarded not only as religious but as monumental structures, they were built on sites where they could best dominate and be seen from the Forum, public place, or avenue which formed the chief approach. Thus, in the Roman Forum they are found on all the four sides, and consequently face the four points of the compass. The temple of Mars Ultor in the Forum of Augustus, and the temple of Minerva

in the Forum of Nerva, are placed at the farther end, so as to give a larger area in front. This position has apparently ruled the design of the plans, which must, when compared with Greek temples, be studied in conjunction with their surroundings; and in Rome this is even more important than with Greek temples. At Tibur and Præneste a whole hillside was occupied by the temple and its accessory buildings (Plate XXXVI).

Besides the temples already referred to, there were others in which the Romans followed Greek precedents, in that they were isolated and enclosed in areas surrounded by porticoes; such as the temple of Venus in the Forum of Julius Cæsar, the temples of Jupiter and Juno in the Portico of Octavia, the temple built by Hadrian and dedicated to Trajan to the north of Trajan's Forum, the temple of Hadrian, the double temple of Venus and Rome, the temple of Peace in the Forum of Vespasian, the temple of Apollo at Pompeii, etc.

There is still another important difference between the Greek and Roman temples, viz., the increased size given to the cella. For this there may have been two reasons: firstly, the Romans by trussing the timbers of their roofs were able to roof over spans never attempted by the Greeks; and, secondly, the cella of the Roman temple virtually became a museum in which the greater part of the spoils of Greece, consisting of statues in marble and bronze, were placed. The increased size required for the cella may have led the Romans to adopt the pseudo-peripteral plan, in which the cella occupies the full width of the portico, the tradition of the peripteros being retained only in the engaged columns which are attached to the external walls of the cella. The principal examples of this are found in the Ionic tetrastyle prostyle temple of Fortuna Virilis already referred to, and the Corinthian hexastyle prostyle temple known as the " Maison Carrée " at Nîmes, which is the best preserved Roman temple in existence.

The work of the time of Augustus is, as a rule, more refined in its details than that of later times; but there were revivals in the time of Trajan, of Hadrian, and of the Antonines, when monuments were produced which for splendour of conception, magnificence of material, and vigour of execution have never been surpassed. Reference has already been made to the materials employed in Rome up to and during the reign of Augustus. To this Emperor is due the increased employment of marble, which previously had only been occasionally introduced as spoils from Greece. The marbles that were first employed were imported from that country, and, excepting those brought by Sulla[1] from Athens, used in the decoration of the temple of Jupiter Capitolinus, were generally introduced into the mansions of the wealthy. Augustus not only embellished the city with splendid monuments, but induced others to follow his example, and hence his boast that he had found Rome of brick and left it in marble, the brick mentioned (*lateres*) being the crude brick which up to this time was almost universally employed for ordinary structures in Rome (*supra*, p. 27). Marble, however, was not so often used in the construction of the walls as had been the case in Greece. The core of the Roman temple wall (if it was not, as often, entirely composed of ashlar masonry), was concrete

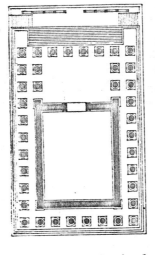

with facing of brick, hard tufa or travertine ; and an external casing (only) of marble, with slabs 2 to 3 inches thick and solid cornices. Nor did the Romans always follow the usual Greek custom of building shafts of their columns in drums. Monoliths of various marbles appealed much more to their sense of monumental effect. The white marbles principally used came from Mount Pentelicus, Mount Hymettus, and the Isle of Paros, in Greece, and from Luna near Cararra, in Italy.

Coming now to the principal temples of which there are remains existing, the temple of Castor, 6 A.D. (Fig. 15, Plate XXXVII), has already been referred to, in speaking of its order, as the most beautiful example in Roman architecture. The temple was octastyle

FEET   METRES

FIG. 15.—PLAN OF THE TEMPLE OF
CASTOR AND POLLUX AT ROME.

and peripteral, with a portico in front three columns deep. There were only eleven columns on the flanks, instead of from fifteen to seventeen, the usual number for a Greek octastyle temple. The temple was raised[2] on a podium 22 feet high, faced with thin slabs

[1] See Penrose's *Athenian Architecture*, 2nd edition, p. 16.
[2] In the Forum at any rate the use of lofty podia was due to the liability to floods of this low-lying site. Horace's *Vidimus flavum Tiberim* . . . *tre*

PLATE XXXVI.

PLATE XXXVII.

TEMPLE OF CASTOR AND POLLUX FROM THE PALATINE.

of Pentelic marble, with a solid marble cornice and base. The three columns still standing and their entablature were of the same material. The temple of Mars Ultor, built by Augustus in 14 B.C., was one of the most sumptuous in Rome ; the columns, of which only three remain (Plate XXV), their responds, and the entablature were all in Luna marble. The cella wall was faced in the same material, with a dado suggested possibly by the vertical slabs round the cellas of the Greek temples. Internally, on each side of the cella were six detached columns raised on a dado, the latter serving as a pedestal for the statues placed between the columns. The columns carried an entablature, but served no purpose beyond that of decoration[1], for the Romans, who were acquainted with the principles of trussed timbers, were able to roof over much greater spaces than the Greeks, who introduced columns inside the cellas of their temples in order to carry the ceiling and roof. A similar employment of the classic orders is found in nearly all the temples in Rome. Sometimes (as here) niches were sunk in the wall between the columns to give more space for the statues and works of art, and semi-circular apses at the further end, opposite the door, for the statues of exceptional dimensions. The sculpture of the foliage of the capitals and in the coffers of the ceiling of the peristyle is extremely vigorous in its execution, but not equal in refinement to that of the temple of Castor. Some of the architecture of the first century is almost as debased as that of the third century, and it would seem to have been a question of the architect employed. The entablature of the temple of Serapis in the Colonna Gardens, on the Quirinal Hill (Plate XXVIII), built by Caracalla, is almost equal in its design and execution to the work in Trajan's Forum, a century earlier.

Although of much later date, the temple of Antoninus and Faustina (142 A.D.) (Plate XXXVIII), bears witness to a purity of

---

deiectum monumenta regis templaque Vestœ was no mere phrase, as was proved by the flood of 1900, when the Forum lay several feet under water : and it has only been saved for the future by disconnecting the Cloaca Maxima with the Tiber and making it discharge into the modern main sewer, which runs inside the river embankment. The podium of the temple of Castor was a mass of concrete, enclosed by walls of blocks of peperino 2 feet in height and thickness, which were used to carry the walls of the cella and the front and back lines of columns : while at the sides the columns were actually carried by blocks of travertine, the remainder of the projecting walls which supported them (for between each wall there was a small chamber in the side of the podium) being of peperino. The blocks of stone were quarried in the Middle Ages, leaving the concrete standing (Plate XXXVII).

[1] In the cella of a Greek temple the columns were introduced to assist in carrying ceiling and roof.

style similar to that which characterises the work of Augustus ; and as the frieze is a reproduction of an ancient Greek frieze at Delos it is probable that in this case a Greek artist was employed.   It has not always been possible, therefore, in Roman work to decide, as in the case of Greek architecture, the approximate period of its execution.

Of the temples in the Forum, the temple of Concord, built against the Tabularium, departs from the usual plan, the width of the cella being nearly twice its depth.   The portico also only extended across the centre portion, leaving one bay on each side, in which a niche with a statue in it is shown in the medal of Tiberius. The temple was rebuilt by Augustus in B.C. 7, and the carving of the capitals and entablature (now in the Tabularium) is of great beauty, though exception may be taken as to the propriety of introducing into the capitals rams' bodies of the order inside the cella, with their heads and horns taking the place of volutes.   The plan of the temple is of interest as suggestive of the type adopted by Agrippa for his temple dedicated to all the gods, the Pantheon, to which reference will be made later on.   The temple erected by Augustus in honour of the deified Julius Cæsar was very similar in plan (Fig. 16)[1], both being hexastyle prostyle, owing, as in the case of the temple of Concord, to the restricted site available.   In this particular case the niche in the centre of the front of the podium is a unique feature ; it enclosed the actual paving stones upon which the body of the great dictator had been burnt, and the base of the memorial[2] which had been erected on the spot.   On each side of and behind the niche was a space for the orators—the so-called Rostra Julia.[3]   A less-known temple of the Augustan era is that of Minerva at Assisi, the capitals of which

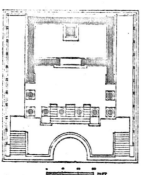

FIG. 16.—PLAN OF THE TEMPLE OF JULIUS CÆSAR.

---

[1] From Richter, *Jahrbuch des Instituts*, IV (1889), 137 sqq.

[2] Our authorities differ as to whether this was a column, a statue, or an altar : it may have been a combination of some or all of them.

[3] The walls which carried the columns and cella walls have been quarried, as was the case in the temple of Castor and Pollux, leaving only the concrete which they originally enclosed.

belong to the Græco-Roman type found in the temple of Castor and Pollux at Cora.   Perhaps for want of space in front, the steps at Assisi are carried back between the columns, which are raised on pedestals, the only instance of this arrangement in Italy, though examples are occasionally found in Syria.   Outside Italy, the most perfect Roman Corinthian temple existing is that known as the Maison Carrée at Nîmes, built by Antoninus Pius and dedicated to his adopted sons Lucius and Martius (Fig. 17, Plate XXXIX).   Hexastyle, pseudo-peripteral, with a portico three columns deep, it is well-proportioned and its sculpture is comparatively pure for provincial work.   The temple measures 59 feet by 117 feet, and is raised on a podium 11 feet high, with a flight of nineteen steps.   The columns are 30 feet 6 inches high, with a diameter of 2 feet 9 inches, and inter columniation of two diameters.

FIG. 17.—PLAN OF THE MAISON CARRÉE, NÎMES.

Nothing definite is known as to the nature of the ceilings of the Roman temples, which may have been horizontal, with deep coffers (a type of design which would be in harmony with the marble ceilings of the peristyles), or else open roofs richly decorated, such as are seen in the earliest Christian basilicas of Rome.[1]   The roof of Trajan's basilica is described by Pausanias as being of bronze, but whether that referred to its external covering in the place of tiles, to the ceiling cased inside with bronze plates, or to the employment of trusses in bronze, is not known.   The roof of the Portico of the Pantheon, rebuilt by Severus and Caracalla[2] consisted of three trusses of bronze plates, two vertical and one horizontal, riveted together with bronze bolts.[3]   Considering the great risk of destruction

[1] The discovery of fragments of a flat ceiling of painted plaster in the fourth century edifice which occupied the site of the basilica at Aquileia, the mosaic pavement of which was brought to light a few years ago, renders it not improbable that the basilicas of Rome originally possessed similar ceilings.

[2] The propylæa of the portico of Octavia, rebuilt by these same Emperors, still shows remains of the marble tiles with which it was roofed, with marble antefixes decorated in relief.

[3] This is the description given in Prof. Lanciani's *Ruins and Excavations of Ancient Rome*, 485, in which a drawing is published made by Dosio, an Italian architect, prior to its destruction by Urban VIII.   There is also a drawing of the trusses wrongly attributed to Andreas Coner, in the Soane Museum (*Papers of the British School at Rome*, II, Pl. 65 : cf. VI., p. 202), and a third by Philibert de l'Orme, a reproduction of which was published in the *R.I.B.A. Journal*, Vol. XXI, 3rd series.

tion by fire to which such roofs (whether in bronze or wood) were
exposed, it is singular that the Romans, who already in their amphitheatres, palaces and thermæ, had shown the most perfect acquaint-
ance with the science of vaulting, should not have considered it
essential to adopt this method of roofing their temples, which
contained by far the richest treasures, for it is a fact that there
are hardly any Roman temples in Europe known to have been
vaulted over before the time of Diocletian.[1]   One example which has
generally been attributed to an earlier date, the temple of Venus
and Rome, was originally built by Hadrian, but the brickwork shows
clearly that the superstructure belongs to the restoration by Maxentius after its destruction by fire at the beginning of the fourth
century A.D.   It was one of the most magnificent of the Roman
temples.   It had two cellas, each with apses set back to back, and
a pronaos, the whole being surrounded by a single peristyle, with
ten columns at each end, and twenty on the flanks.   The side walls
of the cella were of extra thickness to carry the vaults, and niches
were sunk in them to hold statues, with the usual decorative
treatment of columns between ; the apses were vaulted in coffers
(Plate XL).   The temple was enclosed in a peribolus, with porticus
all round, the columns being in granite or porphyry, the whole
being raised on an artificial platform in accordance with the advice
of Apollodorus.   Although far smaller in size than some of the
sacred enclosures in Syria, this temple and its enclosure occupies
the largest area of any in Rome, measuring 541 feet by 337 feet.

The temple at Nîmes, known as the Baths of Diana, is in its construction the most advanced in the science shown in its vaulting,
and might fairly in that respect be taken for an eleventh century
church in Provence.   The cella is spanned by a transverse ribbed
vault, virtually a barrel vault with stone ribs underneath, rising
above the detached columns on each side of the cella, the definite
purpose of which would seem to have been to lessen the span of the
ribs, as they are brought forward to the same plane as that of the
architrave below.   Outside the cella walls are narrow aisles, over
which a barrel vault is thrown to resist the thrust of the cella
vault, an arrangement adopted in French Romanesque churches
of the eleventh and twelfth centuries.

---

[1] The building known as S. Urbano, just outside Rome, belongs to the
sepulchral type.

M

PLATE XXXVIII.

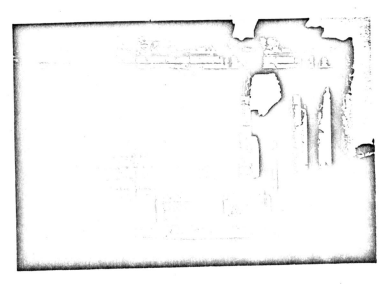

TEMPLE OF ANTONINUS AND FAUSTINA.

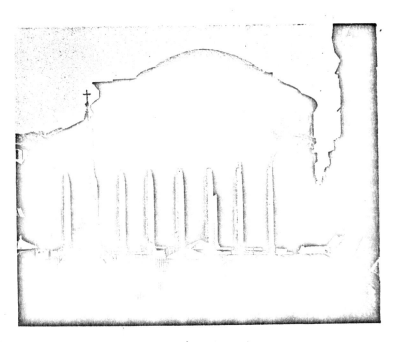

THE PANTHEON AT ROME.

PLATE XXXIX.

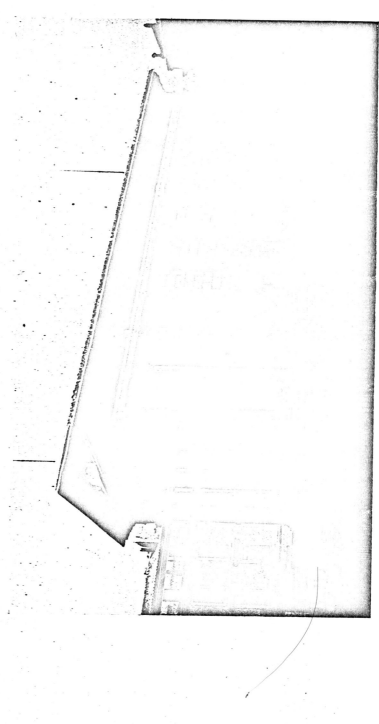

THE MAISON CARRÉE AT NÎMES.

If the architect of the temple of Bacchus[1] at Baalbek (see Plate XXXV) had utilised the semi-detached columns and piers in the same way as in the temple above-mentioned at Nîmes, viz., by bringing the vault forward, it is quite possible the cella might have been vaulted. The columns there, however, as in Rome, were used only for a decorative purpose : there would be no height for a circular vault, as shown in Wood's restoration, and a segmental one could not have stood.[2] The temple itself is one of the best preserved in Syria, and is built in masonry of great size. It is difficult to understand why the architrave and frieze of the great doorway should have been constructed as a flat arch with voussoirs, seeing that in other parts of the temple there are stones of far greater dimensions than the width of the doorway. The temple was octostyle, peripteral, with a portico of four columns deep, and a double row of columns in front, the inner row being fluted. The cella was decorated with semi-detached Corinthian columns (Frontispiece, Plate I) against piers, the entablature returning round both columns and piers. Between the piers were niches in two tiers. At the western end was a square sanctuary, about half the width of the cella, the floor of which was raised 10 feet above the ground, with a flight of steps in front ; steps on each side led down into a vaulted chamber below the square apse. It should be noted that in this temple, as possibly in the great temple of the Sun, the intercolumniation of the two central columns is greatly in excess of the others, so that there is every reason to suppose that it was spanned by an arch instead of an architrave.

The temple of the Sun at Palmyra departs from the usual plan of Roman temples in Syria, in that its main axis is north and south, and that one of the long sides, viz., the west, becomes the principal front. The temple is octostyle and pseudo-dipteral, with fifteen columns on the east and west sides. The principal entrance doorway on the west side (probably added by Aurelian when he restored or rebuilt the temple) is not quite in the centre of the main front, and has been emphasised, first, by adding engaged columns to the central column of the peristyle and its neighbour (towards the north) and breaking the entablature round them ; and, secondly,

---

[1] Judging by the sculptured friezes lately discovered the temple was probably dedicated to Bacchus, and the older attribution to Jupiter has therefore been abandoned.

[2] The same remark applies to the vault shown over the portico. In Wood's work the cornice in the cella is drawn 6 feet too low down, as the entablature of the portico and cella are on the same level.

by building the architrave and lintel of a great doorway between these engaged columns. This doorway, though not in the centre of the great court or of the temple, lies on the central axis of the Propylæa. The columns (65 feet high) were probably of the Corinthian order, but the ornamental portions of the capital, including the abacus, have disappeared, leaving only the bell, the holes in which suggest that it was encased with metal decoration.

There are other temples in Palmyra of smaller size. In one, the temple of Neptune, the six Corinthian columns of the portico are raised on pedestals, which stand on a stylobate of three steps. Reference has been made already to other temples in Syria in which the same arrangement is found ; unfortunately none of these temples have yet been properly examined or described.

Among the temples in North Africa there is one example at Sbeitla (Sufetula) which varies from any we have hitherto described. The group consists of three sanctuaries standing side by side (about 16 feet apart), each on a separate podium, with flights of steps in front. All three structures are tetrastyle, prostyle and pseudo-peripteral, but the central temple, of the composite order, has semi-engaged columns round the cella, the side temples having pilasters only of the Corinthian order round the cella walls. The three temples are placed at the end of the Forum, an enclosure surrounded by a peristyle, with a series of small chambers at the back. The whole area covered measures about 200 feet wide and 240 feet deep, and the entrance is through a fine gateway with centre and side arches, flanked by columns on pedestals. The central intercolumniation of the middle temple was, according to Bruce, spanned by an arch instead of an architrave. The temples belong to the age of Antoninus Pius, in whose time this change from the custom in Rome seems to have been very general in provincial work.

CIRCULAR TEMPLES.

.The celebrated temple of Vesta was near the Forum, close to the house of the Vestals. This was traditionally founded by Numa, and frequently destroyed and rebuilt. The latest temple was that built by Septimius Severus about 206 A.D., of which the remains have lately been found. It consisted of a circular cella with peristyle of twenty Corinthian columns, raised on a podium 50 feet in diameter and 6 feet 6 inches high, the total height to the top of cornice being 28 feet (Fig. 18). The mouldings of the

entablature, as also those of the cornice and plinth of the podium, were elaborately carved. On the podium were projecting dies, forming pedestals to the columns, the moulding of cornice and plinth being returned round them—a peculiarity not found in the temple at Tivoli.

The circular temple in the Forum Boarium, formerly known as the temple of Vesta, is perhaps that of Portunus, though often attributed to Mater Matuta, and although of early foundation was probably rebuilt in the Augustan era. The whole of the temple is built of Parian marble, including the flight of eight marble steps, some of which are buried ; originally there was a podium 6 feet in height. The peristyle consisted of twenty Corinthian columns, of which only one is missing.

There are two other small examples of circular temples, besides the temple of Jupiter at Spalato, viz., the temple of Roma and Augustus on the Acropolis at Athens, which rested on a square podium and consisted of a peristyle of nine Ionic columns with a diameter of 23 feet, and the temple of Venus at Baalbek (Plate XXXIII) with a tetrastyle portico leading to a circular cella round which are detached columns carrying a cornice which sweeps back with segmental curves, designed to meet the difficulty of the junction between the entablatures of a circular temple and a rectangular portico. This last is a characteristic example of the baroque tendencies of Roman imperial architecture represented by Hadrian's architect Apollodorus in Rome, and especially in Hadrian's villa, where curved lines predominate.

The largest circular temple, and in most respects the most remarkable monument ever built, is the church known as the Pantheon, which consists of an immense rotunda 142 feet in diameter and 140 feet high internally, with a wall surrounding it 20 feet thick.

The rotunda is preceded by a Corinthian portico (Plates XXXVIII, XLI), 101 feet wide and 59 feet deep in the centre. The portico is octostyle and three columns deep, there being two additional rows of two columns each behind the third and sixth columns. The three columns on the east, which had been damaged in the Middle Ages, were replaced in the seventeenth century. The masses of wall which form the responds (if they may be so called) of the portico have two large niches sunk in them in which are staircases to the roof, and were built and bonded into the rotunda during the course of its erection.

On the right and left, west and east of the central axis of the rotunda, are two apses (see Fig. 19) in the thickness of the wall, each rising to the height of the main cornice of the lower order, and having two columns in antis in front. At the farther end of the rotunda is a similar apse, but of greater height, as the cornice of the lower order becomes the impost of the hemispherical vault which crowns it. The entrance doorway has a barrel vault of similar height. In the axes of the four diagonals are four rectangular recesses, with two columns in antis in front of them. There are curved niches between these several recesses, lessening the amount of solid and wall. The hemispherical dome of the rotunda has vertical horizontal ribs, forming a series of deeply-sunk coffers[1]. There are thirty-two vertical ribs and five ranges of coffers, which rise to where the horizontal diameter of the dome is 80 feet. Above this

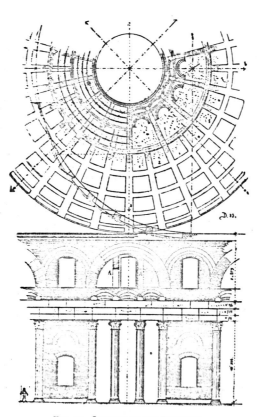

FIG. 19.—SECTIONS OF THE PANTHEON.

[1] The upper and lower set-backs of these coffers, which were probably decorated with carved mouldings, are inclined upwards, so as to display them to the spectator in the church.

PLATE XL.

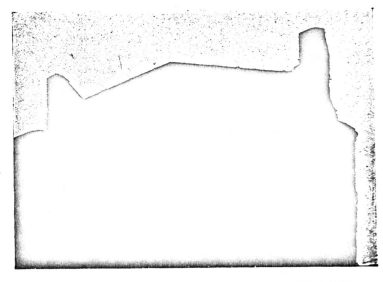

VAULTED APSE OF THE TEMPLE OF VENUS AND ROME.

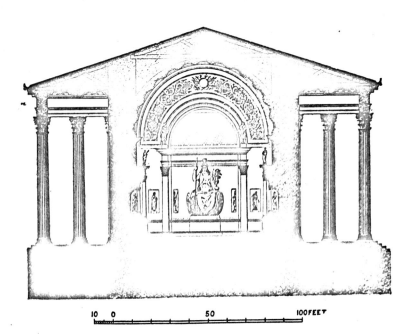

10 0   50   100 FEET

TRANSVERSE SECTION OF THE TEMPLE OF VENUS AND ROME.

PLATE XLI.

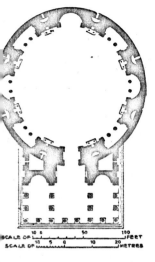

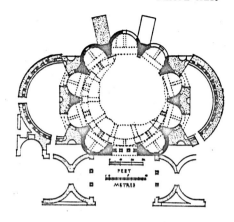

PLAN OF THE SO-CALLED TEMPLE
OF MINERVA MEDICA.

LAN OF THE PANTHEON.

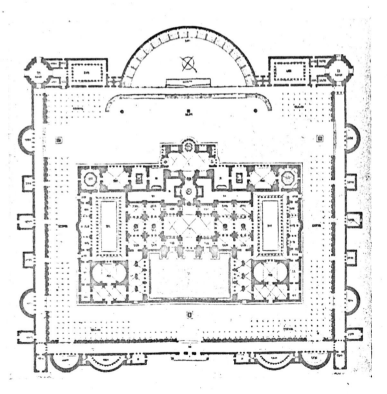

PLAN OF THE BATHS OF DIOCLETIAN.

the vault is not coffered, but there is a central opening 30 feet in diameter through which the building receives its only light. The effect produced by this great opening to the light of heaven is most impressive, and, as Fergusson says, " it is by far the noblest conception for lighting a building to be found in Europe." The lower order is 42 feet 6 inches high (Plate XLII), and the attic order 28 feet 6 inches.

Externally the walls are faced with brickwork and divided by two strings of cornices. Up to the lower string the walls were originally faced with marble, and above this string with stucco, decorated with pilasters.

The Pantheon was originally considered to have been built by Agrippa in consequence of the inscription on the portico, and the style and character of the order. But the discoveries made by M. Chedanne in 1892 proved that the rotunda was erected by Hadrian 120-124 A.D., and that the portico was partly built of the materials of Agrippa's temple, which was erected to form the entrance portico to the Pantheon[1]. Subsequent excavations have shown : (1) that the temple built by Agrippa consisted of an oblong cella with a portico of ten columns facing the south[2] ; (2) that in front of this temple, viz., on the south side, was an immense circular piazza, of which a portion of the enclosing wall concentric with and contiguous to the rotunda has been found ; (3) that this circular piazza was uncovered, as its pavement, found 8 feet below the floor of the Pantheon, sloped downwards from the centre to the circumference[3] ; (4) that the rotunda was built on the site of the circular piazza[4], some 7 or 8 feet above the pavement of the same ; and (5) that at a subsequent period Agrippa's temple and its portico were taken down and rebuilt at a higher level, to form the portico of the existing Pantheon facing north.

In rebuilding the portico it was made octostyle instead of decastyle[5], the eight columns of the front resting on what must have been the rear wall of Agrippa's cella. The entablature, with the

---

[1] Durm : *Baukunst der Etrusker und Romer*, ed. ii, p. 550 sqq., maintains that the portico is later than the rotunda, though it must be previous to the time of Septimius Severus.

[2] The present portico faces north.

[3] It is probable that this piazza was surrounded with a portico, the foundation walls of which were uprooted when the rotunda was built.

[4] This may have suggested to Hadrian or to his architect the idea of a rotunda to occupy the whole site of the piazza.

[5] The foundation walls of travertine are one bay or intercolumniation wider on each side than the present portico.

inscription on the frieze, and the pediment also belonged to Agrippa's temple, and with reference to the latter, M. Chedanne made a singular discovery in the course of his minute examination. Agrippa's pediment, belonging to a decastyle portico, was of less pitch than the existing pediment, and the marble blocks of its cornice re-employed were inclined at a steeper angle; consequently the sides of the modillions, which originally were vertical, have a slight inclination towards the centre of the portico.

M. Chedanne's discovery of the actual date of the rotunda was due to his having obtained permission to examine the brickwork of a portion of the vault in which great cracks had appeared, and a special scaffolding having been erected, he was able to take out some of the bricks, which, to his surprise, bore stamps known to be of the time of Hadrian. Further examination was then made in other parts of the structure, in every case resulting in the discovery of similar stamps. M. Chedanne's researches, however, did not end there. He had already noticed that the cracks came over one of the rectangular chapels, and from this and other observations he came to the conclusion that the columns forming the front of these chapels were part of the original construction, and were not decorative features inserted afterwards. These cracks necessitated the removal of some of the stucco facing of the attic storey and revealed : (1) that above the entablature of these columns there was an immense relieving arch of similar dimensions to those over the entrance doorway and the principal apse; (2) that above the columns were vertical piers[1] of brickwork rising to the soffit of this relieving arch ; and (3) that between each of the three divisions were small discharging arches. In a restoration made in 1747 the architect had cut through all the central discharging arches in order to obtain a greater depth for his niches, being unaware that they were integral portions of the main construction. This was the origin of the cracks, which had become so serious in 1892. Carrying his researches further, M. Chedanne found that above the cornice of the attic storey was a second relieving arch[2] of similar size to the one below, with vertical piers over those below, and other small discharging arches. The wall, therefore, was vertical up to the inner coffer of the second range, so that the vertical ribs already referred to, and the

---

[1] The existence of vertical ribs in the dome is denied by Rivoira (*Roman Architecture*, 127), see below.

[2] All these relieving arches were not, as has been suggested, skin deep, but carried back some 8 feet.

first horizontal rib, were actually built out in front of this vertical wall.

M. Chedanne also found that the whole thickness of the vault was built in brick laid in horizontal beds[1] up to the level of the fourth range of coffers (or about two-thirds of the height of the dome), and also in the proximity of the central opening in the vault. It was not possible to examine the vault between the fourth range of coffers and the central opening, and here, where the diameter is reduced to about 80 feet, according to M. Chedanne, a series of arches may have been built on a regular centering.[2]

It has hitherto been assumed that the marble decoration of the interior was originally carried out during a restoration by Septimus Severus and Caracalla ; but we have already shown that the columns in front of the chapels form an integral part of the structure. From this it may be inferred that the construction and decoration formed part of the original conception of Hadrian's architect, for both the responds of these columns and the entablature formed a necessary sequence. The marble wall decoration between the chapels may have been completed at a later period, and the niches with columns, entablature and pediments added afterwards. The attic storey was originally decorated with a series of marble pilasters, with panelling between, the design of which is shown in Palladio's *Architectura*, and in two of Piranesi's plates. Piranesi in his description says that the pilasters were in porphyry, and the panels in giallo antico, pavonaz zetto and serpentine—*i.e.*, green porphyry. The capitals were in white marble.[3]

All this marble panelling on the attic storey was taken away in 1747, and the present decoration in stucco (Plate XLII) probably dates from that time, as it is shown in a later engraving of Piranesi's. The coffers of the vault were all gilded with bronze flowers in the centre, and M. Chedanne found the bronze bolts in the vault. The great circular opening in the centre of the vault still retains its bronze cornice, a drawing of which by Philibert de l'Orme is given in the Baron de Geymuller's work, *Documents inedits sur les thermes d'Agrippa*, 1883. The external roof, part of which is stepped, was originally covered with plates of

---

[1] The so-called horizontal beds slope down outwards about 1 inch in 2 feet.

[2] Once the concrete was set, the whole dome formed one homogeneous mass without thrusts. Its weight was decreased by the use of pumice stone in the skin—the earliest example known (Rivoira, *op. cit.*, 126).

[3] Eight of the capitals of these pilasters are in London, viz., six in the British Museum, one in the Royal Academy, and one in the Soane Museum.

gilded bronze.   These were, however, stripped off, and subsequently replaced with lead.   The massive doors (Plate XXIX) with their fluted Doric pilasters on each side, and the grating above, all in bronze, and originally plated in gold, are the best preserved examples in Rome.   They were, however, practically cast over in the time of Pius IV (Lanciano, *Ruins and Excavations*, 486), though this must have been done without altering the original form, which is shown in the *Codex Escurialensis* f. 29 (about 1490)[1] the doors are framed with large plates of cast bronze, the cyma recta mouldings and the decorative bosses being also cast.

The so-called temple of Minerva Medica (Plates XLI, XLIII) which served the purposes of a nymphæum in the Horti Liciniani, one of the great private parks of Rome, has a considerable importance in the development of the dome.[2]   The absence of any flue tiles in the walls, or even of the hypocaust, is a clear proof that it could not have been a sudatorium, which has been suggested on account of its decagonal form.   Its principal interest is to be found in the vault, in which the use of ribs is important—and in which an early example of the pendentive is found.   The corbelling out, however, is of the rudest kind, and was probably entirely masked by the decoration.   The windows lighting the interior are of considerable size, so as to give plenty of air and light (necessary for the plants and flowers), and are in two rings[3]—that is to say, an outer and an inner arch, the former of greater radius than the latter.

A simple dome of the time of Diocletian in which amphoræ are used to lighten the weight of the vaulting is the so-called Tor de Schiavi, probably a mausoleum (Plate XLIII).   Its internal diameter is 47 feet.   The stucco facing makes it impossible to see any ribs ; it is closed at the top, but has four circular windows.   It is exactly analogous in construction to the Mausoleum of Romulus on the Via Appia.

Compared with the nymphæum of the Horti Liciniani, the mausoleum of Helena shows a notable advance in the principles of construction.[4]   The former is a hemispherical vault, with its

---

[1] Egger, *Codex Escurialensis*, Text, p. 92, who points out that there are various copies from the same original in existence (Bartoli, *Monumenta di Roma nei disegni degli, Uffizi*, Pl. LXIV, LXV and text to Pl. CCCLIX).

[2] See *Builder*, Vol. LXXXVIII (1905), p. 529.

[3] In the larger Thermæ (hitherto called the Palace) of Treves, are windows with three rings of arches, one set behind the other.

[4] Besides, the Tor de'Schiavi, the use of amphora may also be noted in the Circus of Maxentius, and a good deal earlier in a reservoir near the Via Latina, near a villa of the time of Hadrian, known as the Ruderi delle Vignacce (*Papers of the British School at Rome*, IV, 74).

PLATE XLII.

PLATE XLIII.

THE SO-CALLED TEMPLE OF MINERVA MEDICA.

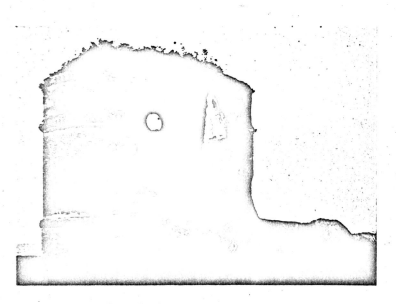

TOR DE SCHIAVI, NEAR ROME.

framework composed of ten radiating ribs meeting at the ring which enclosed the central opening in the crown of the dome, resting on a lofty polygonal drum lighted by large windows, and strengthened on the outside by powerful buttresses between the niches corresponding to the reentrant angles inside, and raised somewhat by means of steps above the impost of the cupola in order to be the better able to resist its thrust. (Rivoira, *Roman Architecture*, 182.) In the latter, there is a vaulted dome, lightened by concentric rings of amphorae[1]; the dome was thus able to be set up without any buttresses, upon a lofty drum, lightened by niches on its exterior, and pierced by windows. The prototype of the vaulted aisled rotunda (S. Costanza, the Mausoleum of Constantia, dating from the early part of the 4th century, Plate XLIV) is simply the Mausoleum of Helena set on an open arcade.

BASILICAS.

The first basilica built in Rome was the basilica Porcia, erected in 184 B.C. by Porcius Cato, who provided it to relieve the over-crowding of the Forum. A portion of it was set apart as a court of justice, and the remainder served as an exchange for merchants. A second basilica, the Fulvia, followed in 179 B.C., and a third in 170 (the Sempronia), which again was pulled down in 54 B.C., to make way for the basilica Julia, the complete plan of which is now laid bare in the Forum. The central area of the basilica Julia was 260 by 60 feet, and as rebuilt by Diocletian, it was surrounded by a double aisle of arches resting on piers, with transverse arches carrying quadripartite groined vaults (Plate XXX) with angle supports for their springing (an anticipation of the compound pier of Lombardic and Gothic architecture)[2]. The nave was lighted by a clerestory[3]. Over the outer aisle was a flat roof on one side overlooking the Forum, and probably occupied by spectators when meetings were held there, and above the inner aisle a gallery overlooking the central area. Externally the lower storey was decorated with engaged columns of the Doric order between the arches, and the upper storey with Ionic pilasters.

The nave of the basilica Aemilia on the north side of the Forum measured as much as 221 by 100 feet (70 by 29 metres). It had a nave and three lines of columns, one on the S.W. and two on the

---

[1] Rivoira, *Lombardic Architecture*, II, 22 : *Roman Architecture*, 230.
[2] Rivoira, *Lombardic Architecture*, I, 24 : *Roman Architecture*, 203.
[3] See the reconstruction in Hülsen's *Roman Forum*.

N.E. (the irregularity in the central hall may have been due to the desire to make the roof central), and, like the basilica Julia, had no apses. The nave had two orders of Corinthian columns of Africano (Chian marble), with bases, capitals and entablature of white marble: the decoration of these architectural members is extremely fine. The façade facing on the Forum had a Doric arcade below with a massive entablature (Plate XX); of the upper arcade no remains are preserved. Inside this were tabernæ, between which three entrances led into the S.W. aisle. Like the basilica Julia, it had a clerestory, and the pilasters which divided its double windows show some of the finest decorative carving that has come down to us from the Augustan period.

The Ulpian basilica, though covering a slightly smaller area, had in addition two great semi-circular halls which constituted the courts of justice. Architecturally its interior must have presented a much finer appearance than the basilica Julia, as monolithic columns took the place of the arcade piers. The plan was similar to that of the basilica Julia, with a central area with double aisles all round and enclosure walls on the two longest sides. All the shafts of the columns of the ground storey were of red granite from Syene, in Egypt, with Corinthian capitals of white marble. Galleries are supposed to have been carried over both aisles. As regards its roof, Canina in his restoration shows a horizontal ceiling with deep coffers and a trussed roof in timber, and he lights the interior by clerestory windows above the galleries. Pausanias' statement that the roof was all in bronze probably refers only to its decoration, not to its construction.

The third great basilica was commenced by Maxentius and completed by Constantine (Plate XLV, Fig. 20). It is half as large again as either of the other two just described, and is totally different in its nature and construction, being virtually a reproduction of the vaulted central hall of the Thermæ hitherto (but wrongly) known as the Tepidarium[1]. It consists of an immense hall 266 feet long (exclusive of the apse) by 82 feet wide and 114 feet high, divided into three bays, and covered with an intersecting barrel vault, and aisles or side halls 55 feet deep. The huge columns which stood in the nave were merely ornamental, and did not support the vault. Between the walls contrived to resist the thrust are three rectangular halls on each side; these communicate one with the other

---

[1] Compare the description of the central hall of the Thermæ of Diocletian (*infra* p. 107).

through large doorways, so that they virtually constitute aisles. The vault of these halls or aisles on the north side still exists, and displays deep coffers all built in brick (Fig. 20). There were two apses, one (added subsequently) opposite the later main entrance in the centre of the south front, the other at the west end, opposite the original entrance, which was at the east end, where there was a portico one storey high. Above this were two rows of huge windows, which gave light to the nave ; while the aisles were lighted

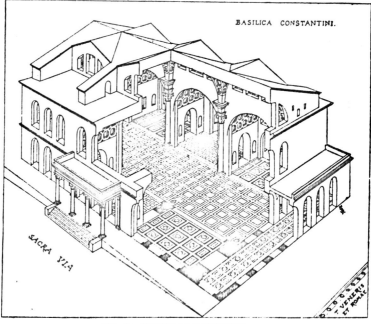

FIG. 20.—BASILICA OF CONSTANTINE.

by two rows of windows (reduced to one on part of the north side, where the level of the ground outside was higher). This great vault is one of those instances to which reference has been made in Chapter III as of construction by means of ribs of tiles, the interstices (with which the large coffers coincide) being filled with lighter material : this method was possible only with pozzolana ; and the homogeneous nature of the vault is shown in the fact that an immense mass of overhanging concrete has stood unmoved for ages.

Of provincial basilicas, that at Pompeii shows the simpler type adopted, consisting of a central area enclosed by a single aisle, the columns, 3 feet 6 inches in diameter, are built of brick, each horizontal course consisting of nineteen bricks radiating round a central core of rubble work, the flutings being added afterwards in stucco.   The height of the columns was probably from 32 to 33 feet. On the aisle wall are engaged columns of the Ionic order, 2 feet 4 inches in diameter, and about 20 feet high.   At the farther end of the basilica was a rectangular recess, raised some 4 feet above the aisle and entered by steps on the east side.   This served as the law court, and the columns in its front supported beams whose ends were let into the sides of the great columns, thus inclining us to think that the aisles were similarly roofed over at a low level, and that there was no gallery, except over the entrance porch, access to which may have been obtained by the staircase provided to reach the upper storey[1] of the portico round the Forum.   The central area of the basilica was probably covered over by a horizontal ceiling carried by the great columns and lighted through clerestory openings above the aisle roof.[2]   As the rain may occasionally have beaten in, a drain round the interior at the base of the columns was provided to carry off the water.   The basilica at Fano, built and described by Vitruvius, seems to have been lighted in a similar way, but above a gallery.   The columns were monolithic, over 48 feet high and 5 feet in diameter ; and as both Choisy and Rivoira remark, the conception of the whole building shows him to have been a man of considerable talent.

The basilica at Treves is interesting in that it shows how the Romans designed their structures in accordance with the climate. Here the basilica was simply an immense hall with an apse, the whole building being lighted by two tiers of windows, and the " lesene " or pilasters between the windows being united by round arches at the top.   The double tier suggests that originally there was a gallery round the interior, carried on columns.   It belongs either to the time of Diocletian or, less probably, to that of Constantine.   It is as much as 180 feet long and 90 feet wide, and was originally about 100 feet high.   It is built entirely of brickfaced concrete.

---

[1] Of this upper storey the Ionic columns have been found, but no architraves ; it is probable, therefore, that it was covered with a timber roof with projecting eaves.

[2] A more recent theory maintains that the central space was unroofed (Sogliano in *Memorie dell'Accademia di Napoli*, Nuova serie, Vol. II (1913), part I, pp. 117-129).   The basilica at Palestrina, which was certainly roofed, should therefore not be cited as a parallel. (*Papers of the British School at Rome*, IX, 225).

PLATE XL

MAUSOLEUM OF CONSTANTIA (S. COSTANZA).

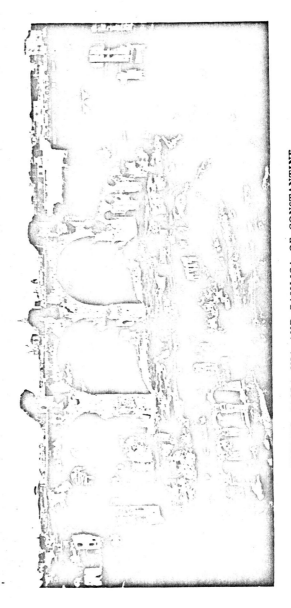

EARLIER SACRA VIA AND BASILICA OF CONSTANTINE.

THEATRES.

The tendency in the later development of the Greek theatres was to bring the stage forward into the orchestra, so as to place the actors nearer to the spectators. In the Roman theatre the orchestra was reduced to a semi-circle, on the diameter of which was the front of the stage. In the old Italic theatre from which the Roman theatre was derived there was no chorus, so that the stage was always slightly raised. At first the spectators stood, and then sat parallel to it, and the orchestra and auditorium were only added later from the Greek type of theatre (Fiechter, *Baugeschichtliche Entwickelung der Antiken Theaters*, 75). This work should be considered for information in regard to the architecture of the ancient theatre. He divides its development into five stages (p. 84) :—

1. Primitive stage—no seats.
2. Stage with space behind ; seats in front.
3. Combination of the two into a rectangular building.
4. Rectangular building with curved seats.
5. Open semi-circular building after Greek plan but with Roman construction and façade.

The greatest change, however, is found in the scæna, which was raised to a great height[1] and decorated with great sumptuousness. The Greek theatre was generally excavated in the side of a hill, so that no substructure was required for the rising tiers of seats in the auditorium. The Romans occasionally availed themselves of similar opportunities, as found in the theatres of Asia Minor and Syria. In Rome, however, the introduction of vaulting enabled the Roman architect to build tier above tier of corridors, with staircases leading to the various parts of the theatre. These corridors, whilst serving as communication between the staircases, were probably used as refuges in case of heavy rain, and that is suggested by the fact that in most of the theatres excavated in the side of a hill there are great porticoes which might be used for that purpose.

---

[1] The proscænium of the Greek theatre (cf. Fiechter, p. 100 : Fig. 7, from *Amer. Journ. Arch.*, VII, Pl. XI—Theatre at Eretria) was abolished ; it has no connexion with the Roman *scænæ frons*, inasmuch as its colonnade stood, not behind, but under the stage, which it supported. The origin of the decoration of the *scænæ frons* is, however, Hellenistic (the back of the stage having large openings in which paintings gave an idea of a distant perspective), as we learn from a study of the paintings of Pompeii ; but it became more and more magnificent as time went on. Little or no scenery was therefore required except scenes hung on to the back wall (Fiechter, 118).

The outer corridors on the several tiers were lighted by open arcades, the walls between being decorated with columns of the Doric, Ionic and Corinthian orders, one above the other. That which was first designed and developed as a constructive feature became one of the finest architectural compositions it was possible to devise, and, coarse as are the mouldings of the Colosseum and incorrect the relative proportions of the orders, there is no more impressive monument in the world. The only example existing of a theatre in Rome is that of Marcellus (Fig. 21), already referred to (see p. 44). Unfortunately, the two lower storeys only remain, the upper portion having been rebuilt for other purposes, and whether there was a third arcade or a blank wall with engaged Corinthian pilasters is not known. The substructures of the auditorium exist, and have been measured; but nothing remains of the scæna, so that reference must be made to other examples to determine its structural and decorative treatment. The theatre at Orange, sadly defective as regards its auditorium, still retains its scæna wall to its full height, and

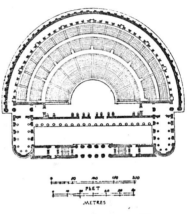

FIG. 21.—PLAN OF THE THEATRE OF MARCELLUS.

sufficient of the returns on either side to show that whilst in the Greek theatres there was a complete break between the scæna and the auditorium (so far as enclosure walls were concerned), in the Roman theatre the two were brought into one architectural whole. Fiechter (*op. cit.* 83) traces this to the prototype of the Roman theatre—the rectangular wooden roofed theatre, the seats of which were originally parallel to the stage. The stage was deep and low, not narrow and high as in Greece, and was framed by side walls—derived again from its rectangular prototype.

The total width of the theatre at Orange was 343 feet, inclusive of walls; the stage being 203 feet wide, and 42 feet deep. In the side wings next to the stage were staircases, and beyond these, on the right and left, halls about 40 feet square, which seem on the ground and first floor to have been " foyers " for retreat in case of rain. In

the rear of the stage, and running the whole width of the theatre, was an immense portico for the same purpose. Vitruvius (v. 9) refers to these porticoes which should be built " behind the scenes, to which in case of sudden showers the people may retreat from the theatre " ; they were also utilised for the rehearsals of the chorus. Throughout Asia Minor and Syria porticoes always formed essential adjuncts to every theatre. The apsidal halls at the back of the theatre of Marcellus were probably covered vestibules to a terrace behind the long narrow stage. Protection from rain led to the carrying of a sloping roof, with ceiling under, over the whole stage. In the side walls of the theatre at Orange are seen traces of the roof, and on the rear wall the sinkings in which the timbers rested. This roof consisted of ceiling beams rising from the back at an angle of 30°, and forming cantilevers tied in by the rafters of the roof, and partly carried by projecting piers of the scæna wall as at Aspendus. In Caristie's[1] restoration the slanting ceiling is shown as enriched with coffers. Such a construction, 203 feet long, could not have been self-supporting ; at the back of the rear walls, therefore, and carried on corbels, were masts with iron chains attached to the upper timbers of the ceilings. The scæna wall exists to its original height, and the sinkings at various levels show that it was decorated with three storeys of niches flanked by marble columns and entablatures, and these were also carried on the two return walls of the stage. The account of a wooden theatre erected in Rome by M. Scaurus as ædile in 58 B.C., which was large enough to contain 70,000 spectators, shows that the scæna wall was divided into three orders. In order to understand the nature of these decorations it is necessary to examine other examples, and in Asia Minor there are some in which the lower storey of columns still remains. At Aizani, in Asia Minor, the scæna is more or less perfect ; the original building is Hellenistic, but it was altered in Roman times, probably under Hadrian (Fiechter, p. 91); the auditorium was horseshoe in form, and there was no junction between the walls of the auditorium and the stage buildings. The depth of the stage was 20 feet ; and the scæna, 60 feet in length, was decorated by a series of columns standing 6 feet from the wall and carrying a second storey of columns. These columns were arranged in pairs, with doorways between them, the central doorway being flanked by columns of greater size. The lower storey was of the Composite order, the upper

[1] Caristie (A.), *Monuments à Orange*. 1856.

Corinthian, and the covered portico seems to have been under the stage. In still better preservation (when visited by Fellows in 1841) was the theatre of Aspendus (Fig. 22), also in Asia Minor, built by Zeno, the architect, in the reign of Marcus Aurelius. The illustration shows the auditorium with two ranges of seats, twenty-one in the lower and eighteen in the upper, with an arcaded gallery round, as at Bosra, in Syria, and elsewhere. The stage is similar to

FIG. 22.—THE THEATRE OF ASPENDUS

the one described at Orange, and the line of the roof of its ceiling is seen in the illustration, with the sinkings in the rear wall in which the rafters and ceiling beams were fixed. It also shows the decorations of the scæna, the columns only being missing. In a better known example, at Taormina, some of the columns still remain, so that with these three examples the exterior of the theatre of Marcellus, and the upper storey of the Colosseum, it is possible to arrive at a complete conjectural restoration of the Roman theatre.

Of other well-known examples, the Odeion of Herodes Atticus (166 A.D.), at the foot of the Acropolis, and, like the theatre of Dionysus, partly hewn out of the rock, still preserves portions of its outer walls and some of the marble casing of the seats. The roof is stated to have been of cedar wood. This, however, can only refer to that over the stage, which may have resembled those at

PLATE XLVI.

VIEW OF PART OF THE REMAINS OF POMPEII FROM THE SOUTH (FROM A MODEL).

PLATE XLVII.

THE SMALL THEATRE AT POMPEII.

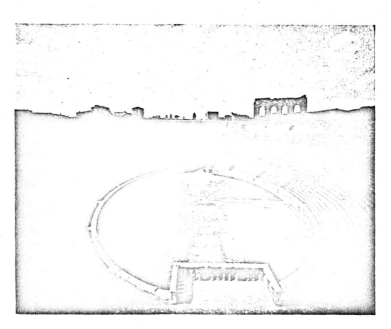

THE AMPHITHEATRE AT VERONA.

Orange and Aspendus, to which we have already referred. Without internal supports, of which there is no evidence, it is impossible that the Romans could have covered over the entire area, which had a diameter of 240 feet.

There were two theatres in Pompeii, both of them partially excavated in the rock. In the large theatre (Plate XLVI) the stage,[1] owing probably to its comparatively small size, is not brought forward as in most Roman theatres, and the seats are carried in parallel lines beyond the diameter of the orchestra. In the smaller theatre (Plate XLVII) nearly all the seats are perfect ; in those of the upper rows the irregularities of the cut rock are made good by fixing slabs of tufa 7 inches thick and 1 foot wide to serve as seats. In both theatres are raised platforms, close to the stage, called tribunals, occupied by the provider or censor of the play. The parapet wall which separates the tribunals from the cavea or ordinary range of seats on each side of the theatre, is terminated by a kneeling figure of Atlas, and at a lower level the favourite device of the winged hind leg of a griffin.

Many other examples of theatres exist in Asia Minor, of which the chief, after Aspendus, already referred to, are Aizani (external diameter 380 feet, stage 156 feet), Side (external diameter 409 feet): Telmessus ; Alinda ; Ægæ; and in Syria those at Amman (external diameter 428 feet, with forty-three rows of seats), Gerasa, where the scæna still remains complete, Shuhba (external walls perfect), and Beisan, said to be the best preserved in Palestine.

AMPHITHEATRES.

It was thought at one time that the Romans derived their amphitheatres from the Etruscans, but the example at Sutri, where the seats, corridors and arena are all cut in the solid rock, is now considered to be of later date than the Colosseum. Again, it has been suggested that the temporary wooden theatres of Curio, 50 B.C., gave the original model. Curio's amphitheatre consisted, according to the description given by Pliny, of two large theatres built in wood and made to run on wheels working on a central pivot (hence the name), so that whilst the two theatres in the morning were used for dramatic representations, in the afternoon they were turned

[1] Recent study has shown that it has some relation with the Hellenistic East, and especially with Antioch (Spano in the periodical cited p. 109, sqq.). Fiechter (op. cit., 77) makes out that it was originally Hellenistic, but Romanized in the first century B.C. by the rebuilding of the stage.

round to constitute an amphitheatre. If that had been so, the earliest amphitheatre would have consisted of two semicircular ends with a rectangular portion between them. This is, however, not the case. The earliest example known, the amphitheatre at Pompeii, which dates from not long after 80 B.C., is elliptical. The arena there would seem to have been excavated, so as to save the expense of a lofty enclosure round the seats. The dimensions were

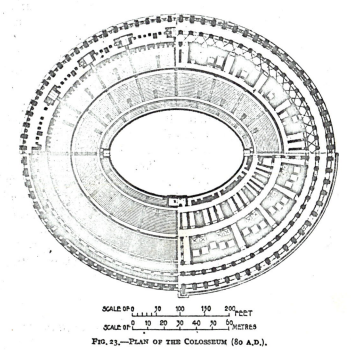

FIG. 23.—PLAN OF THE COLOSSEUM (80 A.D.).

445 feet the major axis, and 341 feet the minor axis—an immense size for a second or third rate provincial town.

The largest amphitheatre[1] is that known as the Colosseum (Plate XLVIII, Figs. 23, 24, 25). Built on the site of Nero's lake, it was commenced by Vespasian, continued by Titus, completed by Domitian, and restored in 222-244 A.D. by Alexander Severus and Gordianus III, and in 249-51 by Decius. The building is elliptical in plan, and measures 620 feet on the longer axis, by 513 feet on the shorter axis. It was raised on two steps in the middle of a great esplanade paved with travertine, the pavement of the

[1] The amphitheatre of Pozzuoli was 10 feet longer but 35 feet narrower.

corridors up to the inner corridor sloping outward, to allow any rain which might beat in to run out. Of the eighty entrances, two of which were reserved for the Emperor and his suite, and two for gladiatorial processions, seventy-six were numbered and gave access

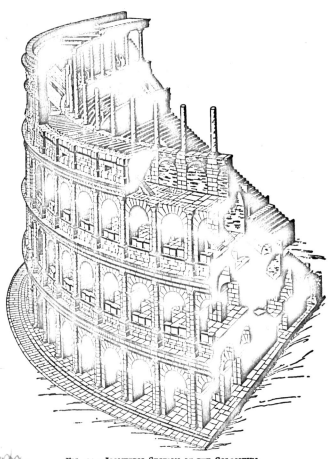

The auditorium of the theatre

FIG. 24.—ISOMETRIC SECTION OF THE COLOSSEUM.

to all parts of the cavea. The cavea was divided into three parts—the podium, a terrace 11½ feet wide; then the main part of the cavea, which was divided into two zones, separated by a passage, and consisted of marble seats reaching up to the bottom of the third external order; then came a wall with doors, windows and niches, and above it a covered colonnade with a flat roof, under

which were wooden seats,[1] while there were doubtless seats on the
roof of it also.   The approaches to the various seats are extremely
well arranged.   Access was given by staircases built between walls
radiating to the arena corridors under the cavea, by passages
between the ranges of seats, and by steps below the seats, the latter
being divided into wedges (*cunei*).   In the lower portion the staircases radiate to the arena ;   in the upper they are parallel to the
outer wall.   Generally the lowest range of seats were occupied by
the more distinguished citizens ; the second by the middle class ; the
third by the poor and by women.   The total number of spectators
cannot have been more than about 45,000.   The whole of the exterior and the principal corridors were built in travertine stone in
large blocks carefully jointed, set without mortar, and secured with
iron clamps run in with lead ;   the inner walls were built of travertine at the points of greatest strain, forming a skeleton extending
as far as the top of the second storey, and elsewhere of sperone,
tufa and concrete, with brick facing ;   and all corridors, staircases
and substructures carrying marble seats were vaulted in concrete.
The two principal entrances, one on each side, were reserved for the
Emperor and his court, ministers and foreign ambassadors, and led
to a platform (Pulvinar) raised above the other seats and protected by a wall on each side.   The arena measured 287 feet by
180 feet, and was surrounded by a wall 15 feet high, with iron grille
and other protection on the top.   The excavations undertaken by
the French in 1811-13, revealed the existence of numerous passages
round the centre communicating with the dens in which the wild
beasts were shut up ; putlog holes exist in the walls of the passages
under the arena in which joists carrying a series of inclined planes
were provided leading from the dens to the arena level, and arrangements for lifts were also to be seen.   The floor of the arena was
carried on joists also.   The system of drainage consists of a series
of drains radiating outwards.   Similar underground arrangements
had long been known at Capua and other amphitheatres.

The exterior is divided into four storeys, the three lower ones
being pierced with a series of arches of equal dimensions, forming,
as it were, a continuous arcade round the building, and divided by

[1] This is the reconstruction adopted by Uggeri and Hülsen, and is justified
by the presence of windows on the fourth storey, which lighted a vaulted
corridor placed behind the colonnade, but would have no *raison d'etre* were
Canina's restoration correct.   The restoration given by Gaudet is wrong in
placing the colonnade too high ;   it should rest direct on the wall, with doors,
windows and niches.

PLATE XLVIII.

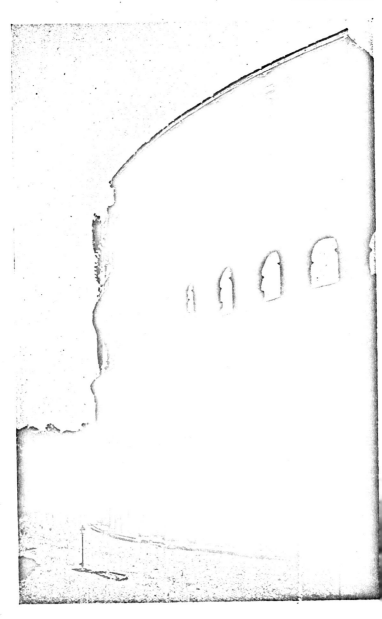

THE COLOSSEUM AT ROME.

PLATE XLIX.

RESTORATION OF THE CENTRAL HALL OF THE
BATHS OF CARACALLA.

three-quarter detached columns of the Tuscan,[1] Ionic, and Corinthian orders, superposed on the respective storeys, and carrying each a complete entablature, the architraves of which are voussoired and carried back into the solid wall. The upper storey is unpierced except by small windows lighting the corridor underneath the upper range of seats or gallery, and its wall is decorated with Corinthian pilasters on lofty pedestals superposed on the other

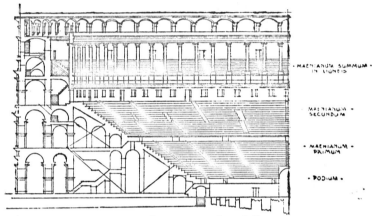

FIG. 25.—SECTION OF THE COLOSSEUM.

orders below. Above the windows outside are three projecting corbels in each bay to carry the masts of the velarium, (the awning by which the auditorium was shaded), which rise through the cornice, while inside there are corbels, which carried flat arches, forming a terrace for the sailors whose duty it was to attend to the *velarium.* The proportion of the lowest order is poor and meagre, the column being 9 diameters high and 7½ diameters centre to centre. In consequence of the height of the vault over the ground floor corridor the pavement of the corridor above is raised considerably above the cornice of the order, and a podium or plinth is introduced, the cornice of which ranges with the first floor pavement ; a similar arrangement exists on the next floor. Under the columns the mouldings of the plinth return on each side, and constitute pedestals, and it may be in consequence of this arrangement that the Ionic column is only 8½ diameters in height, as also the Corinthian column above. The results are very fine, and compensate for the

---

[1] There are no triglyphs in the frieze of the lower order, the capitals have Etruscan mouldings, and the bases are Etruscan.

poorness of the ground storey. In order to afford protection to the first and second floor corridors, solid balustrades are carried within the imposts of the arcades.

The complete entablature of each order is carried round without a break, and this and the sturdy nature of the three-quarter detached columns give a monumental effect to the Colosseum which it would be impossible to rival. The applied decoration of the orders, their superposition, and the jointing of the architraves, in principle are all wrong, and should be condemned ; but the portions of the external wall which remain, rising to their full height of 157 feet, and the splendid nature of the masonry, disarm all criticism and constitute the Colosseum as one of the most sublime efforts of Roman architecture.

The velarium, the stretching of which was done by sailors who were placed on the roof of the peristyle gallery round, extended over the whole of the space reserved for the spectators. The arena was certainly omitted, for there are arrangements for fixing the poles at the lower end all round the edge of it ; and it is most likely that this enormous awning was made in strips and not in one piece.

A second example in Rome, the Amphitheatrum Castrense, was built not earlier than the second century[1], perhaps for the soldiers of the imperial palace close by. It was built of concrete and faced with brick, with brick pilasters and Corinthian capitals in moulded terracotta built in courses ranging with the bricks. Originally there were three storeys, the two lower ones with arcades, as shown in a drawing by Palladio in the Burlington-Devonshire Collection (see also *Topographical Study in Rome in* 1581, Roxburghe Club, 1916. Among other amphitheatres of importance taken in order of dimension, are those of Capua, Verona, El Djem, Pola, Arles, Nimes, and Pompeii. The amphitheatre at Verona (Plate XLVII) has preserved nearly the whole of its stone seats, but retains only four bays of its external walls. In the example at Pola, on the other hand, the external walls exist, but the seats have all gone, though their foundations still existed in the eighteenth century[2]. In both these cases the masonry is rusticated, with flat pilasters only between the arcades, so that the superposed orders are not sufficiently emphasised and the general effect is poor.

---

[1] Hülsen (*Romische Topographie*, i, 3, 249), conjectures that it may have been built by Trajan, and Van Deman agrees; (*A.J.A.*, xvi (1912), 417).

[2] Durm. (*op. cit.*, p. 689), notes that they were drawn by Stuart and Revett (pt. 15, pl. X).

In the amphitheatre at Pola there are, on the diagonal axes, four projecting bays, 43 feet wide and 10 feet projection, forming on the ground storey open arcades, and containing staircases in the two upper storeys.

In the amphitheatre at Nîmes there were only two storeys and an attic which supported the masts for thevel arium. The lower storey had three-quarter detached piers, and above three-quarter detached columns of the Doric order. The floor of the first storey arcade was level with the cornice, and the mouldings of the entablature on both storeys break round the pilasters and columns. The arch of the arcade of the upper storey is carried as a barrel vault across the corridor, which has a fine external effect, but destroys the continuity of the corridor.

The amphitheatre of El Djem (Thysdrus), south of Carthage in North Africa, ranks next in size to the example at Verona, and was evidently built in imitation of the Colosseum, though it differs from it in the orders employed for the three arcaded storeys, the first and the third storey being decorated with Corinthian columns, and the second storey with those of the Composite order. The intercolumniation, nine and a half diameters, is so wide that it scarcely carried out the principles of the Roman order as already described, and the columns being semi-detached only, have not the vigour and boldness of the Colosseum design. On the other hand, the masonry is of great excellence. The stones were obtained from a quarry 20 miles distant, and all the courses are of the same height, viz., 20 inches. The building was erected by the Emperor Gordianus III, but was never completed. There were sixty-four arches, and three storeys rose to a height of 85 feet. The fourth or attic storey required to carry the velarium was commenced on the inner wall of the external gallery, but never terminated.

THE STADIUM.

In imitation probably of the Greek stadium, Domitian built an example in the Campus Martius, of which one of the piers was discovered in the Piazza Navona, which now occupies its site and preserves almost exactly its shape and size, and perpetrates its plan. Its seating capacity is estimated at about 15,000. The so-called Stadium of Domitian on the Palatine was in reality a garden.

N

The Roman Circus.

There are scanty remains of the Circus Maximus, built in the valley between the Palatine and Aventine Hills, and dominated by the Palaces of the Cæsars on the north side; the valley was drained (as was that of the Forum) as soon as the original settlement of the Palatine expanded into the City of the Seven Hills, and set aside for public games and sports.   The seats were at first of wood, but

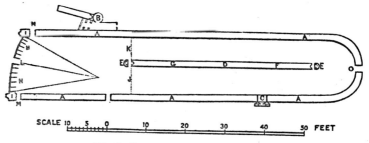

SCALE 10   5   0   10   20   30   40   50   FEET

FIG. 26.—PLAN OF THE CIRCUS OF MAXENTIUS.

were frequently destroyed by fire.   The restoration by Augustus after a fire in 31 B.C. seems to have been of permanent importance. The area measured about 2,000 feet in length by about 460 feet in width, and could hold 380,000 spectators.

The circus of Nero was destroyed by Constantine in the fourth century.

Of the circus of Romulus, built by Maxentius 311 A.D. (Fig. 26), there still exist sufficient remains to determine the plan, the arrangement of the seats, the spina, carceres, and the Emperor's tribune. The area covered was 1,620 feet long by 245 feet wide, and the spina was 1,000 feet in length.

O

CHAPTER VI.

THE THERMÆ OR BATHS.

THE term Thermæ is given to those immense bathing establishments built by the Emperors in order to ingratiate themselves with the people.[1] They were devoted not only to the baths, which were of exceptional size and magnificence, but to every kind of gymnastic pursuit—wrestling, boxing, racing, jumping, etc.—to the training in the same for both youths and athletes, and to various games. Beyond this, the Thermæ were the resort of the poets and philosophers, who held forth and made known that which in our day is printed in the daily newspapers or in books. Here, also, poets and authors could read in public their latest works.

Admission to the men's baths was either free, or very cheap; women paid a somewhat higher price. In some cases there were separate baths for men and women; but in Rome mixed bathing seems to have been prevalent. The bath was considered as a part of the daily routine, and was generally taken in the afternoon after the siesta, but in Rome itself not after sunset until the third century A.D.; though in Pompeii and elsewhere we have evidence of the use of baths after dark. Large private town and country houses had baths of their own (see the Chapter on Private Life).

There has always been some difficulty in assigning the right names and purposes to the several halls, principally owing to the fact that, although baths are frequently mentioned in ancient authors, no adequate description has been given of the various processes which had to be gone through when taking a bath, or of the other purposes of the Thermæ. One of the best illustrated works on the subject is that of the Thermæ of Caracalla, by Abel Blouet,. of the French Academy, published in 1828, and based on

---

[1] Of smaller public baths there are said to have been in Rome over eight hundred.

excavations made in 1824-1826. Iwanoff's Studies (1847-9) were
only published in 1898, with text by Hülsen. A later work by
M. Paulin, 1890, on the Thermæ of Diocletian, contains further
information, and in his conjectural restoration suggests even
greater magnificence than that shown in Blouet. The plans of the
great Thermæ were measured and drawn by Palladio about 1560,
when the remains were far more extensive than at the present day.
These plans were published by Lord Burlington in 1730, and by
Cameron in 1772. The original drawings, which have been deposited
by the Duke of Devonshire in the R.I.B.A. Library, are, however,
of considerable importance notwithstanding, as Palladio sometimes
indulged in arbitrary restorations.

The principal value of the study of the plans of these Thermæ,
however, lies chiefly in the principles observed in the setting out,
and in the aggregation of a number of halls together, of different
dimensions and varied heights, a problem which at the present
day has constantly to be solved, and from this point of view the
actual purpose and use of each hall is of minor importance.

The earliest Thermæ were those built by Agrippa about 20 B.C. in
the Campus Martius, about 200 feet south of the first Pantheon.
They were restored and in part added to chiefly by Hadrian and
Severus, and were preserved till the sixteenth century.[1] Of other
examples sufficient remains exist or have been discovered of those
of Nero (dedicated in 62 A.D. and restored by Alexander
Severus), Titus (79-81 A.D.), Trajan (98-118 A.D.), Caracalla (211-217
A.D.), Diocletian (284-304 A.D.), and Constantine (306-337 A.D.) to
enable fairly accurate conjectural restorations to be made of them.
The most complete are those of Caracalla, whilst of Diocletian's
Thermæ two of the great halls still exist in the Church of S. Maria
degli Angeli, and others are now occupied by the National Museum.

Although in detail the plans of the several Thermæ vary, they
are all set out on the same principle, and as this is best illustrated
in those of Caracalla, its plan may be taken first. Attention has
been already drawn, when speaking of the Forums, to the maintenance of the axis in the scheming out of the plan. This is found in

---

[1] Nothing of what exists can be attributed to the period of Agrippa.
Palladio's reconstruction is in great part fantastic and the large central hall, in
particular, is a pure invention. See Hülsen, *Thermen des Agrippa* (Rome,
1910), 13, who gives the plan as far as it can be recovered from Renaissance
drawings and from existing remains : it is not at all a normal plan but bears
a striking resemblance to that of the larger Thermæ at Treves (Trier), as the
reconstruction by Mr. E. Williams, Jarvis Student of the British School
at Rome, will show.

all the monumental work of the Romans, and can even be followed in the smaller houses at Pompeii. A second principle is the establishment of some central important feature, and the subordination of all the other parts to it. In the Thermæ the *central hall* (*generally, but quite wrongly, called the Tepidarium*)[1], *constituted the nucleus which governed the plan and around which all the other halls and rooms were grouped.*

The main block of the Thermæ of Caracalla (Figs. 27, 28)[2] has an area of about 270,000 square feet—greater than either the Houses of Parliament, the Law Courts or the British Museum. The central hall (No. 2 on plan and Plate XLIX) measures 183 feet by 79 feet in the clear between the brick walls. It was covered with an intersecting barrel vault apparently springing from columns, the function of which was, however, mainly ornamental; the soffit was 108 feet above the pavement of the hall. The hall was divided into three bays, and in order to resist the thrust of the vault on the four central piers,[3] walls 14 to 16 feet wide, were provided on the north side, and extended on the south side to 80 feet in depth by arches thrown across the Tepidarium. The spaces between these walls, on both sides of the central hall, were utilised for baths, and on the side of the Frigidarium were developed into large, semi-circular recesses which constituted very important architectural features. On each side of the Frigidarium, and separated from it by a line of columns, were halls for the spectators of the sports in the cold bath; and again, beyond these, on right and left, were other rooms, some on two floors, which were used either for dressing rooms (*apodyteria*), or for the oiling and sanding of the body. Looking at the comparative importance of a similar room at Pompeii, the entrance and side rooms in this plan would serve better the purpose of the *apodyterium* than that of a library as suggested by Blouet. At the end of the central hall were

---

[1] It has been pointed out by Hülsen that it would have been quite impossible to keep up even a moderate temperature in a hall with so many large openings: and, further, investigations made in 1900 have made it clear that it was not heated, as there are no hypocausts under it.

The name tepidarium must therefore be transferred to a much smaller room between it and the calidarium : and the same applies to the Thermæ of Trajan, Diocletian, etc.

[2] Reproduced from Middleton's *Remains of Ancient Rome*, by permission of the publishers (Messrs. A. & C. Black). For more recent information see *Relazione dell'officio Tewico per la Conservazione dei Monumenti* (Rome, 1903), p. 108, *sqq.*, and Plates I, II, and *Notizie degli Scavi*, 1912, 305.

[3] The thrust at the four angles was amply resisted by walls on the right and left, 108 feet long, and in the front and rear 80 feet and 54 feet respectively

other great halls separated from it by a screen of columns, so that from one end to the other there was a vista of 313 feet. Beyond these were semi-circular halls of considerable height. On the south side of the central hall was the Tepidarium, a comparatively small antechamber to the Calidarium, with two baths in it. The

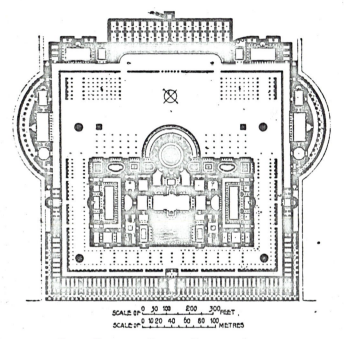

SCALE OF 0 50 100   200   300 FEET
SCALE OF 0 10 20 40   60   80 100 METRES

FIG. 27.—PLAN OF THE BATHS OR THERMÆ OF CARACALLA.

Calidarium was a large circular hall covered with a dome which is about 20 feet too high in Blouet's reconstruction (see on Fig. 28).

The four other rooms on each side of the Calidarium facing the xystus or garden, were probably used by poets and philosophers for recitation, and for conversation. We have still to note the open courts on right and left of the block, with porticoes round them, generally called *pælaestræ*, with separate baths for athletes, in the exedræ of which were found the two mosaics with figures of athletes, now in the Lateran Museum. This completes the main block of the Thermæ of Caracalla.

When we come to compare it with other examples, the theory we have put forward relative to the central hall constituting the nucleus

round which all the other services were grouped will become evident. For the moment we pass on to the immense enclosure in which the block of buildings above described was situated, the entrance to which was on the north-east side. Outside this enclosure was a portico.

Passing through the entrance gate between the walls of these private baths and the central block was a promenade 131 feet wide, which was laid out with alleys of trees. This left an open space at the further end of the site, of about 400 feet in depth and

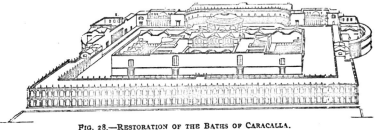

FIG. 28.—RESTORATION OF THE BATHS OF CARACALLA.

1,100 feet long, in which the exercises and games took place. At the farther end of the enclosure, and in front of the series of reservoirs (in two storeys, supplied by the Marcian aqueduct), was the Stadium, where the racing and athletic contests took place. The two halls in the centre of each side were libraries, the niches in the walls serving to contain the presses in which the manuscript books were kept.

To the right and left of the enclosure were projections with semi-circular porticoes, each enclosing a group of rooms, consisting of a room heated by hypocausts (not a piscina), an open portico and an octagonal domed room. In this an interesting example of the spherical pendentive may be seen (Fig. 29); and it also provides, as Rivoira notes (*Roman Architecture*, p. 209), the earliest example of a window in the drum of the dome. The corridor behind perhaps served as an apodyterium.

In front of all these halls there was a colonnade running round three sides of the garden space.

Returning again to the central block; the central hall (Plate XLIX), rising much higher than the adjoining halls, was lighted by clerestory windows above their roofs, and this is generally the case with every group of halls—the central hall always rising higher than the side ones (Plate L) (even when in the latter there are two storeys), and obtaining its light by clerestory windows.   It was always supposed that the Frigidarium was open to the sky, but the discovery of many tons of L or T-shaped iron below the pavement of the bath, bolted together in the form of a St. Andrew's cross, has raised the question as to whether it was not partially covered over by iron girders encased in bronze, answering to the description of the author of the *Vita Caracallæ* (297 A.D.), who referring to the *cella soliaris* says, " Cross beams of brass or copper are said to have been placed on the top, to which the whole ceiling was entrusted, and so great is the span as to make learned mechanicians say that this very construction is impossible."   A more recent interpretation of the name *cella soliaris*, however, based on the discovery of an inscription in North Africa, would make it mean a hall in which there were hot baths for single bathers, so that the reference would be to the *calidarium* (which had such baths, not a central pool) and not to the *frigidarium* at all.   In this case we may take it that our author, writing nearly a century after the construction of the thermæ, is merely repeating a story to account for the huge span of this lofty dome ; for there is no trace of metal girders in the vaulting of the *calidarium*.[1]   Thus it seems very probable that, as in the case of the baths of Diocletian, the Frigidarium was not roofed at all, except for the halls at each end.   The outer wall is without buttresses in both cases and could hardly have supported the weight of a vaulted roof.   The Calidarium had a very lofty dome, which provides the first example known of the use of dolia for lightening its weight.

Before passing to the other Thermæ there are two important points which still require some description, viz., the service of the Thermæ and their heating.   In order to follow the first, it should be noted that the whole of the Thermæ of Caracalla, including the enclosures, were raised on an artificial platform 20 feet high.[2]   The portico to which reference has been made as existing on the main front, and returning some 370 feet along the two sides, was in two storeys, the lower storey on the level of the street, the upper on the level of the platform.   In the centre of the open space between

---

[1] *Mél. Ec. Francaise*, xxix (1909), 40, *Architectural Review*, Oct., 1919 (xlvi., 80) ; *Architectural Water Colours and Etchings of W. Walcot*, 36.

[2] In one instance, on the left of the central block, a chance discovery revealed the remains of a house—which showed that the site was then already occupied—which were covered over and formed part of the substructure of the platform.

the main entrance and the central block was a triple service corridor (see Blouet), 58 feet wide, which was lighted and ventilated by circular openings at the top, these probably covered over by bronze gratings. Similar vaulted corridors were carried on each side of the central block to the farther end of the enclosure, with cross corridors to the open courts and other halls where service was required in the central block. These and vaulted chambers for stores of various

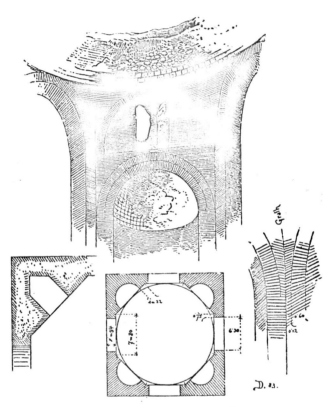

FIG. 29.—DETAILS OF AN OCTAGONAL DOMED ROOM IN THE BATHS OF CARACALLA.

kinds occupied a considerable portion of the artificial platform and at a still lower level ran the outfall drainage system. Corridors for storage also ran under the north-western annexe along the south-west front of the main building (where three of them run side by side) and along the front of the peristyle which surrounded

P

the garden. In fact, the planning of the subterranean portion is no less admirable than that of the superstructure.[1]

The hypocausts of the Thermæ of Caracalla may be best understood by reference to a drawing by Choisy (our Plate XVIII).[2] From 3 to 4 feet below the pavement of the baths, on a bed of concrete, were laid the ordinary Roman tiles (2 feet square and averaging 1¾ inches thick). On this floor were built small piers, 2 feet high, of smaller tiles, 8 inches square. These piers carried a concrete floor about 12 inches in thickness, on which was floated first a layer of pounded tufa and potsherds, and then a thin course of marble cement in which the mosaics were embedded or on which marble slabs were laid. The furnaces, stoked and lighted from the inner courts, were at a lower level than the hypocaust floor, and the smoke and heated air passed under the floor to flues in the walls on the farther side of the several halls. The flues consisted of socket-jointed clay pipes, about 12 inches in diameter. For the halls which required an exceptional heat the walls were virtually lined with these flue pipes. In rooms of smaller size the tile piers were sometimes dispensed with altogether, the whole of the concrete floor resting on ledges or corbels in the wall. Middleton gives one instance in the house of the Vestals where there is a concrete floor 14 inches thick with a bearing of 20 feet. In such cases the floors were filled in on some temporary support of wood planking, which will naturally have left an impression on the under surface of the concrete.

The Thermæ of Diocletian (290 A.D.), (Plates XVII, XLI, L, LII, LIII) resemble very closely those of Caracalla, the principal differences being (1) instead of the hall and hemicycle on the right and left of the central hall there are two halls of equal size ; (2) the Tepidarium is circular, with a circular opening at the top ; (3) the Calidarium is a hall of the same plan as the central hall, with hot baths between the buttresses ; (4) the Frigidarium is two bays wider and was certainly open to the sky ; (5) the entrance to the baths is on the chief front at each end, and consists of a large vestibule leading to the apodyterium ; and (6) the oiling and sanding rooms are placed on each side, at the farthest end of the building. The Thermæ of

---

[1] In one of these halls on the N.W. side of the enclosure a large Mithræum was placed in the third century A.D.

[2] Where piers of tiles were used, there was generally (if not always) a layer of square 2-foot tiles between them and the under side of the concrete floor, as shown in the drawing.

PLATE L.

SECTION THROUGH THE CENTRAL HALL OF THE THERMAE OF TRAJAN, AS RESTORED
BY CHARLES A. LECLERC.

PLATE LI.

TEPIDARIUM OF THE BATHS OF THE FORUM AT POMPEII.

STUCCO CEILING OF THE TOMB OF THE VALERII ON THE
VIA LATINA NEAR ROME.

Diocletian are remarkable, according to Rivoira,[1] both as summing up the principles of construction and statics attained by the architects of Imperial Rome, and as the inspiration of the builders of succeeding ages.

He mentions the system of thrusts and counter-thrusts which may be seen in the central hall (now the Church of S. Maria degli Angeli)—the pierced flying or ramping buttresses which may also[2] be seen in the Basilica of Constantine,[3] the rectangular buttresses on the eastern face, enclosing stairs, and the chambers with quadripartite vaulting, strongly ribbed, which close the two ends of the hall ; and finally, the surrounding of the Tepidarium with four towers containing staircases, two circular and two rectangular, which last serve also as the outer buttresses of the central hall.

In the Thermæ of Trajan (Fig. 30, Plate L) the Frigidarium was much larger than that of Caracalla, and was enclosed with a peristyle on three sides. The central hall and the halls on the southwest side are similar to those of the Thermæ of Diocletian, and in the central hall we have the earliest example known of concrete cross vaulting supported by columns, though we find simple vaulting resting in columns in the Œcus Corinthius of the Casa delle Nozze d'Argento at Pompeii. The vaulted hemicycles (the earliest examples known) are placed on the extreme right and left of the central block, beyond the peristyle court. In front of the central block, on each side, is a circular room, with a bath in the centre similar to that described in the baths at Pompeii as the Frigidarium, and on the right and left of the latter are the private baths. The enclosure in which the main block is built is not so large as in the Thermæ of Caracalla. Passing through the entrance gateway, we enter the north peristyle of the Frigidarium, and the corridor is carried to the right and left, affording covered access to various halls, to two great hemicycles with circular promenades in the rear, and to other private baths. On each side of the central block there were wide promenades with bosquets, with exedræ or semicircular marble seats and avenues of trees. The Stadium, at the farther end (built over part of the Golden House of Nero), was semi-circular. In this case, as also in the Thermæ of Constantine, on the right and left of the enclosure were a series of halls and two other hemicycles.

---

[1] *Roman Architecture*, 204 *sqq.*
[2] It is the only large ancient interior (except the Pantheon) still existing in Rome in a good state of preservation.
[3] The prototype may be traced in the Forum of Trajan.

Among the other Thermæ, in those of Nero and Constantine, the central hall constitutes the principal hall round which the other services are grouped, the longitudinal and transverse axes of the central hall being the leading lines of the setting out in all cases. In the Thermæ of Titus the central hall takes the form of a cross with an intersecting barrel vault.

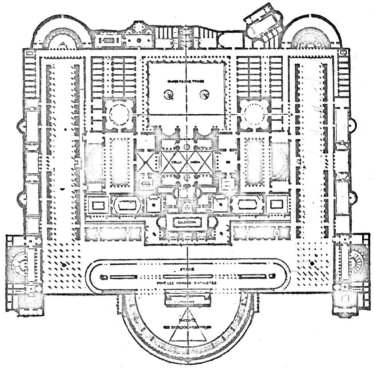

Fig. 30.—Plan of the Baths of Trajan as Restored by Charles A. Leclere.

The architectural decoration of the Thermæ in its nature and in the principles of its design seems to have been so similar in all the examples quoted that no separate description of each is required. Palladio seems to have confined his attention to the main forms of structure, including only the columns which formed essential constructional features, so that all appear to be the same in the series of elevations and sections given.   There is no doubt that in many cases Palladio's sections are purely conjectural, and indicate only a type of vaulting which he conceived likely to have been adopted

when comparing them with other plans of similar design. It was reserved, therefore, for the students of the French Academy to publish in two important works the most complete sets of drawings of two of the Thermæ, already referred to, showing the actual remains existing and conjectural restorations, which not only corroborate one another so far as the decoration of the Thermæ is concerned, but suggest the type which was adopted in Roman monumental edifices of the third and fourth centuries after Christ.

With regard to the decoration of the principal halls and courts we may note that the series of two or three tiers of niches, flanked by marble columns carried on corbels and supporting entablature and pediment, were securely fixed to the wall by these corbels and by the entablature blocks built into the wall (Plate L). These solid blocks of marble being sunk two feet into the wall, must have been built-in whilst the carcase was being constructed. Owing to their height, many of these marble blocks have escaped the plunderer and some still exist in the outer walls of the Church of S. Maria degli Angeli. Again, all the niches were regularly constructed in brick of the required depth. These facts proved that the whole design was conceived by the architect prior to the commencement of the work, and that as soon as the plan was set out, it ruled the whole of the structure both constructively and decoratively.

For this reason it is not necessary to describe each set of Thermæ separately, nor is any lengthy account required. The columns employed throughout the Thermæ were generally of marble, as also their entablatures; the shafts of the same, whether large or small, were all monoliths, and of various kinds. The great shafts of the central hall of Caracalla, 38 feet high and 5 feet 4 inches in diameter, were in granite; others of smaller size were of porphyry, oriental alabaster, giallo antico, and numerous other marbles from the Greek islands. The larger columns supported the vaults or the floors of the balconies overlooking the central hall, or formed screens between the halls; they likewise constituted the frontage to the halls round the xystus, or carried the roofs of the numerous peristyles, so that they were all constructional features. The smaller columns of the niches and the whole of the marble facings were decorative, and were not fixed till after the completion of the carcase. The halls and courts were all paved with marble mosaic in diverse patterns, with figures of gladiators, athletes, tritons, and geometrical designs and borders. The steps, linings of baths, seats, bases, capitals, entablature, etc., were all in white marble. The walls were lined with marble of various colours and panelled like those of the Pantheon, up to a certain height, and above that in white marble up to the springing of the vault. The upper portion of the walls and the vaults were decorated in stucco with arabesque ornament. The internal decoration of a Roman tomb may give some idea of this ornamentation (Plate LI), for it is noticeable that while the scale of the buildings increased, that of the decoration was not adapted to it for some time, and indeed appears to have re mained under the influence of the style used in the columbaria of the early first century A.D.[1] The paintings in the Golden House of Nero, for instance, are so minute in proportion to the height of the rooms that the details must have been invisible. As in the larger vaults, such as those of the central hall, the inner lining was already of tiles (for the constructive reasons given in Chapter II), it was not possible to have the deep coffers like those constructed in brick in the aisles of the Basilica of Constantine. The panels, in consequence, could not be of any depth, and were therefore filled with glass mosaic, to accentuate the small figure subjects, which otherwise, at their great height, would not have been distinguishable. Blouet contents himself with reproductions of the panel subjects found in the Roman tombs and at Pompeii ; whilst Paulin suggests large figure subjects in mosaic (Plates LII and LIII)[2] for both walls and vaults. The walls enclosing the Frigidarium were decorated with tier above tier of niches, flanked by columns carrying entablatures and pediments, circular as well as triangular. The existence of these in the Thermæ of Diocletian is shown by the niches sunk in the brickwork and by the marble corbels ; Paulin's restoration is corroborated by the drawings of an Italian artist of about 1475 A.D. in the Uffizi Collection, Florence, published in the Baron de Geymuller's work. These represent not only the niches, but the actual decoration of the immense buttresses of the central hall.[3]

Whilst in the interior of the Thermæ the decorations in marble

---

[1] See my remarks on the columbarium style in *Papers of the British School at Rome*, vii, 123.

[2] Plates LII and LIII are reproduced from M. Paulin's fine work, entitled *Les Thermes de Diocletien.*

[3] A further corroboration of Paulin's restoration of these buttresses will be found in drawings by Palladio in the Burlington-Devonshire Collection, now in the R.I.B.A., with the exception of the crowning feature, which is shown as a solid buttress and without the canopy drawn by Paulin.

PLATE LII.

SECTION THROUGH THE CENTRAL HALL, BATHS OF DIOCLETIAN IN ROME.

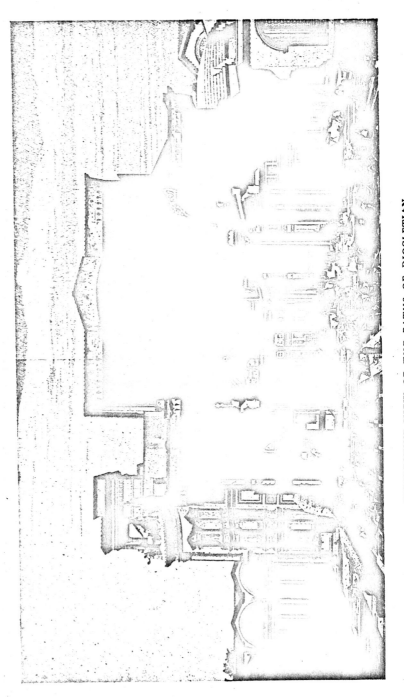

PERSPECTIVE VIEW OF THE BATHS OF DIOCLETIAN.

and mosaic were of the most elaborate and sumptuous character, the Romans do not appear to have attached the same value to the external appearance, and they contented themselves with covering the walls with the fine stucco we have already described, which, from its resemblance to marble and its great durability, required only the imitation joints of stone to give it a certain monumental character. This is the type of wall surface which has been adhered to by Paulin in his conjectural restoration of the outer walls of the Thermæ of Diocletian,[1] and the same was probably adopted to protect and decorate the concrete walls faced with brick which from the time of Augustus, became the favourite method of construction in Rome. Even the upper portion of the Pantheon and the pilasters decorating the upper storey were coated with stucco. A divergence from this custom has been pointed out by Blouet, who found the remains of stucco, 3 inches thick, inlaid with mosaics, which covered the upper portion of the front of the central block of the Thermæ of Caracalla. Sufficient existed to show that the decoration adopted was that which was found in the Thermæ of Trajan, and is better known to us by the paintings in Pompeii, representing imaginary courts with porticoes and verandahs, such as may have been derived from the ephemeral decorations of the solaria or terrace roofs of the houses. This type of design is shown in the conjectural restorations by Blouet of the external wall of the central block facing the xystus, and in Paulin's interior of the sphæristerium. The lower portion of the walls of the central block Blouet considers to have been faced with marble, so as to accord in richness with the granite columns of the various halls facing the xystus. All the other walls, which were partially hidden by the groves of trees, were simply covered with stucco.

But few remains have been found in Rome of the smaller public baths, but in Pompeii there are three examples more or less completely preserved, and therefore of great interest. The "older Thermæ," north of the Forum (so called because they were the first discovered), included, besides a complete establishment for men, a small set of baths for women; the hot rooms of both were heated by the same furnace, in accordance with Vitruvius's description (v. 10). They covered an area of about 171 feet square, exclusive of shops, which occupied two sides of the enclosure, and consisted

---

[1] The Curia Julia, restored by Diocletian, in the Forum, was certainly decorated externally in this way, and so was the Basilica of Constantine.

of an open court with peristyle on three sides, a vestibule, ante-
room, Apodyterium, Frigidarium, Tepidarium, and Calidarium.
Of these, the most interesting is the Tepidarium (Plate LI), which
has preserved its vault richly decorated in stucco, and a series of
niches sunk in the wall round the room, the piers between being
decorated with figures of miniature Atlantes, 2 feet high.   There
was no hypocaust under the room, and it was heated apparently
by charcoal in a large bronze brazier found *in situ*.   The Calidarium
was heated by a hypocaust and flue tiles in the walls.   It consisted
of a hall 42 feet by 16 feet wide, with a barrel vault decorated in
stucco, and a semi-circular recess at the farther end which originally
held the labrum ; above the same, in the vault of the recess, being
an opening which could be shut or closed at pleasure.   The other
end of the Calidarium was occupied by an oblong bath.

The Stabian baths, discovered in 1857, were the oldest, having
been erected towards the close of the second century B.C., though
remodelled in later times.   They covered an area of about 164 feet
square, including a court 100 feet long by 70 feet wide, sufficiently
large, therefore, for various exercises.   The two large stone balls
which were found lying in the court were used for games (perhaps
a sort of bowls).   The peristyle was on two sides only ; on the third
were rooms opening into the court, which may have been used for
exercises or games in bad weather ; on the fourth side[1] was a swimming bath 50 feet wide, and 6 feet 6 inches deep, which in the Roman
Thermæ would have constituted the Frigidarium, a title which here
is given to a circular room covered with a conical roof with opening
at the top, and fitted with a central circular tank with marble
linings and seats round.   The conical roof was plastered over,
painted blue and studded with gold stars.   The same kind of Frigidarium existed in the Forum baths.   Here the square niches in the
wall are found in the Apodyterium, where they would seem to be of
more use.   The labrum, consisting of a circular marble basin
resting on a stone pedestal, still exists in the Calidarium, as also the
oblong bath at the other end of the hall.   Apparently these baths
were originally heated by braziers only, and in the restoration
of the first century A.D. hypocausts were introduced beneath the

[1] Plate LXXXV shows the south end of the south-west wall, which was
decorated with reliefs in stucco representing those architectural fancies to
which Vitruvius (Bk. 7, chap. 5) takes such great exception.   He condemns
them when painted even, but executed as they are in relief, they would have
troubled him still more had they been carried out during his lifetime.

floors of the Tepidarium and Calidarium, and the walls of the latter were doubled with flue tiles. As in the other example, there was a separate and smaller set of baths for women, both sets heated from the same furnace. The third establishment, known as the Central Baths, was in course of erection at the time of the eruption, and is interesting therefore as showing the latest developments. It occupied about the same area as the Stabian baths, but the porticus round the open court had not been built. Here the swimming bath stands outside in the open court, as in the Roman Thermæ. The circular room in this case was arranged for heating with hypocaust flue tiles, and was probably intended for the laconicum, as described by Vitruvius (v. 10). The circular room in the Stabian baths was covered over with a conical roof, built in masonry laid in horizontal courses. The dimensions of this room are small, but as no centering was required there could have been no difficulty in its erection, and it might possibly account for the construction of the hemispherical dome of the Pantheon described on p. 80, where the bricks were laid in horizontal beds. The two circular halls in the baths of Trajan, were probably roofed in the same way.

CHAPTER VII.

ARCHES OF TRIUMPH, AQUEDUCTS, BRIDGES, TOMBS.

THE Roman monumental arch (the term triumphal arch only occurs quite late in the Roman period) consists of a large freestanding base for statues, bas-reliefs and inscriptions (either of the Emperor, of members of the Imperial family, or of private individuals) pierced by one or more passage ways, and placed generally over a road. The façades visible from the road are decorated with pilasters or columns, which, until about the time of Hadrian, were engaged, but at no time had any real structural value, and served to frame the decoration of the openings. In a few cases city gates have the form and decoration of monumental arches; and in other cases an earlier arch has been included in the line of a later city wall. Thus in the two gateways at Verona we find a series of enrichments in the form of semi-detached columns and shafts, and pilasters carrying pediments within pediments, enclosing semi-circular openings, which are quite inconsistent with the object of defence.[1] We have Pliny's testimony that the use of columns to carry honorary statues had been in vogue in Rome long before arches began to be used for the purpose; so that the usual assumption that triumphal arches derive their origin from primitive constructions in wood is not justified. Indeed, the representations on coins of the Arches of Trajan and Domitian suggest that they were regarded primarily as pedestals to carry large groups of sculp-

---

[1] There were in fact earlier structures included in the line of the city walls by Gallienus in 265 A.D. (the arch of the Gavii is now attributed to the end of the Republic, and would thus be the earliest triumphal arch known (Anti in *Architettura ed Arti Decorative*, I (1921-2), 122 *sqq.*). See Curtis, *Roman Monumental Arches* in *Supplementary Papers of the American School of Classical Studies in Rome*, II (1908), 26 *sqq.*, with a revision and correction of two earlier lists (Graef in Baumeister's *Denkmaler*, art. Triumph-Ehrenbögen and Frothingham in *Amer. Journ. Archæol.*, VIII (1904), 1. I have taken it as a guide in the present chapter.

PLATE LIV.

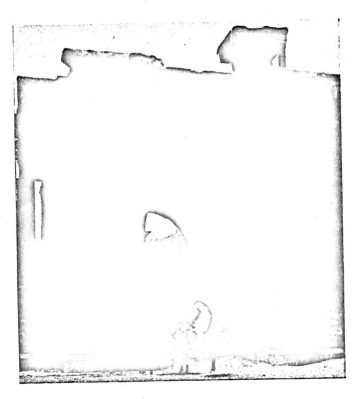

EAST FRONT OF THE ARCH OF CARACALLA AT
TEBESSA (THEVESTE), NORTH AFRICA.

PLATE LV.

ARCH OF TITUS AT ROME.

ARCH AT AQUINUM.

ture ; the central feature consisting of a triumphal car with four to six horses, or, as in the Arch of Domitian, with elephants ; in both cases flanked with statues.

But few arches of the Republican period are known to us even in literature, and we have not even the fragments formerly attributed to the Arch of Fabius in the Forum at Rome, since these have re-rently been assigned to the portico of Nero's Golden House (p. 134). We may therefore begin with the Arch of Augustus at Rimini (27 B.C.), erected to celebrate his restoration of the principal highways of Italy, which forms a link between gates and arches, inasmuch as, while its sides were connected with the city wall, the similarity of its outer and inner façade and the variety of orna-mental detail give it a monumental character. It is a single arch of very fine proportions ; we may note the great size of the voussoirs, the impost moulding without angle supports, as well as medallions in the spandrels and the small tympanum over the arch, a sign of an early date. It served Alberti as a model for the façade of the cathedral (1450). The Arches of Aosta and Aquinum (Plate LV), in both of which we may note the com-bination of capital and impost moulding, may be connected in date with it ; while that of Susa (9-8 B.C.), a simple, though dignified structure, is the first which has the frieze decorated with reliefs (Plate LVI). They represent the conclusion of an alliance between Augustus and Cottius, who was made præfect of the Alpine tribes of the district, over which his father had ruled as king. The bases of the pilasters supporting the archivolt are on a level with the base of the pedestals of the columns.

Besides a number of smaller arches in Italy and France,[1] the arch at Orange (Plate LVI) is also to be attributed to the Augustan, period. The beginning of an inscription in honour of Tiberius has been made out, the bronze letters of which were affixed after the monument was completed, inasmuch as they cover the decorations of the architrave.[2]

It is thus the earliest example of an arch with three openings, the

---

[1] That of Fano dates from 9-10 A.D. It has two side passages and serves also as an entrance gate to the town.

[2] It has been placed very much later on stylistic grounds (e.g., in the pre-vious editions of the present work), but to go as far as German critics do, and to say that "the architect cannot follow the dating given by the epigraphist" is tantamount to throwing overboard the evidence of contemporary documents, and sets up an arbitrary method of subjective criticism, which, if generally applied, would lead to utter chaos (Durm., *op. cit.*, 725, 727, cf., Senz, *Jahrbuch des Instituts*, III (1888), 1).

smaller passage ways being doubtless transformed niches, which were made to serve for the convenience of foot passengers. The general heaviness of the proportions, owing to the addition of an extra storey (rendered necessary by the fact that the pediments were carried up into the attic) is probably an indication of early date, as are the pediments themselves. Among the unique features of the arch is the elaborate decoration of the sides, which bear, in addition to the angle columns, two similar columns ; they also have a tympanum above the columns (the ends of which destroy the line of the cornice on the front) and are decorated with reliefs. The semi-engaged columns between the arches and the three-quarter detached columns at the angles are raised on pedestals and are all Corinthian.

The reign of Tiberius provides us with the earliest example (17 A.D.) of an arch with two passage ways, at Saintes, in France. Only one other example is known, at Announa in N. Africa (third century, A.D.)[1], though in town gates the type is familiar enough, and there are sometimes two lateral arches for foot passengers as in the Porta Augustea at Nîmes. Otherwise there are almost no arches of the first century A.D. remaining until we come to the Arch of Titus on the Sacra Via in Rome (Plate LV), erected in 82 A.D., after his death, to commemorate the taking of Jerusalem. There is only one central archway, and the columns which flank it, and those on the angles, are only semi or three-quarter detached, so that they form part of the actual core of the structure, and are not purely decorative adjuncts as in the Arch of Constantine. The ornamental faces of the pilasters supporting the impost are now turned towards the passage-way instead of towards the façades. The beauty of the figure sculpture is greatly enhanced by the simplicity of the masonry[1] throughout, when contrasted with that of the Arches of Constantine and Septimius Severus. The barrel vault of the archway is sunk with deep coffers and enrichments, in the centre being a relief of the apotheosis of Titus. The famous reliefs on each side below the vault represent on one side the Emperor drawn in his triumphal car led by Roma and crowned by Victory, and on the other the spoils taken from the Temple of Jerusalem. The execution of the sculptures in the frieze is far inferior. The columns decorating the archway are of the Composite Order, and are the earliest examples

---

[1] The sides were restored in 1822, the arch having been up till that time embedded in mediæval fortifications.

PLATE LVI.

ARCH OF TIBERIUS AT ORANGE.

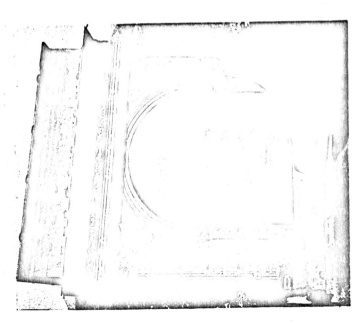

ARCH OF AUGUSTUS AT SUSA.

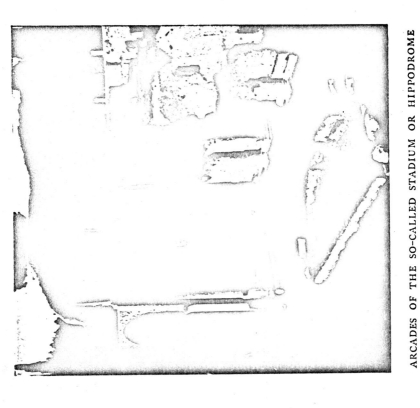

ARCADES OF THE SO-CALLED STADIUM OR HIPPODROME
ON THE PALATINE.

FRIEZE AND KEYSTONE OF THE ARCH
OF TITUS.

PLATE LVIII.

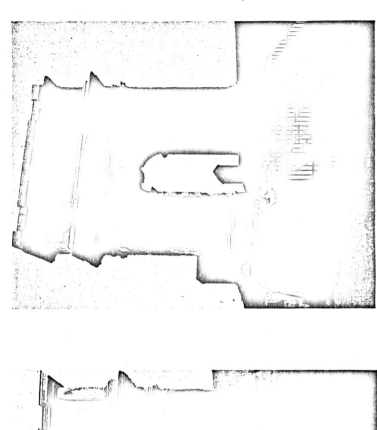

PLATE LIX.

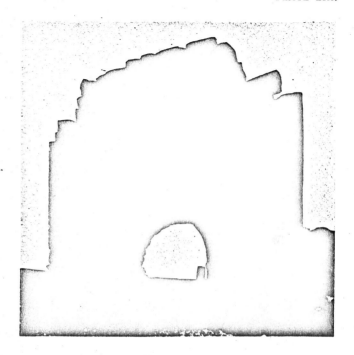

ARCH OF TRAJAN AT MAKTAR.

SO-CALLED ARCH OF TRAJAN AT TIMGAD.

known of its employment in Rome. As the entablature is carried across between the two central columns, some visible support seemed to have been required in the centre, and this was met by the accentuation of the keystone and its projection beyond the plane of the architrave (Plate LVII). The figures carved on the keystones are those of Roma on one side of the arch, and of Fortuna on the other. Great solidity is given to the base of the structure by having a simple podium on each side to carry all the columns, instead of a series of pedestals, as in other arches.

The fate of Domitian led, as in the case of Caligula and Nero, to the subsequent destruction of all honorary monuments which bore his name ; but we have a number of arches belonging to the reign of Trajan, though two of the most important (both erected in Rome) are known to us only from coins.

As a frame for sculpture the arch at Beneventum (Plate LVIII), built in 114 A.D., is the finest example, as the columns flanking the arch and at the angles, being only semi and three-quarter detached, interfere less with the sculptural bas-reliefs between them than in some other cases. The subjects of these reliefs and of the friezes represent the Dacian wars and triumphs, and the order employed is the Composite, the columns resting on a podium, as in the Arch of Titus.

The Arch of Trajan at Ancona (Plate LVIII) was set up in 112 A.D. at the entrance to the harbour which he built. It is raised aloft and approached by a flight of steps, and must be regarded as a pedestal to carry a group of sculpture, now gone. As a pedestal it is a fine conception ; but as an archway its proportions are too elongated.

To the reign of Trajan belongs the earliest example of a dated arch in North Africa, that of Maktar (116 A.D.) (Plate LIX). Its principal characteristics are the framing of the opening by two pairs of engaged Corinthian columns, the smaller of which carries an entablature and a pediment, and the prolongation of the impost moulding around the piers, which we find later in the Arch of Septimius Severus in Rome.

In the reign of Hadrian an important innovation was made— that of freestanding columns. As Curtis points out,[1] " the result was far from satisfactory from an artistic standpoint. The columns

---

[1] *Op. cit.*, p. 55.

are thrust forward with no reason for their existence, since they have nothing to support but the few inches of the entablature which projects over them.   The wall assumes its true supporting function, and the inordinate mass of the piers is revealed with no relieving features.   Moreover, the play of light and shade becomes so pronounced that it is out of all proportion to the size of the monument." We find ourselves, in short, confronted by the beginnings of the baroque architecture of the later Roman Empire.

Reference has been made in Chapter IV to the most important archway in Syria which probably belongs to the period of Hadrian (Curtis p. 56), viz., that which was erected to form the junction between the main colonnaded street and that leading to the Propylæa of the Temple of the Sun at Palmyra ; throughout the country, however, in every town built by the Romans, entrance gateways are found which in their design resemble Arches of Triumph, but were built to give more importance to the entrance to a town or to some temple.   The sculpture is, however confined to the capitals and bases of the engaged columns with which they are decorated, or, as at Petra, to the pilasters on each side of the principal archways.

The arch at Timgad, though generally attributed to Trajan, more probably belongs, as Curtis thinks, to the period of Marcus Aurelius. It has three openings, the central arch being much larger than the two lateral ones ; over them are rectangular niches flanked by small supported columns on projecting corbels, while the main entablature is supported by four unfluted Corinthian pilasters, in front of each of which, on the same high pedestal, is a detached fluted Corinthian column.   Each pair of these columns supports a curved pediment which is carried over the space above the lateral niches (Plate LIX). It is more elaborate than the great majority of the numerous triumphal arches of N. Africa, where the absence of sculpture is very noticeable.   There is, however, a little on the recently restored Arch of Marcus Aurelius at Tripoli.

The most remarkable example in the country is the quadifrontal Arch of Caracalla at Tebessa (Theveste), which was probably erected, like the Arch of Janus in Rome, at the intersection of two streets. It consists of a single archway (Plate LIV) on each front, flanked by pairs of Corinthian columns raised on pedestals.   The frieze is made of unusual depth, so as to allow of space for inscriptions, and it is, perhaps, in consequence of this that no attic storey was provided. On the other hand, in its place, and still existing over the north

PLATE LX.

ARCH OF THE SILVERSMITHS AT ROME.

PLATE LXI.

ARCH OF CONSTANTINE, ROME (312 A.D.).

PORTA NIGRA AT TREVES, GERMANY.

front, is a canopy consisting of four columns carrying an entablature. A second canopy is mentioned as formerly existing on the south front, and there were perhaps four such constructions in all with arched openings between, and above them all a cupola. The inscription on the south face is in honour of Caracalla (214 A.D.).

The most elaborate arch of the period is the Arch of Septimius Severus in Rome (203 A.D.), built to commemorate his Parthian victories, and decorated with bas-reliefs of the various episodes of the wars. The arch is similar to that of Constantine, with centre and two side arches flanked by detached columns and responds (but here of the Composite order), resting on pedestals which are also decorated with reliefs. The frieze, which in such a structure ought to be of greater depth than usual, is here so narrow that the whole entablature seems to consist of mouldings only. On the other hand, greater breadth is given to the attic storey, which is unbroken, so as to give abundant space and more importance to the dedicatory inscription.

The gateway built by the silversmiths in honour of Septimus Severus (Plate LX), in the Forum Boarium, though of great richness in sculpture, is an extremely debased conception.

The triple arch at Reims should also be attributed to the third century A.D. if we are to judge by the style of its reliefs. It is unusually broad (108 feet) and consists of three archways, the central one wider than the others, but all springing from imposts at the same level. On each façade are four pairs of engaged Corinthian columns, one on each pier, with niches between them, and at each end are two similar columns.

The entablature has disappeared except for portions of the architrave, and so has the attic.[1]

The Arch of Janus in the Forum Boarium is one of those structures, of which there are many in Syria, built at the junction of four streets as a shelter. It is attributed to the age of Constantine, and consists of a square mass of masonry pierced on each face with an archway (above which an attic originally rose), the interior being covered by an intersecting barrel vault. The construction of this vault is interesting, because, according to M. Choisy, it shows that the same centering was used for both the intersecting groins. These groins were built in two rings of Roman bricks (Fig. 31). As soon as one of them had set, the hollow space between the two rings was

---

[1] Curtis, p. 74, 75.

filled in with concrete, and the centering having been shifted round, the other double ring was constructed, butting on each side against the first groin. Another similar arch on the Via Flaminia, 11 miles north of Rome, is attributable to the same period,[1] and was indeed built to commemorate Constantine's victory over Maxentius. But the most important monument of this is the famous arch near the Colosseum (312 A.D.) and consists of a central archway and two side ones (Plate LXI), flanked by detached columns and responds of the Corinthian order, raised on pedestals and carrying an entablature which returns above each column. The attic is hollow, and is reached by a stairway in the west pier.

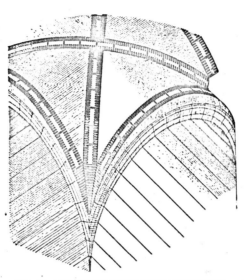

FIG. 31.—INTERSECTING BARREL VAULT OF THE JANUS QUADRIFONS IN THE FORUM BOARIUM AT ROME.

The sculptured decorations of the arch are in great part taken from earlier monuments ; at each end and on each side of the central passage are fragments of a frieze representing Trajan's victories in Dacia ; the circular medallions probably belong to the period of Hadrian, though the question has been much discussed ; the reliefs on the attic were taken from an Arch of Marcus Aurelius and even those of the frieze have been thought to have originally served for a monument of Diocletian.[2]

The remainder of the sculptural decoration, which belongs to the time of Constantine, is poor in execution, but the general effect is little inferior to that of earlier monuments.

---

[1] Toebelmann, *Bogen von Malborghetto* (Heidelberg, 1920) : See *J. R. S.*, xiii (1922).

[2] Stuart Jones. *Papers of the British School at Rome*, iii, 225, *sqq.* : Wace, *ibid.*, iv, 270 : Bulle in *Jahrbuch des Instituts*, xxxiv (1919), 144 : Wilpert in *Bull. Comm. Arch.* (1924).

No imperial arches of any subsequent date are preserved to us ; and we may now turn to an examination of city gates properly so-called.

The entrance gateway known as the Porta Nigra, at Treves (Trier), is one of the most important examples existing, and is still in good preservation (Plate LXI). It consists of an inner and outer double gateway, with two storeys of arcades with attached columns between. It is flanked by two towers, which are four storeys in height. On the entrance, or north, side these towers have a semi-circular front. Internally they measure 55 feet by 22 feet wide, constituting, therefore, important halls. At first sight, the arcaded galleries seem to have served the same purpose as those at Autun, and their wide openings impair the defensive value of the whole structure, but as the central court between the inner and outer gateways is unroofed, they formed the only means of communication between the wings, and the open court might have been of service in defending the entrance if the outer gateways were forced. As the gateway formed part of the external walls, the entrance to the halls on each side may have been from the ramparts, with an internal staircase in wood leading from floor to floor. An apse was added on the east side when the building was converted into a church in the middle ages, and may have caused the destruction of an external stone staircase on that side.

It dates either from the reign of Postumus, who detached Gaul from the rest of the Empire, and made Treves the capital, or from that of Gallienus, or from that of Valentinian I ; but it closely resembles the Porta Prætoria at Aosta[1] and the two city gates at Turin, though these last examples belong to the reign of Augustus. The latter had a decagonal tower flanking the double arcade on each side.

As examples of city gates of the simpler type we may take the Porta Romana at Aquino (Plate LXII), or the Porta S. Maria at Ferentino, both belonging to the Republican period, or the double-arched Porta Romana at Ascoli.

Next in importance to the arches of triumph come the memorial structures, such as the columns of victory set up in Rome and else-where, which, by the sculptured bas-relief decoration of their shafts in the Trajan and Antonine columns at Rome, gave even a better record of the campaigns undertaken than that which could be

---

[1] Durm., *op. cit.*, 438 *sqq.*

obtained in the panels of a triumphal arch. César Daly's interpretation of the spiral bas-relief of the Trajan column as the unfolding of the volumen or papyrus scroll was a happy suggestion of the origin of this conception. We have already referred in Chapter IV to the Trajan column (Fig. 10). Its construction is very remarkable. It is composed of twenty-nine blocks of marble, of which eight form the pedestal and eighteen the shaft, the other three being those of the base, the capital and the pedestal which supported the statue of Trajan. The pedestal on which the column stands is nearly a cube, measuring 16 feet 6 inches wide and 18 feet high. It is decorated on three sides with sculptural trophies of victory ; on the fourth is the doorway and dedicatory inscription. The lower diameter of the shaft is 12 feet, and the spiral staircase of one hundred and eighty-five steps is carved out of the solid marble, and lighted by forty-three loopholes.

The Antonine column, erected sixty-three years later (c 176 A.D.), by Marcus Aurelius in memory of his victories over the Germans, was copied, so far as its general design is concerned, from Trajan's column. Its height, 96 feet 6 inches (100 Roman feet), including base and capital, is the same as that of the Trajan column, its diameter being slightly in excess of that of the latter. In both cases the column was of the Doric order, the echinus of the capitals being carved with the egg and tongue. The base, 12 feet high, but now buried, was composed of three degrees or steps.

The column built to the memory of Antoninus Pius, 162 A.D., by his adopted son Marcus Aurelius, consisted of a monolith of granite, 47 feet high ; it no longer exists, but its pedestal, carved with the Apotheosis of Antoninus and Faustina, now in the gardens of the Vatican, is one of the finest examples of the sculpture of the period.

Outside Rome, the columns set up at Alexandria in Egypt, Brindisi in Italy, and Cussy in Burgundy, have no special value as architectural designs, but there are two other examples of memorial structures which should be mentioned.

The first, near Treves (Plate LXIII)[1], is known as the Igel monument. It is a remarkable design, and were it not for its history might be fairly ascribed to the period of Francis I of France. The pilasters which decorate each face have a very slight projection, and the sculpture of the capitals and panels recalls the work of the Chateau de Gaillon panels, now in the court of the Ecole des Beaux

[1] Strong in *J.R.S.*, i (1911), 24 and Pl. V.

PLATE LXII.

AQUEDUCTS NEAR PORTA FURBA.

AQUINUM, PORTA ROMANA.

PLATE LXIII.

THE TOMB OF ABSALOM
AT JERUSALEM.

MONUMENT AT IGEL,
NEAR TREVES.

MONUMENT AT ST. REMY,
PROVENCE, FRANCE (*left*).

PLATE LXIV.

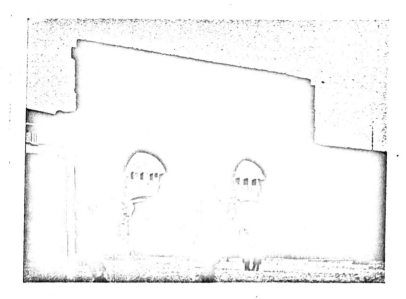

PORTA MAGGIORE, ROME.

THE PONT DU GARD, NEAR NÎMES.

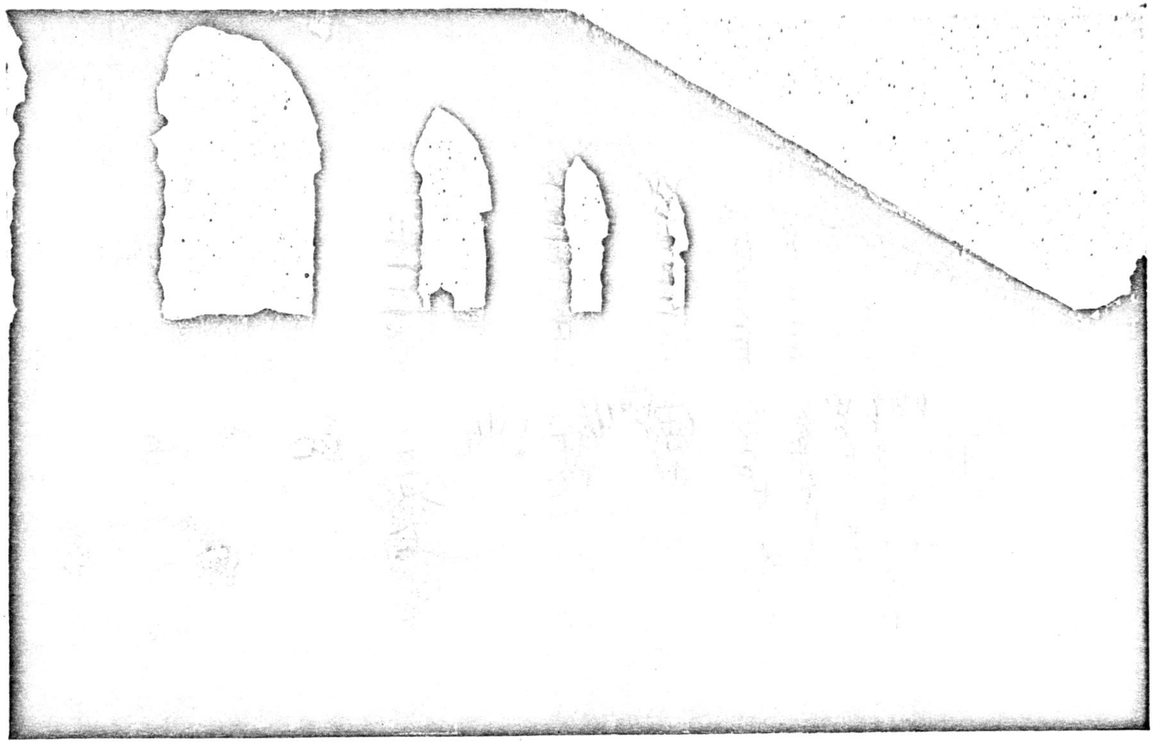

THE AQUEDUCT AT SEGOVIA.

Arts at Paris.   The monument was set up by two brothers named Secundinus, and the sculpture decorating it represents various scenes drawn from family history and from religious symbolism. It dates from the third century A.D.   The second example, the monument at St. Remy (Plate LXIII), which dates from just before the birth of Christ, in Provence, is square on plan, and decorated with engaged Corinthian columns at the angles carrying their entablature, and an archway in each face.   The whole is raised on a lofty pedestal decorated with bas-reliefs and is surmounted by a circular structure consisting of ten columns[1] carrying an entablature and a conical roof in stone.

AQUEDUCTS AND BRIDGES.

Among the monumental works of the Romans, though probably regarded by them purely as engineering works of a utilitarian character, were the aqueducts by which the thermæ, baths and fountains were supplied with water.   These structures were by no means confined to Rome, for throughout the Empire, and more especially in the eastern portion of it, the proper supply of water to the cities taken or founded would seem to have been the first steps taken by the Romans in civilising the barbarous tribes they had subdued.   Throughout North Africa and Syria there still exist extensive remains of the arches which carried the channels by which water was brought, sometimes from long distances.

It should be observed that the Romans were well acquainted with the hydraulic principle that water in a closed pipe finds its own level, and Vitruvius (VIII, 7) describes the leaden pipes used, and the precautions to be taken so as to regulate the fall and rise of the water.   They often found it, however, much less costly to build level water channels, as the materials employed belonged to the State, and the labour was that of slaves.   Lead pipes, according to Pliny, were used extensively as rising mains to supply the upper floors.

In the four aqueducts which supplied the city of Lugudunum (Lyon) no less than eight (or nine) inverted syphons have been found, in most cases crossing deep valleys ; they were supported by massive arches, and provided with a reservoir at each end.   The difficulty was, however, that the Romans were unable (or afraid) to make a syphon of concrete lined internally with hydraulic cement,

---

[1] This would seem to have been the prototype of the turrets of the churches in the Charente, and of St. Front at Perigueux.

and that they were equally unable to make a cast-iron pipe ; and, as a result, they required nine or ten lead pipes of $1\frac{1}{2}$ inch bore to take the contents of a concrete channel about $1\frac{1}{2}$ feet wide and 2 feet high (from which fact we can further see that the latter was generally only about half full). It has been well pointed out[1] that for the great aqueducts of the city of Rome the channels of some of which are as much as 4 feet wide and 6 to 9 feet high, an almost prohibitive amount of lead would have been required in the construction of the descent under pressure which would have been necessary had they descended direct from Tivoli (as the modern Aqua Marcia does, instead of making a great circuit) ; and that the pipes would have rapidly become choked with calcareous deposit. On the other hand, they do not seem to have realised that the water would have formed a less heavy deposit in a closed conduit, and preferred therefore to introduce shafts at frequent intervals for inspection and cleaning.

The earliest aqueduct built to bring water to Rome was the Appian (312 B.C.), which was carried underground for eleven miles, and this system was largely, but not entirely, followed in the Aqua Virgo and in the aqueduct (34 miles long) built by Trajan (109 A.D.) to supply his Thermæ, and in other cases. It was no doubt for military reasons that the Aqua Appia and the Anio Vetus (272 B.C.) were carried underground as far as possible, and even the Aqua Marcia (144 B.C.) was originally carried on arches only in the neighbourhood of the city. The loftiest arches are found in the Anio Novus, some of which rise over 100 feet in height. This and the Claudian Aqueduct (both 38-52 A.D.) were raised so as to supply water to the highest hills in Rome. One reason for suggesting that the Romans regarded them as engineering works only is based on the absence of any attempt to introduce architectural features of a decorative nature. They depended on their superb construction alone for their monumental character (Plate LXII). Attempts were made to enrich them only where they served as entrance gateways of the city, by the additions of niches, with pilasters, entablatures, and pediments (as at the Porta Maggiore) (Plate LXIV). The construction of the piers of the Marcian Aqueduct, which is one of the finest examples, is of the type described by Vitruvius as " opus quadratum," viz., with regular courses of headers and stretchers

---

[1] C. Germain de Montauzan. *Les Aqueducs antiques de Lyon* cf., T. Ashby, in *Builder*, xcvii (1909, ii), 357.

2 feet by 4 feet and 2 feet high.   Round the face of each stone is a draft about $1\frac{1}{2}$ inches to 2 inches wide, worked with a chisel ; the centre is left rough and worked with a pick.   The arches are set back at their springing behind the impost, leaving a ledge on which the centering was carried.   The stone employed is peperino, with travertine when greater strength was required.   Many of the aqueducts built in stone have been restored or added to in concrete with brick facing.[1]   The Aqueduct of Nero (a branch of the Aqua Claudia which ran to the Palatine, probably crossing the valley between it and the Cælian by a syphon) was in brickwork of the finest kind.   The remains of the four most important aqueducts of the city of Rome, the Anio Vetus and Novus, the Marcia and Claudia, were recently levelled by the late Professor Reina and two of his assistants (*Livellazione degli Antichi Acquedotti romani,* reprinted from *Memorie della Societa Italiana delle Scienze,* detta (dei XL), Series 3, Vol. XX) with the co-operation of the present author, who will shortly publish a full account of them from the architectural and archæological standpoint.

Of aqueducts in other countries, those of Segovia and Tarragona, in Spain, where they cross valleys, are of greater height than any in Italy, and in consequence, the arches are built in two storeys. The upper arches of the Tarragona Aqueduct are 42 feet in height, and the lower ones 58 feet, with drafted masonry similar to that of the Marcian Aqueduct above described, and the piers diminish in width and depth as they rise.   In the Segovian Aqueduct (Plate LXV) the upper arches are about one-third only of the height of the lower ones, the contrast giving scale to the latter.   The piers of the lower arches have offsets which take away much of their monumental effect.

By far the finest aqueduct is the Pont-du-Gard (Plate LXIV), near Nîmes, in the South of France.   Its length across the valley is 882 feet, about the same as that of the two examples in Spain ; but its height, 160 feet, is greater, and it is divided into two ranges of large arches and an upper row of smaller ones " which gives," as Fergusson says, " to the structure the same finish and effect that an entablature and cornice gives to a long range of columns."

---

[1] The Alexandrine Aqueduct, which supplied the Thermæ of Alexander Severus, was built, from the first, in concrete with brick facing : and there is an example in opus reticulatum of the Augustan period at Minturnæ, a town of the Volsci, where a decorative effect has been given to the wall surfaces by the employment of different coloured tufa in geometrical patterns.

Much of its present charm is probably due to its position in the great valley of the Gardon, and to the exquisite colour which in the course of ages the stone has acquired ; but in point of design it is certainly the most remarkable building of its kind, and this seems to be owing to two characteristics : firstly, in its erection the architect renounced all those architectural superfluities with which the Romans were accustomed to surcharge their buildings ; and secondly, it is the result of an attempt to simplify, to fulfil and meet the requirements of a well-defined programme.   The stream, which has worn its way in the solid rock, is not quite in the centre of the valley ; in other words, the slope on one side is less steep than on the other, and this gives variety to the design.

Roman water cisterns are remarkable for the solidity of their construction, and a large number of them have been preserved in and around Rome.   They are generally rectangular in plan, with vaulted aisles, which in the case of the larger reservoirs are divided by pillars ; and are lined with very hard hydraulic cement.

Not very many of the larger road bridges constructed by the Romans have existed to the present day.   Of the Pons Æmilius in Rome, built by Æmilius Lepidus in 179 B.C., only the foundations exist in the Ponte Rotto, but the Pons Fabricius (62-21 B.C.) is preserved intact, as was until recently the Pons Ælius (the modern Ponte S. Angelo) (Plate LXVI) constructed by Hadrian as an approach to his Mausoleum, with three main arches in the centre, and three smaller ones on the left, and two on the right bank.   The Ponte di Nona, at the ninth mile of the Via Prænestina, with its seven arches, is also finely preserved, while the Ponte Amato is a good example of a small bridge.   One of the best preserved in Italy is the bridge built by Augustus and Tiberius at Rimini, with five arches the three central ones of the same span (each measuring 27 feet), and the side ones about 20 feet (Plate LXVII).   The spandrels of the arches are decorated with niches, flanked with pilasters carrying entablature and pediment.   Following the usual Roman custom,[1] the bridge is not carried through on the same level, there being an ascent and descent at either end.   One of the finest bridges in Italy must have been the so-called Ponte d'Augusto on the Via Flaminia at Narni in Central Italy, only one of the four arches of which still exists, and is shown in Plate LXVIII.   Two examples of smaller bridges are shown in Plates LXVIII and LXIX, a two-arched

---

[1] See *J.R.S.*, xi (1921), 170.

PLATE LXVI.

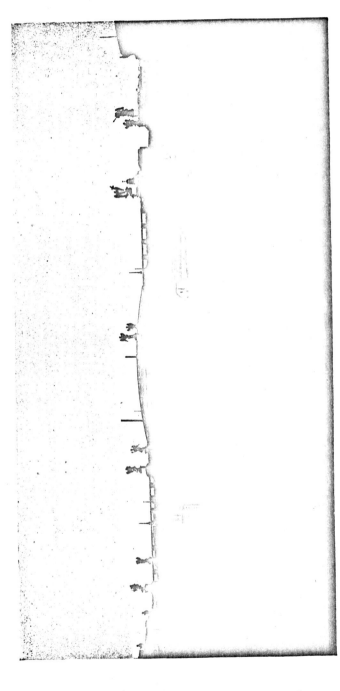

PONS AELIUS, ROME.

PLATE LXVII.

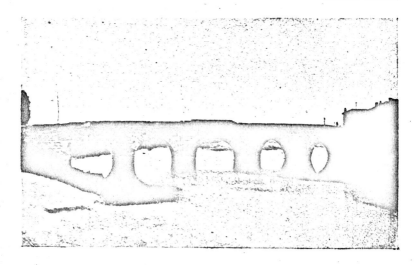

BRIDGE OF TIBERIUS AT RIMINI.

BRIDGE AT ST. CHAMAS (SO-CALLED PONT FLAVIEN).

PLATE LXVIII.

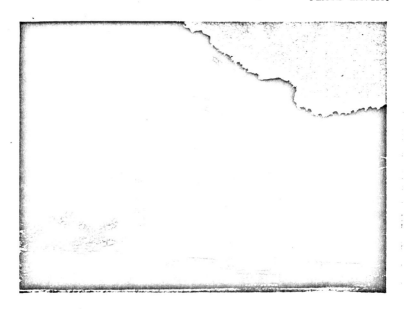

DETAIL OF THE BRIDGE OF AUGUSTUS AT NARNI.

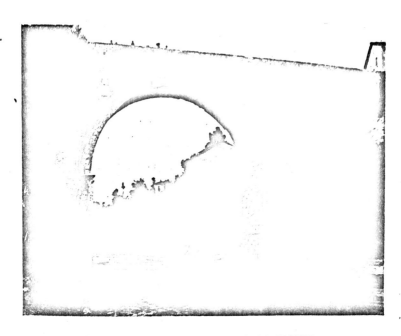

PONTE DEI CAPPUCINI, ASCOLI PICENO.

PLATE LXIX.

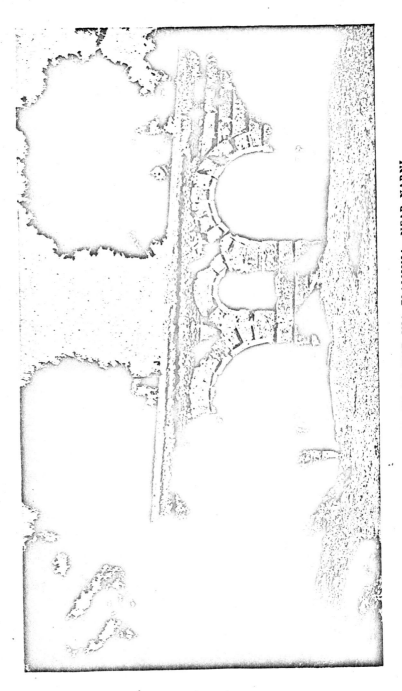

THE PONTE CALAMONE ON THE VIA FLAMINIA, NEAR NARNI.

bridge on the Via Flaminia near Narni (the Ponte Calamone) and a single-arched bridge with a 71-foot span at Ascoli Piceno (the Ponte dei Cappuccini).   The elegant profiling of the archivolt, seen in the first and third examples, is not often met with.   The construction is here, as in most cases, of finely-laid massive stonework, and road bridges in concrete faced with brick or small stones are somewhat rare: an example on a branch road not far from Hadrian's Villa may be noted, and another at Sessa Aurunca between the Via Appia and the Via Latina is shown in Plate LXX.

The finest example of a Roman bridge is that across the Tagus at Alcantara, in Spain (Plate LXXI).[1]   The length of the bridge is 650 feet, with a level roadway through.   It consists of six archways, the two central ones about 100 feet span, those on either side 60 feet, and the outer arches 50 feet.   As the sides of the valley rise on either side, the relative proportion of width to height is maintained, and scale is given to the central arches by those on either side.   Here also, as in the Pont-du-Gard, the arches spring from different levels. With the exception of an archway which is erected on the central piers, there are no architectural superfluities.   The qualities of the design are based on its superb masonry and the graceful proportions generally of the piers and arches.   The bridge at St. Chamas in France, which belongs to the Flavian period, is decorated with a simple but tasteful arch at each end with Corinthian pilasters (Plate LXVII).

TOMBS.

The Romans, in their larger tombs, imitated the great sepulchral tumuli of the Etruscans (p. 7) but gave greater importance to the enclosing ring of masonry, as in the tomb of Cæcilia Metella, of which the upper portion, consisting of a large circular drum about 93 feet in diameter, still remains more or less perfect on the Via Appia, outside Rome.   It is faced in fine masonry and crowned by an entablature with frieze decorated with ox skulls and festoons of fruit and flowers hanging between them.   The square podium on which the circular drum rested has been entirely stripped of its external masonry, so that we have no clue to its architectural design. The circular nucleus of the tomb of Augustus in the Campus Martius still exists, but we know little of its architecture.[2]   Of the tomb of

---

[1] From Stuart Jones' *Companion*, Pl. xii.

[2] A reconstruction by Mr. R. A. Cordingly, Rome Scholar in Architecture of the British School at Rome, will shortly be published in collaboration with Mr. I. A. Richmond, Craven Fellow in the University of Oxford.

Hadrian there still exists in the castle of S. Angelo the whole of the core and a portion of the great circular drum, which, as in the tomb of Cæcilia Metella, rested on a podium.   Here, however, the podium was 340 feet square and 30 feet high.   In the centre of the drum is the sepulchral chamber, approached by a spiral passage ; above it a square tower-like structure rises from the centre of the drum ; and above this is a cylindrical structure, which has recently been found to be ancient, so that previous reconstructions have been proved incorrect.[1]   There is a tomb on the Appian Way called the Tomb of Cotta (Casal Rotondo), which dates from the Augustan era, and in its design also recalls the early Etruscan tombs.   According to Canina's restoration, it consisted of an immense mole, 342 feet in diameter, with a pyramidal roof of marble slabs and a lantern rowning the summit.

Another class of tombs are those, which are known as Columbaria.   These were, however, usually below the ground, though in many cases an upper storey existed.   This very often took the form of a small temple with a portico of four columns or of two columns in antis, and of these there were many examples on the Via Appia.   They were often of fine ornamental brickwork in two colours (cf. Plate XI).   The ground on each side of the road was set out very much in the same way as in our cemeteries, and there were often small branch roads behind the main road, where the lines of tombs were three or four deep.   Spaces of so many feet frontage and depth were allotted to the purchasers, and enclosed with a low wall or boundary, in the centre of which was built the tomb, square, oblong, or circular, carved sometimes with figure sculpture in the same way as in Athens, but more frequently decorated with pilasters or panelling surmounted by a cornice and raised on a podium or on steps,   Sometimes the area would be surrounded with a richly decorated wall, and marble seats.   On the Via Appia nearly the whole of the marble decoration of the tombs has been stripped off, leaving only the concrete and tufa core ; but in Pompeii, outside the Herculaneum gate, a large number of tombs have been found *in situ*, and are now exposed to view, suggesting similar types to those outside Rome.   Here at Pompeii, as in Rome, the street of tombs was divided off on each side, and the enclosures still remain, there being in addition, in

---

[1] See that of S. R. Pierce in *J.R.S.*, XV (1925).

PLATE LXX.

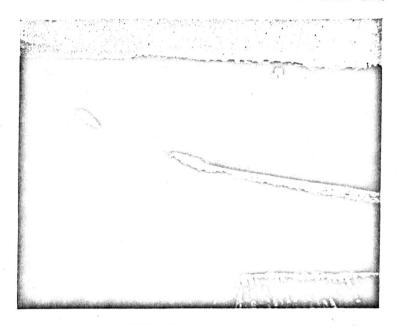

FONTE RONACO AT SESSA.

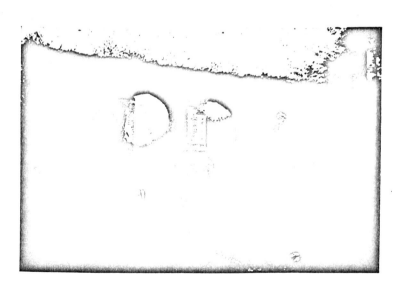

(DETAIL OF THE ABOVE.

PLATE LXXI.

ROMAN BRIDGE AT ALCANTARA.

the rear, small sepulchral chambers with niches to hold the urns containing the ashes of the deceased. The cinerary urns, often in the form of elaborately decorated altars, are of singular beauty (Plate LXXII). Exedræ in marble and semi-circular niches with seats were provided for the repose of those visiting the tombs.

There are but few examples of Roman tombs in Asia Minor, but in Syria they are found in great numbers. The most ancient are probably those in Palmyra. It is true that many of them were erected before the submission of the city to Rome, but their internal decoration with Corinthian pilasters shows the full development of the Roman Corinthian order. These tombs take the form of square towers from 70 to 90 feet high and 30 to 32 feet square, resting on a podium with no cornice, and two or three steps. Internally they are divided into three or four storeys, each storey having a series of recesses one above the other to hold coffins. On the ground storey these recesses are divided by Corinthian pilasters, and the cornices and ceilings of the chambers, all built of stone slabs, are richly decorated. The upper storeys are simpler. In one example given in Wood[1] the three storeys are suggested outside by a slight diminution in the width of each, otherwise the sides are vertical.[2] The towers are built of fine masonry with a simple cornice, and externally the only decoration consists (half-way up the tower on the principal front) of a projecting canopy over a recumbent figure resting on a slab supported by corbels.

The tombs at Jerusalem, all of which date from about the middle of the first century of our era, are too mixed in their style to allow of their being classed as Roman work. They are all cut in the solid rock, with the exception of the upper part of the so-called Absalom tomb (Plate LXIII), which has been built in masonry. One of these tombs, known as that of St. James, consists of a portico in antis of two columns between wings projecting slightly on each side. These wings are carried up a considerable height above the cornice of the portico, and in Cassas' work[3] are shown as towers with a cornice on the top, suggesting a similarity to the front of the temple of Jerusalem, where the pillars of Jachin and Boaz formed a similar portico between lofty towers, as described in the Bible. There are three

[1] Wood (R.), *Ruins of Palmyra*, fol. 1738.
[2] The example as drawn in the Marquis de Vogüé's *Syrie Centrale* is shown as diminishing in width towards the top. It has apparently been reproduced from a photograph taken with a tilted camera. A photograph of the same tomb in Mr. Spier's possession showed the sides absolutely vertical.
[3] Cassas (L. F.), *Voyage Pittoresque de la Syrie*, fol. 1799.

R

other tombs in Jerusalem, known as the Tombs of Jehosaphat, of
the Judges, and of the Kings. In each case a court has been excavated and sunk in the solid rock, and the entrance to the tomb cut
on one side of it. In the two first cases the entrance consists of a
portico with moulded jambs and lintel, surmounted by a pediment
enriched with debased Greek foliage. The tomb of the Kings—now
identified as the tomb of Helena, Queen of Adiabene, c. A.D. 75—is
entered through a porch consisting of a portico in antis, the face of
the jambs and lintel being enriched with carving; above is a Doric
frieze with triglyphs and a cornice. A bunch of grapes in the centre
and a palmette on each side have been carved in the place of three
of the triglyphs. The entrance to the tomb is on the left-hand side
of the portico, and the rolling stone by which the opening was
closed still remains.

In other parts of Syria there are Roman tombs, which vary in
size from 25 to 40 feet square, and are decorated externally with
Corinthian pilasters of the angles. Internally they are covered
with barrel vaults or with domes on pendentives, the latter consisting sometimes of stone slabs placed across the angles. Examples
of triangular spherical pendentives may be found in Rome[1] in
various second century tombs. Some of the tombs in central Syria
are sunk in the rock, and over them are built groups of two or more
columns held together by their entablatures. Others follow the
arrangement typified by that of the Tomb of the Kings: viz., a
portico in antis and occasionally a pediment.

The most important of the rock-cut tombs are the magnificent
examples at Petra (Plate LXXIII). Cut in the vertical sides of a
cliff, and rising sometimes to over 100 feet in height, the artist was
freed from the trammels of ordinary construction and was able to
realise his conceptions much in the same way as a painter produces
a theatrical scene. One of the examples which was commenced
but never finished, shows the method employed in the setting out of
the design. The steep slope of the rocky cliff was cut away, leaving
a vertical face of the intended height and width of the tomb. The
artist commenced by drawing, on the rock itself, the various features of the proposed design, and then (working from the top down
to the base) cut back into the solid rock to the depth required to
leave his conception in relief. In some cases, as notably in the
Khasne, a portico of two Corinthian columns in antis was sunk on

---

[1] *Infra*, Ch. xv, p. 11.

S

PLATE LXXII.

CINERARY URNS IN THE FORM OF ALTARS.

PLATE LXXIII.

THE TOMB OF THE KHASNE AT PETRA.

the lower storey, in the rear of which was the entrance door and the sepulchral chamber.   The principal tombs are those of the Khasne (called by the natives the Treasury of Pharaoh), and of El Deir: the Corinthian tomb, and the tomb with the urn.   The finest and best-preserved is that of the Khasne (Plate LXXIII),[1] divided into two storeys, the upper one with a circular pavilion in the centre and two side wings with half pediments, all carved with the Corinthian order. The lower storey has a tetrastyle portico in the centre, the angle columns, however, not entirely detached, and two side wings.   All the mouldings and ornament suggest the employment of Greek artists, and the remarkable resemblance of the central pavilion to the Choragic Monument of Lysicrates suggests that it was inspired by that building.   The ornaments on the acroteria of the broken pediment would seem to be representations of eagles: those of the pediment of the portico are not distinguishable, but the figures on pedestals between the columns on the upper storey, show that an artist of some repute must have been brought over to execute them. Perhaps the most remarkable feature in connection with these tombs is the exceptional care which must have been taken, in cutting away round the projecting features, as there are no instances recorded of new blocks being inserted where too much had been cut away.   The projection of the abaci, which is greater than that usually given, was probably regarded by the artist as a *tour de force*.   The illustration shows the very slight inclination of the sides of the cliff, and how little had to be cut away to procure a vertical plane for the setting out of the design.

The tomb of El Deir and " the Corinthian tomb " are of similar design, the latter having a more solid ground storey,   The front of the " tomb with the urn " was carved in imitation of the tetrastyle portico of a temple, but with semi-detached columns only ; the urn crowned the top of the pediment.   This tomb was preceded by an open court with a porticus on each side, also cut in the rock, and a platform partly built in masonry.   There is a fifth tomb, of a most decadent type, with three storeys of Corinthian pilasters.   As a rule the sepulchral chamber was not decorated internally.   In one instance only semi-detached Corinthian columns are carved round the chamber.   As evidence of originality of design and richness of

---

[1] Dalman in *Annual of the Palestine Exploration Fund*, 195 *sqq.* (with drawings by the late F. G. Newton), who considers it possible that it may be the monument of one of Petra's last kings, erected not very long before the Roman Conquest of 105 A.D.

execution, these tombs are remarkable examples of the Roman style, of probably the second century of our era ; but the absence of any constructive character takes them out of the range of serious architectural developments.

CHAPTER VIII.

PALACES AND HOUSES.

THE Palatine Hill had become, towards the end of the Republic, the most desirable site for the residences of the great, owing to its nearness to the Forum, the centre of the political life of the city. Here dwelt Cæsar, Cicero, and his rival Hortensius: and it was from the latter that Augustus purchased the house (now generally known as the house of Livia, his widow, to whom it passed at his death) which still exists near the western angle of the hill. Though he added to it considerably on the south-west side, it always remained a comparatively modest residence, and is an interesting specimen of the domestic architecture of the latter half of the first century B.C. It is interesting to note how this historic house was respected to the end despite the huge substructures which were needed on the other side of the hill. Remains of two other houses of the same period containing, just as it does, important mural paintings, have been in part rediscovered, in part newly excavated, under the north-east portion of the Flavian Palace.

Tiberius, when he became Emperor, set himself to the construction of a far larger palace on the north-west summit of the hill (Plate LXXIV), which must have led to the destruction of more than one private house. It was reached from the much lower level of the Forum by a monumental approach, added by Caligula, of which few traces are now left except for a large open piscina, measuring 85 by 30 feet, which must have formed the central point of a peristyle serving as the vestibule to this approach. The statement of ancient authors that Caligula considered the temple of Castor and Pollux as the vestibule of his palace is thus no mere rhetorical exaggeration. It was perhaps Claudius, but more probably Nero, who erected a palace on the south-east summit of the Palatine, connected with the other palace, and with the house of Livia, by a cryptoporticus.

This palace, which was in two storeys, has also been rediscovered in recent years—for it was in part known in the early eighteenth century,[1] and the ceiling paintings of two of its rooms, known as the Baths of Livia, were the subject of frequent drawings, the best, perhaps, of which are to be found in the breakfast room of Sir John Soane's Museum, in Lincoln's Inn Fields; while another room, beautifully decorated with fountains and pergolas supported by small marble columns, was known to Breval, who travelled in Italy in 1721.[2]   More paintings of great beauty and delicacy of execution have recently come to light; while on the upper floor, a pavement of marble inlay has lately been found, which is the finest specimen of its kind which has come down to us.

The second of these palaces appears to have been destroyed in the fire of Nero (64 A.D.).   After the fire, whatever be the exact degree of his responsibility for it, he at all events took advantage of it to build for himself an enormous palace, the so-called Golden House, the area of which, including the park in which it stood, has been calculated to have been greater than that of S. Peter's and the Vatican with its garden.   He constructed a monumental approach to it from the Forum—a colonnade[3], starting at the temple of Vesta and leading right up to the ridge of the Velia, where the vestibule was situated.

On the Palatine he had but little time to restore the palaces of his predecessors; but some concrete foundations under the triclinium of the Flavian Palace may be attributed to him.   After the accession of Vespasian, the site of the Golden House was gradually restored to the Roman people, and Domitian employed his architect Rabirius to restore the imperial palaces on the Palatine; that of Tiberius having probably been destroyed by the fire of Titus in 80 A.D. As had been the case under Tiberius, the approach from the Forum was on the north of the hill, close to the temple of Castor and Pollux.   Three great halls were constructed, one of them the building which has till recently been known as the temple of Augustus, and the other two (under which the piscina of Caligula has been found) converted in the sixth century into the church of S. Maria Antiqua.   Behind the latter four inclined planes (perhaps, however, due to Hadrian) ascended to the Clivus Victoriæ immediately

---

[1] *Papers of the British School at Rome*, vii, 36, 60.
[2] Engravings by E. Kirkall separately, and in Breval's *Remarks on several parts of Europe.*
[3] Little more than the foundations of it exists.

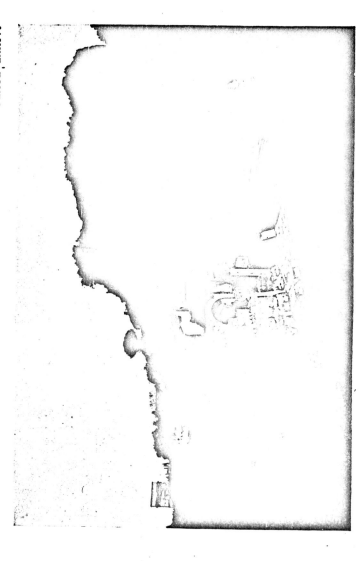

PALACE OF TIBERIUS (LACUS JUTURNAE IN FOREGROUND).

PLATE LXXV.

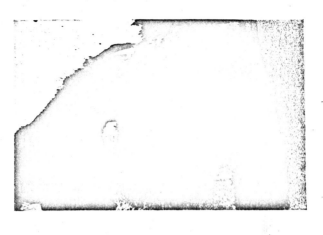

BALCONY OF THE PALACE OF
TIBERIUS AS RESTORED
BY DOMITIAN.

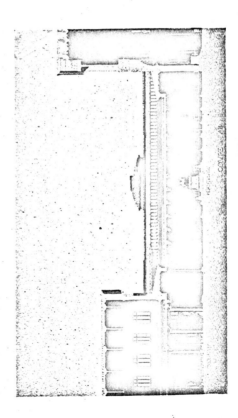

SECTION THROUGH THE PALACE OF DOMITIAN
ON THE PALATINE HILL AT ROME
(RESTORED BY DUTERT).

below the angle of the substructures of the palace on the north-west summit of the hill. These substructures were extended by Domitian, so that in Plate LXXIV the whole of Tiberius' work is concealed; and what has by many been called Caligula's bridge is simply the ornamental balcony, supported by corbels and decorated with stucco and painting, which ran along the outside of a considerable part of the substructures of the palace (it may also be recognised at the eastern angle) (Plate LXXV), while the great arches by which the area of the palace was further extended over the road, until it came almost immediately over the Atrium Vestæ, were probably the work of Hadrian. The cryptoporticus which runs along the south-east side belongs to the time of Nero (the original one, which is much smaller, has recently been found running parallel to it, but is no longer accessible); it was covered with a barrel vault, and lighted by a series of windows on one side formed in the springing of the same. The vault was enriched with painted stucco reliefs, portions of which are still preserved, and the walls were lined with slabs of marble of different kinds, affixed by clamps of iron and bronze, some of which still remain. A branch leads to the Flavian palace. Of the palace itself nothing is left, and we know very little about its plan; but the case is very different with the south-east summit of the hill. Here Domitian built an enormous palace, which falls into five main parts : (a) The state apartments on one floor only, grouped round a peristyle, which, with the triclinium on its south-west side, was constructed over the remains of the older palace, so that the latter were entirely obliterated. (b) The private apartments, with a huge staircase descending to a peristyle at a lower level, which gave on to a segmental portico overlooking the Circus Maximus ; the Villa Mills is built into the remains at the upper level. (c) A large walled garden (the so-called Stadium) at the lower level with a great semi-circular exedra on its south-east side (Plate LVII). (d) The thermæ on the south-east side of it at the upper level, which were partly rebuilt by Septimius Severus, who added considerably to the palace on this side, extending the side by the huge arched substructures which form so prominent a feature from below, and building the Septizonium, a huge sham façade, to conceal them. (e) The so-called gardens of Adonis, at the east angle of the hill, where, according to some authorities, the temple of Apollo is to be placed.[1]

---

[1] The above is an extract from my article on *Rome* in the *Town Planning Review*, x (1923), 23 *sqq.*, and my best thanks are due to the Editors for leave to reprint it.

The excavations on the Palatine Hill, commenced systematically by Napoleon III under Signor Rosa in 1863, and continued since 1870 by the Italian Government, have laid bare the walls of the greater portion of this palace. Although in the centre (see Plates XCIII, XCIV), on the site occupied by the Villa Mills, there still remain other researches to be made, the restorations here shown of the plans of the palaces of Domitian and Severus are based on the walls actually found. The restoration shown in the section by Dutert (Plate LXXV)[1] of part of Domitian's palace is based on portions of the walls still existing, on similar halls found in the Roman Thermæ, and on the records of the marbles discovered in 1720 and described by Bianchini. Portions of the pavements of almost every hall in the palace still exist, and in many cases the lower part of the walls.

In this palace, as in the thermæ, the two chief principles on which the Roman architect set out his plan are clearly set forth : first, the maintenance of the axis ; and second, the selection of some leading features which ruled its design. With reference to the first principle it will be noted that the walls of the several palaces and other buildings are not always parallel or at right angles to one another. Where there is a variation in the parallelism of the axis, as in the case of the temple of Apollo, built 36-28 B.C., with that of the palace of Domitian, the irregular juxtaposition of the two is masked by the rooms on the left of the triclinium, so that anyone approaching the temple from the south-west should not recognise that the temple and the palace were not in parallel planes. The second principle is shown in the palace of Domitian by the adoption of a central feature or set of features, such as the throne-room, the peristyle court, and the triclinium, with a room of peculiar shape, the nymphæum, on each side, the space at the back of the latter being filled in with small service rooms. At the back of the triclinium are two small rooms of irregular shape, which allow the south wing (containing the two halls of the " library ") to align with the axis of the temple of Apollo[2] and its approaches. Again, on the right-hand side of the plan, the central axis of the south-eastern portion (thermæ, etc.) was not at right angles with the Stadium. This was masked by an immense

---

[1] The columns of the triclinium were as a. fact far larger than he shows them : apparently there was only a single order in the interior, and the line of columns separating it from the peristyle was equally large.

[2] I refer to the temple facing the Aventine, often called (Axis Bradshaw, who follows Hülsen), the temple of Jupiter Victor.

PLATE LXXVI.

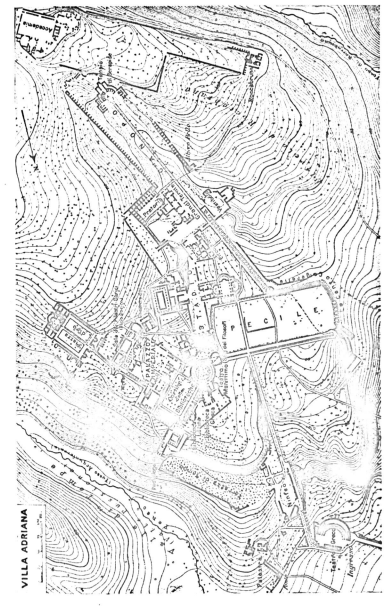

PLAN OF HADRIAN'S VILLA.

PLATE LXXVII.

HADRIAN'S VILLA : THE SO-CALLED HOSPITIUM.

HADRIAN'S VILLA :
THE "AVIARY" (SO-CALLED TEATRO MARITTIMO).

PLATE LXXVIII.

HADRIAN'S VILLA : ROOM IN LARGE THERMAE.

PLATE LXXIX.

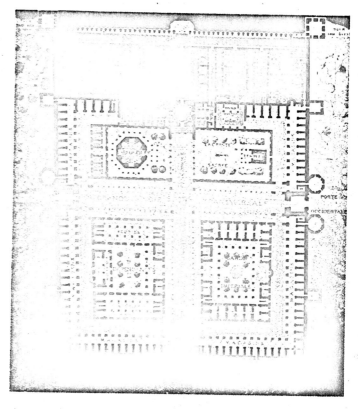

PALACE OF DIOCLETIAN AT SPALATO.
RESTORED PLAN BY M. E. HÉBRARD.

PLATE LXXX.

THE PALACE OF DIOCLETIAN, SPALATO.
GENERAL VIEW OF MODEL FROM THE NORTH-WEST.

THE PALACE OF DIOCLETIAN, SPALATO.

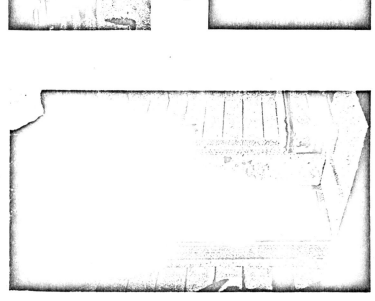

PORTAL OF THE TEMPLE.

PLATE LXXXI.

PORT AUREA, SPALATO.

hemicycle which formed a tribune from which the Emperor and his suite viewed the races in the Stadium.

One of the most remarkable features in the plan is that which is shown in the portion overlooking the Circus Maximus, where the two side wings have their fronts placed at a slight angle to one another, and are united by an immense segmental corridor in several storeys, the effect of which must have rendered this palace one of the finest compositions of Roman architecture.

The principal approach to the Palatine Hill was by the Clivus Palatinus, a road which started from the Sacra Via, on the west side of the Arch of Titus, and led to an arch which gave access to the sanctuary of Apollo on the one side, and to the palace of Domitian on the other. In ascending the road, close to the Arch of Titus, on the east side, stood the temple of Jupiter Stator, of which the foundations only have been found.

The palace built by Domitian had a portico on the north, and another on the west, the entrance being on the latter side only. The central hall, assumed to have been the throne-room, was covered by a barrel vault, which had the widest span of any in Rome, the hall being 100 feet wide by 131 feet long. That of the triclinium was about as wide. The walls were 10 feet thick on each side, but the thrust of the wall would seem to have been resisted by the halls on each side, there being buttresses outside the basilica on one side and piers inside the lararium on the other side.[1] There were three great niches in the wall on each side of the throne-room, in which were colossal statues in porphyry, and between these and the doorways were detached columns of pavonazzetto and giallo antico monoliths 24 feet in height. Opposite the central doorway was the throne, in a recess. All the walls were cased with marble up to the springing of the vault, about 60 feet above the pavement.

On the west side of the throne-room was the basilica, with a row of six columns on each side, forming aisles, and in this respect corresponding to the Egyptian Œcus[2] which is described by Vitruvius (VI, 5). At the south end of the basilica was an apse. On the opposite side of the throne-room was the so-called lararium. In the rear was a staircase leading to an upper

---

[1] Buttresses were added along the whole of the west façade by Hadrian, who also found it necessary to add them inside the basilica and to thicken its apse wall.

[2] The title of Egyptian Hall given to the great banqueting hall in the Mansion House is probably derived from Vitruvius's definition.

T

floor, and beyond a square hall. It might here be noted that the lararium and rooms behind it were not of the same width as the basilica : the most important room, therefore, the throne-room, which rose in height above the others, was not in the central axis of the front.[1]   Beyond the throne-room was a great central court surrounded by a peristyle (Plate LXXV), with columns of pavonazzetto marble and halls on either side.   In the centre, on the south of this, was the triclinium, or state dining-room, which opened on each side to what was virtually a conservatory, as in the Nymphæum, were fountains, plants, and flowers, with niches at the back in which were statues ; the centre portion perhaps being open to the sky.   All these halls, as also the walls of the peristyle, were lined with rich marbles.   The pavement of the triclinium was of the description known as " opus sectile," which consisted of thin pieces of marble and porphyry cut in shapes to suit the pattern.

The north portion has not yet been entirely excavated, so that the plan of that portion can only be recovered from Guattani's drawings, made before the Villa Mills was erected.   All the south portion has been excavated, and the rich marble work of the lower part of the walls and the mosaic pavements were found *in situ*.   Portions also of the vaulting retained their rich decoration in stucco work.   The domed rooms below the Villa Mills are extremely interesting.   Two are octagonal with curved and rectangular niches alternating ; while the third has been thought to offer the earliest examples known of spherical pendentives (Rivoira, *Roman Architecture*, 108, Fig. 124), but is probably an example of an intersecting barrel vault.

The eastern part of the palace of Domitian built in the rear of the great tribune which he constructed, facing the stadium,[2] is incorporated with the later palace of Severus.   Of the latter little is left but the substructions, and of these only a portion remains, the rest having been thrown down by earthquakes in the Middle Ages. The palace was, thus, once an edifice of great size, raised at a great height above the Via Appia on huge arches, which were masked by the Septizonium.

---

[1] We may note in these halls for the first time the combination of a vaulted interior with a rectilinear exterior, which becomes so frequent in Christian architecture.

[2] The name Stadium has been given by modern archæologists—a late classical authority calls it Hippodromus Palatii ; but this name it owes to its shape, for we find that Pliny the younger already uses it for a garden of this particular form attached to a Roman villa ; and there are two actual examples in the Villa of the Quintilii on the Via Appia.

U

Hadrian's Villa at Tivoli.

The great dissimilarity between the many conjectural restorations of the plan of Pliny's Laurentine villa, based on his description alone, shows the great difficulty which is experienced when there are no actual remains upon which to base any conception.[1]

In this respect we are more fortunate when dealing with the Villa of Hadrian near Tivoli ; for although excavated and ransacked for treasures from the sixteenth century onwards (in which operations considerable portions were further destroyed), there still remained sufficient in the middle of that century to allow of fairly accurate plans being made by Ligorio, and in the eighteenth by Piranesi. Other plans were made by Nibby and Canina in the first half of last century, and since then, in 1865, a much more careful and systematic survey by M. Daumet, *Grand Prix de Rome*. Still more recent are the plans of Winnefeld [2] and Reina, and the reconstruction by Boussois (*Monuments Antiques, Supplement*, Pls. 26-37). On all these is based the plan (Plate LXXVI) which is taken from the new volume of the *Guida d'Italia* (Italia Centrale IV), published by the Touring Club Italiano.

The site selected by Hadrian for his villa is situated to the south of Tivoli, and consists of a ridge running from north-west to south-east, and of varying heights, between two valleys, one of which, called by him " the Vale of Tempe " (in recollection of the beautiful Thessalian valley which in the course of his extended travels he had visited), is much deeper than the other, and still preserves its natural features.

The total area which was occupied by the Villa is said by Nibby to have been over seven square miles, but this is an exaggeration. We propose to confine our attention to the most important portion only, *viz.*, the Imperial Palace and the various structures in its vicinity, shown on the plan (Plate LXXVI).

The Villa was commenced thirteen years before Hadrian's death in 138 A.D. Opinions differ widely as to the exact purpose of some of the various edifices, and whilst some archæologists maintain that in them Hadrian attempted to reproduce some of the more remarkable monuments which he had seen in the course of his

---

[1] The latest and most correct is that of Winnefeld in *Jahrbuch des Instituts*, vi (1891), 200.

[2] H. Winnefeld. *Die Villa bes Hadrian kei Tivoli*, Berlin, 1895. (III, Ergän-zungsheft des Jahrbuchs des Instituts) : Reina's plan is published in Lanciani's *La Villa Adriana* (Rome, 1906), cf., also P. Gusman *La Villa Imperiale de Tibur*, Paris, 1904 ; Rivoira, *op. cit.* 132 *sqq*.

travels, others (and among them M. Daumet) are of opinion that the names only of these monuments were given to buildings, which were carried out in the Roman style.   In some cases, as in the Stadium and Palæstra adjoining, in the Greek Theatre, and in the Pœcile, these may have been intended as reproductions of similar constructions in Greece ; but as the Roman vault figures in most of them, it is evident that the general scheme only was Greek, the construction Roman.   In the Imperial Palace and the great terraces (portions of which were raised on immense substructures on the side of the Vale of Tempe) the Roman and not the Greek treatment of such work is very apparent, and even in Canopus, built in recollection of the famous resort of the Egyptians near Alexandria, the whole of the building is essentially Roman, and its only connection with Egypt was the name given to it and the treasures brought from that country with which it was enriched.

The plan shows the general configuration of the site on which the principal buildings were erected.   The highest point of the ridge is occupied by the Golden Peristyle (Piazza d'Oro), so called on account of the richness of its marble decoration.   Thence the ground falls gradually about 12 feet to the terrace of the Libraries (Cortile delle Biblioteche).[1]   Beyond that, towards the north, the ground sinks rapidly, rising again farther on, so that the Theatre (Teatro Greco) is partly excavated in the sides of a hill, and an elevated plateau gives a prominent position to the so-called Palæstra.   On the west side of the ridge the Pœcile is only 6 or 8 feet below the Library terrace, but the ground sinks again towards the south to the Canopus, where an artificial lake was excavated in the tufa rock.

There are three different orientations in the main group of buildings, which should be borne in mind in the study of the remains ; and that of the smaller palace is different again ; but the various levels of the site, and the prospect and aspect thought requisite for some of them, may have accounted for this.   As regards the theatres, the Romans often availed themselves of a hilly slope in which the cavea could be excavated,[2] and the sites selected here at Tivoli accounted for their position, as also for that of the gymnasium. The two so-called libraries faced north ; the walls remaining of these buildings still rise to a considerable height, and in the western

---

[1] The name is in reality quite arbitrary.

[2] The theatres of Balbus, Pompey and Marcellus in the Campus Martius at Rome, are exceptions.

library some are so thick as to suggest that they carried a tower used as an observatory.

The position of the terraces overlooking the Vale of Tempe would seem to indicate that the residential part of the palace occupied the range of buildings and courts from the courtyard of the libraries to the Golden Peristyle, where the state receptions were held ; and it was from these terraces that the finest views were obtained—views which to the present day, in consequence of the preservation of the natural features, are still a source of admiration to the traveller. The various courts of the palace are all planned regularly. The best preserved portion is the so-called hospitium, to the north-east of the Cortile delle Biblioteche, a central hall with small rooms on each side of it, in each of which are three alcoves sufficiently large to hold a bed. The black and white mosaic pavements are extremely well preserved throughout (Plate LXXVII). A well-preserved latrine is annexed : and there is another to the north-east. To the south-east of the Cortile was a nymphæum, which, with the exception of the vaulted hemicycle at the west end was open to the air.

Judging from the mosaic pavements found, and portions of the columns of the portico and the walls, the Golden Peristyle must have been one of the richest monuments of Hadrian's time. The octagonal hall on the south side, with four recessed niches in the angles and a semi-circular apse on the south side, held many of the most celebrated Greek sculptures and bronzes, and, according to M. Daumet, was lighted from the top in a special manner in order to display them to the best effect. The dome is interesting, as being divided into compartments (as is also the semi-dome of the Canopus, which has alternatively concave and flat divisions) ; this is a new feature, and so is the addition of blind arches externally, which spring from the piers and serve both to strengthen and to decorate the dome.[1] A series of terraces and peristyles at various levels led down to the valley. All the walls and substructures cease, however, about 200 feet from the stream, so that nature again asserted itself there, as she does at the present day.

The so-called Ninfeo near the theatre on the plan has been

---

[1] Other new features noticed by Rivoira (*Lombardic Architecture*, ii, 102) in Hadrian's Villa are—cross vaulting springing from corbels, angle pendentives or raccords, external decoration with pediments supported by columns resting on corbels and the use of external pilasters for purely decorative purposes. Other domes broken up into compartments may be seen in an earlier building later included in the Villa of the Gordiani and in the circular temple at Porto (ib. 40) cf. also the same author's *Roman Architecture*, 166 *sqq.*

ascertained by recent excavations to have been a semi-circular terrace with fountains and a round temple in the centre (*Melanges*, 1913, 261). The so-called Pœcile is believed to have been built in imitation of that at Athens described by Pausanias, and decorated with copies of the celebrated paintings by Polygnotus which existed in the Greek example. The remains consist of an immense wall 750 feet in length with a portico on each side, of which the travertine bases on which the columns stood still exist *in situ*, as also the marble panelling of the lower portion of the walls. The west end of it is supported by enormous arched substructions. The portico probably served for walking or driving under in sun or rain[1] and the open space (in the centre of which was an open basin for water) was probably a garden in the favourite shape of a hippodrome. Between the Libraries and the Pœcile, the planes of which form an obtuse angle, there is a large circular building (Plate LXXVII) which seems to have been designed to connect the two. Within the circular wall of the enclosure was a peristyle, and in the centre (with a tank of water round, 3 feet deep, and originally with two movable small bridges across) are the foundations of a structure which, Lanciani thinks, was a pavilion to which Hadrian could retire when he desired to be alone (generally known as the Teatro Marittimo)[2], while Hülsen prefers to consider it an aviary, pointing out that it corresponds to Varro's description, and to the reconstruction after this description by Ligorio.[3] To the east of it was a series of rooms heated by hypocausts, with a south and west exposure, which may provide an example of a *heliocaminus* (the name has often been wrongly applied to another part of the villa), *i.e.*, a place in which the sun's warmth might be used for therapeutic purposes.

To the south of the Poecile is a hall with three semi-circular recesses (interesting as the prototype of the Christian *cellae trichorae*), which recent excavations have shown to be a triclinium for summer use—once very elaborately decorated, but now much damaged.[4] To the east is the so-called Stadium, with a rectangular court to

---

[1] The fact that its length is one-seventh of a Roman mile strongly confirms this view (Hulsen in *Jahrbuch des Instituts*, xi (1896), Anzieger, 47).

[2] There is no better ground for the name Sala dei Filosofi, applied to the hall to the south-east of it.

[3] Cf. Blondel in *Mélanges Ecole Franc*, i (1881), 63 ; and Schultze in *Mem. Amer. Acad.*, ii (1918), pl. 6.

[4] A careful restoration is given by Chilman in *Mem. Amer. Acad.*, iv (1924), 103 *sqq.*

the east, having a piscina in the centre, and a subterranean passage under the portico which surrounded it. To the south are two complete thermal establishments, one (it is supposed) for men (Grandi Terme), the other for women (Piccole Terme). The former has a room with cross vaulting supported by large corbels of travertine at the corners, the first example of this, in which a part of the stucco decoration of the vault is still preserved (Plate LXXVIII). The latter have recently been carefully studied by Mr. Kennedy of the American Academy, whose restored plan, based on new excavations (in the course of which all the pavements were cleared) is published in *Memoirs of the American Academy in Rome*, Vol. III. The vaulting, which is almost everywhere preserved, is interesting, and the planning is remarkable.

Of other buildings there is no distinct record, so that now we come to the most remarkable building, that known as Canopus. Canopus was a suburb about 15 miles from Alexandria, in which there was a temple of Serapis, whither people proceeded from all parts of Egypt, some for religious purposes and others for pleasure; for besides various temples there were numerous hostelries on either side of the canal which led there from Alexandria, and this on festal days was crowded with the light barks not unlike Venetian gondolas shown in Egyptian paintings. Hadrian was apparently attracted by what he had seen at Canopus, and adjoining his villa he excavated an artificial valley 640 feet long by 246 feet wide, along the centre of which ran a canal, and at its south end erected an immense vaulted hemicycle, surrounded by niches in which were placed the statues he had brought from Egypt.[1] Raised aloft in the centre was the statue of Serapis, the great divinity of Canopus. Beyond, as may be seen in Piranesi's etching, was a vaulted passage, down which water flowed in cascades and supplied the artificial lake. On this lake boat races took place, and, in order to recall the hostelries of Egypt there were a number of two-storied halls on the west side where the guests invited by Hadrian took their repasts and probably tarried awhile. The great hemicycle, with a diameter of about 75 feet, was vaulted over, and its walls lined with marbles, with columns between the niches. In front of it was a double portico, on the marble roof of which the principal visitors witnessed the games and races.

The smaller palace (the so-called Accademia or Academy) is a

---

[1] The plan corresponds closely with that of the Serapeum in the Campus Martius.

distinct building to the south-west of the Canopus, with quite a
different orientation; the rooms are grouped round a large courtyard.

The ruins which remain at Tivoli represent only the more solid
portions of the constructions, but the landscapes which decorate
the walls of Pompeii and the famous garden scene of the Villa of
Livia at Prima Porta, suggest that in the Roman gardens there
were many varieties of ephemeral structures in wood (such as small
temples, shrines, nymphæa, etc.), arbours of trellis-work carrying
vines, groves of laurel, streams, fountains, and cascades. Alleys of
trees are frequently referred to by Pliny, as well as box trees cut
into various capricious shapes, which recall those existing at Ver-
sailles and in many of the English formal gardens.

THE PALACE OF DIOCLETIAN AT SPALATO.

The palace of Diocletian at Spalato, to which he retired in 305
A.D., differed from the usual plan of a Roman villa in that it constituted a fortress as well as a palace, the northern, eastern and western walls being protected by towers, and the south front by the sea.[1]
(Plates LXXIX and LXXX.) The palace measured 705 feet from
north to south, the north front 575 feet, and the south front 588
feet. There were four entrance gates, called respectively the
" Porta Aurea," or Golden Gate (Plate LXXXI), on the north side
(Porte Principale on the plan), the principal entrance, facing the
avenue leading to the palace; the narrow " Porta Aenea," on the
south, at a lower level than the rest, giving on to the sea, and communicating with the interior of the palace by an underground
passage; the " Porta Argentea " or Brazen Gate, facing the east;
and the " Porta Ferrea," or Iron Gate, facing the west. Three
avenues, 36 feet wide, with covered arcades on each side, led from
each gate, except the Porta Aenea, up to the centre of the whole
enclosure. South of this was the approach to the palace, consisting

---

[1] Robert Adam, the author of the only complete description of the palace
(published in 1766), until the appearance of M. Hébrard's description, cor·
sidered the towers to have been added as decorative features only; but the
Romans at Palmyra and Baalbec adopted an entirely different method of
decoration when they desired to give a monumental appearance to their structures. Besides, the inner and outer three gates at the entrances with open courts
between show that some kind of defence was intended. The internal plan
may be imitated from that of a Roman camp, or from some Eastern city, such
as Antioch: the numerous mason's marks seem indeed to betray an oriental
origin. Cf. *Mon. Ant.*, iii, 275, and Niemann, *Der Palast Diokletians in.
Spalato* (Vienna, 1910).

on the right and left, of an arcade in which the arches are carried direct on the capitals without any intermediate entablature. In the courts to the rear of these arcades were two buildings—one a small temple, which was tetrastyle, prostyle, with a vaulted cella, with stone coffering—the rich decoration of the portal is also very fine (Plate LXXX); the other the Imperial Mausoleum, often called the temple of Jupiter, circular, with a domical vault, remarkable for its construction, and decorated internally with niches and detached marble columns of the Corinthian [1] and Composite orders superimposed (Plate LXXXII). Externally it was octagonal and surrounded by a peristyle, the whole raised on a podium. The rest of the southern half of the enclosure was occupied by the Emperor's residence; while in the north half were two great blocks of buildings, supposed to have been those of the retainers and servants, of which few traces now exist.

The entrance portico of the palace consisted of four columns in antis, the two central ones wider apart and spanned by an arch, round which the whole entablature is carried in the same way as in the Propylæa at Damascus. This portico led to a circular hall lighted from the top, which is virtually the only great hall still remaining. The plan of the chambers on the lower floor on this side of the enclosure—in the northern portion of the enclosure there were no such chambers, as the level rose considerably going away from the sea—which have been carefully studied by M. Hébrard (they are now used as cellars) show that there was an extensive series of large halls on the south of which was the long gallery erroneously called by Robert Adam the Cryptoporticus,[2] which consisted of a corridor, 520 feet long and 24 feet wide, with a range of 51 windows on the south side facing the sea. This great gallery served to connect all the various halls on its north side, and, being probably filled with works of art accumulated by Diocletian, must have presented a magnificent appearance. Above it was an attic, and upon this a terrace. On the west side of the palace were the baths. The range of windows in the walls forming the external enclosure shows that there were two storeys of rooms (serving as quarters for the Imperial Guard and as storerooms) round the whole

---

[1] The lower has a heavy trabeation like that of the central hall of the Thermæ of Diocletian.

[2] The term cryptoporticus is, as a rule, given to a vaulted corridor underneath the ground, which served either as private communication for the owner of the house or palace, or for the service of an establishment.

northern portion of the enceinte, with a portico in front of them, interrupted only by the open courts between the inner and outer gateways.   There was an open passage between the portico and the main blocks of buildings in the interior.   Externally the design of the southern gallery suggests that at each end and in the middle were halls separated by columns.   These halls were raised higher than the main gallery, and lighted by immense windows, a design being employed in them similar to that in the entrance portico, viz., having a central intercolumniation spanned by an arch. All the columns dividing the windows were semi-detached and carried on corbels.   The same disposition is to be observed in the Golden Gateway (Plate LXXXI), where the upper part is decorated with a series of arches carried on six detached columns, resting on richly-carved corbels.   Within two of the arches are semicircular niches, and under the latter two others which flank the relieving arch of the entrance doorway   The principal interest attached to the palace at Spalato lies in the decadent forms of some of its architectural features, which are looked upon as the precursors of the Byzantine and Lombard styles.   As a matter of fact, the decadence (if it should be so styled) had already set in at least one or two centuries earlier.   It has already been shown that the arch over a wide central intercolumniation dates back to 151 A.D., being found in the Propylæa at Damascus and in the temple at Atil.   Capitals carrying an arch without an intervening entablature are found at Pompeii.[1]   Columns carried on corbels existed in the Thermæ of Trajan, built in the second century A.D., between the niches of the great hemicycles on either side of the enclosure,[2] and the accentuation of the Roman relieving arch over a lintel by enriching it with mouldings, is found in the second century in the synagogue at Kefr Birim (Plate XXXIV) 24 miles east of S. Jean d'Acre, in Syria.

These are the four leading features of the decadence in Roman architectural forms, and although not introduced for the first time in the palace at Spalato, they are certainly exhibited in it in a more striking manner than in any other building.

---

[1] Choisy, *Histoire de l'Architecture*, 515.

[2] Rivoira, *Roman Architecture*, 128 (who cites parallels in the Thermæ of Titus, Caracalla, etc., illustrated in Palladio's drawings at the R.I.B.A.).

PLATE LXXXII.

INTERIOR OF THE IMPERIAL MAUSOLEUM (NOW THE CATHEDRAL),
SPALATO.

PLATE LXXXIII.

FOUNTAIN IN THE HOUSE OF THE
BALCONY AT POMPEII.

THE IMPLUVIUM IN THE HOUSE OF CORNELIUS RUFUS
AT POMPEII.

PRIVATE HOUSES.

The paucity of remains of ancient private houses in Rome, would, even with the descriptions of Vitruvius, give us but a poor insight into their design were it not for the discovery of Pompeii, Herculaneum and Ostia. It is true that the first two were towns of second or even third-rate importance, but a comparison of the design and execution of their houses with the buildings just cited shows that the difference consisted chiefly in the employment of real marble in Rome instead of painted imitations, and in a superior style of execution in the wall paintings. The lavish extravagance in the marble decorations of the mansions of the more wealthy citizens, and the rapid growth in the use of this luxury, are referred to by Pliny (*N.H.* xxxvi, 15), who says " that the house of Lepidus (B.C. 76) was considered the finest in Rome, and 30 years later was not the hundredth." According to Pliny, the extravagance consisted in the employment of monolithic columns of various Greek marbles and the lining of all the internal walls with marble panelling such as is found in the Pantheon and in the palaces on the Palatine.

The detailed descriptions of the Roman house given by Vitruvius, and the names he gives to the several apartments, apply so closely to those found in Pompeii that one is able to follow generally the arrangement of plan, though his attention would appear to have been directed more to the correct proportions of the various rooms than to their relative positions which were fixed by tradition.

The houses at Pompeii seem all to have been arranged on a similar plan, the size and number of the apartments varying according to the rank and means of the owner and to local circumstances. Light was admitted to the rooms (at all events on the ground floor) from the courts in the interior. This was doubtless for the sake of greater privacy, and the same custom still obtains throughout the East.

Recent discoveries have, however, given us an entirely new idea of the appearance of the streets of Pompeii. The excavations in the Strada dell' Abbondanza, conducted with far greater care and success than ever before, have shown us façades richly decorated with brightly coloured paintings below, while the walls of the upper storeys, so far from being blank, as was generally believed, had balconies and open colonnades or windows for the admission of light and the same was the case at Ostia (*infra.* p. 161). The houses of the upper classes were divided into two parts, in accordance with the domestic customs of the Romans and their double life; the first being public and the second private. The public part comprised the prothyrum, atrium, cubiculæ, tablinum, alæ and fauces: the private part, the peristyle, triclinium, œcus, cubicula, bibliotheca, exedra, lararium and offices (see Fig. 32).

The prothyrum, or vestibule, was a passage between the shops leading to the atrium. It was sometimes preceded by a recessed

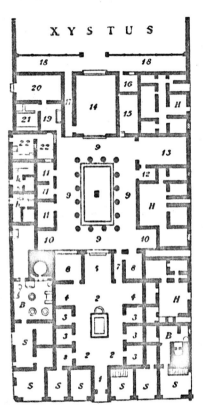

FIG. 32.—PLAN OF THE HOUSE OF PANSA AT POMPEII.

porch. The atrium was the largest hall in the public part of the house, and it was here that the host received his friends and supporters. Except in the case of the poorest houses, the atrium was always lighted through an opening in the centre of the roof called the compluvium, and the rain falling from the eaves direct, or collected in a gutter and passing through spouts, often in the form of lion's heads, was discharged into a tank called the impluvium (Plate LXXXIII), about 18 inches deep and generally lined with marble. At one end of the tank, and opposite the entrance to the atrium, was a small marble table, and a figure in bronze or marble sometimes holding a vase or flower from which water poured into the impluvium (Plate LXXXIII). Of the five varieties of atriums described by Vitruvius, the Tuscan atrium is the one which seems to have been most generally adopted in Pompeii. The roof was probably framed with two transverse beams crossing the atrium, and two longitudinal beams trimmed between them to form the opening or compluvium. These beams

carried the joists and ceiling. Where the width of the atrium was too great to allow of its being spanned by beams, columns were placed at each angle of the impluvium to support them, and this variety is described by Vitruvius as the tetrastyle atrium. In houses of importance, where in consequence of the size and number of rooms round the atrium more space was required, a large number of columns carried the roof with the compluvium enclosure, and this arrangement was known as the " Corinthian atrium."[1]

There was a fourth variety, known as the " atrium displuviatum," where the roof sloped down outwards so that the rain was carried to the outside, away from the compluvium. This sometimes necessitated the employment of trough gutters, with rainwater pipes in the angles of the atrium to carry off the rain. These, however, Vitruvius says (VI, 3), " are constantly in want of repair, for the pipes which receive the water from the eaves being against the walls, and not capable of taking at once the water which should be carried off, it overflows from the check it meets and injures the woodwork and walls in this sort of buildings." A much better light, however, he points out, was given to the atrium and the rooms round. A new type of atrium has recently been discovered in a large fulling establishment in the Strada dell' Abbondanza, with the opening in the centre of a perfectly flat roof.

The " atrium testudinatum " (where there was no opening in the roof) was found only in the smallest houses or where there was an upper storey. In these cases light was obtained from an open court beyond.

The rooms round the atrium were :—

a. *Cubicula*, or small sleeping rooms, generally set apart for visitors or for the male portion of the family.

b. *Alae*, or wings, recesses for conversation or reading.

c. *Tablinum*, a large room facing the vestibule, always opening into the atrium and sometimes into the peristyle or a portico beyond, without any wall or separation. Curtains were probably drawn across this room on either side, and in Herculaneum and Pompeii bronze hooks have been found to which they may have been suspended. This room contained the family archives, statues and pictures.

d. *Fauces*, passages which admitted of passing from the public

---

[1] The title had nothing to do with the Order, in Pompeii, for as often as not the capitals were either Tuscan or Ionic.

to the private portion of the house without passing through the tablinum.

In the private portion of the house were :—

e. *The Peristyle*, which resembled the Corinthian atrium, having a colonnaded portico round it, but it was much larger.   The central court, open to the sky, was planted with flowers and shrubs, with a small fountain in the centre.   The margin round this court was of stone and sunk in the centre, to form a gutter to carry off the droppings from the eaves.

f. *Cubicula*, or sleeping apartments, for the owner and his family.

g. *Triclinium*, or dining-room, the name being derived from the three couches placed round a central table, leaving the fourth side open for the service.   Sometimes these rooms were of large size, so as to accommodate an increased number of guests, and a summer triclinium facing the north is occasionally found.

h. *Oecus*, the largest room in the private portion of the house, usually in the central axis of the house and facing the peristyle. According to Vitruvius, this was the hall occupied by the mistress of the house and where she received her guests, but it was also used as a banqueting room on special occasions, probably on account of its size.

i. *Pinacotheca*, or picture gallery for easel pictures, not often found in Pompeii.

k. *Bibliotheca*, or library, a small room to hold papyri or rolls of manuscript.[1]

l. *Exedræ*, rooms corresponding with the alæ in the public portion of the house, but here occupied by the family or the female guests.

m. *Lararium*, a chamber devoted to the Lares, or household gods.   Sometimes a niche at one end of the peristyle would be considered sufficient.

n. *Culina*, the kitchen.

o. *Xyxtus*, or garden, at the back of the larger houses only, sometimes with a portico facing it, or, as in the Villa of Diomede, on all sides.

The kitchen and storerooms were of small size, and placed on one

---

[1] In the excavations made at Herculaneum in 1753, a library in a private house was discovered with bookcases round the walls and one in the centre of the room.   Although it contained about 1,700 papyrus rolls, the room was not larger than 15 feet by 20 feet, which suggests that the Roman library was probably used as a store only for such documents, which were taken out and read in the exedræ or other apartments of the house.

PLATE LXXXIV.

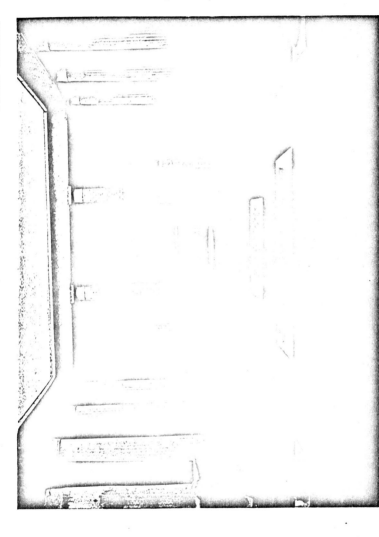

THE PERISTYLE OF THE HOUSE OF THE VETTII AT POMPEII.

PLATE LXXXV.

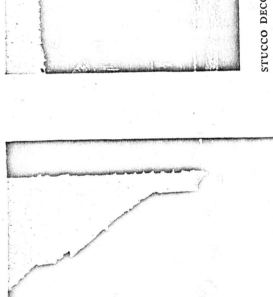

STUCCO DECORATION ON THE SOUTH-WEST WALL OF THE STABIAN BATHS AT POMPEII.

HOUSE FAÇADE, POMPEII.

side of the farther end of the peristyle, with a back entrance. The upper floor of the house (when it existed) was probably occupied by servants or slaves, but sometimes there was a solarium, or terrace.

The house of Pansa is the best representative of the more important residences in Pompeii, as it contains nearly all the rooms which are referred to by Vitruvius. It occupied, with the shops, two bakeries, and three small residences (all apparently let out on lease), an entire block or insula covering an area of about 300 feet long by 100 feet wide. The entrance to the house was in the centre of one end of the block, through a lofty doorway flanked by pilasters in stone with Ionic caps, carrying presumably an entablature and pediment, now gone. Passing through the porch and vestibule (1), one enters a Tuscan atrium (2), with impluvium in the centre, and three small rooms (cubiculæ) (3) on each side, one of which (s) on the left was apparently occupied by the "dispensator," who sold the produce of Pansa's estate, as there is a door between it and one of the shops. Beyond the cubiculæ are two recesses or alæ (4). Opposite the entrance door was the tablinum (5), which opened also to the peristyle beyond,[1] with a passage (7) (fauces) leading direct from the atrium to the peristyle (9) and on the right and left (8), two rooms, the smaller one a library, the other (6) a triclinium. Beyond was the peristyle, with sixteen columns of the Ionic order. On the right and left are two other recesses or exedræ (10), and on the left three more cubiculæ (11). In the centre beyond was the œcus or reception-room of the family (14)—a passage (17) leading to the garden in the extreme rear—and the winter triclinium (15) on the right. Beyond these again was a portico (8) overlooking the garden, and a small room (16) which may have been the boudoir of the lady of the house. To the left of the passage were the kitchen (culina) and offices (19, 20 and 21); a second room of larger size (13) on the right is thought to have been the principal triclinium; (s, s) were shops, the two at the corner of the block being in communication with the bakeries (B) beyond. Besides, on the left, were two rooms (h, h), each with an upper floor, and on the right, three small apartments (H, H, H).

---

[1] In the House of the Silver Wedding fastenings in bronze were discovered *in situ* which showed that curtains attached to them could be drawn across the rear of the tablinum, and similar enclosures were probably provided for other doorways, as no doors except at the entrance of the house have been traced.

Assuming the two doors in the prothyrum or vestibule to be open, and the curtains at the rear of the tablinum and the front of the œcus drawn aside, the passer-by in the street commanded a view of the interior of the house from one end to the other. This seems to have been the leading principle on which all the houses in Pompeii were planned, and may account in some cases for the elaborate nature of some of the sculptural accessories, even in the smaller houses, such as that of which Plate LXXXIII is an example. Even in the case of a small house, where the peristyle terminated in a wall, the wall was painted to represent a garden beyond.

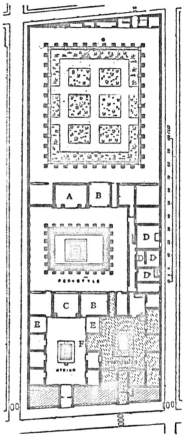

FIG. 33.—PLAN OF THE HOUSE OF THE FAUN AT POMPEII.

Variations from the plan just described are found in the House of the Faun,[1] where the peristyle is turned the other way and its axis is not the same as that of the atrium (Fig. 33). This was apparently in consequence of there being a second residence on one side (probably occupied by some member of the same family, as there are three or four doors communicating between the two). All the bedrooms of the family of the principal house were on an upper floor over the œcus and triclinium.

In the House of the Silver Wedding[2] the atrium was tetrastyle—

[1] The names given to the houses are derived from features found in them, such as works of art or inscriptions with the names of persons.

[2] So called because it was excavated in 1882, in the presence of the King and Queen of Italy, on the celebration of their silver wedding.

that is, with four columns of the Corinthian order supporting the ceiling. The dimensions of the atrium (50 by 40 feet) made it impossible to cover it in any other way.

The House of Epidius Rufus has a Corinthian atrium with sixteen Doric columns, but no peristyle, there being only a portico overlooking the garden at the back.

In the House of the Tragic Poet, remarkable for the paintings it contained, representing scenes from the *Iliad*, the peristyle was enclosed with a porticus on three sides only.

Different from all of these is the House of the Vettii, excavated in the year 1894. Owing to want of space, the atrium adjoins the peristyle, so that the tablinum occupies the position of one of the alæ, and has a wide opening towards the peristyle from which it appears to be mainly lighted. The illustration (Plate LXXXIV) shows the peristyle with its original decorative features, such as pedestals with statues or figures, marble tables, baths, hermæ,[1] etc.

The only two other houses which might be referred to are the House of Sallust and the Villa of Diomede; the former because it apparently belongs to another class of residence, viz., an inn. On the left-hand side of the vestibule is a shop for the sale of drinks, which has a wide opening into the vestibule and a door leading to the atrium. On the right is a second room, which was open to the street, the vestibule and the atrium. There is no peristyle, but a porticus facing a small garden in the rear, where in the farther angle is an open-air triclinium, which still retains its marble table in the centre and three stone couches. The roof consisted of a trellis, over which probably a vine was trained, similar to many such retreats to be found in Italy in the present day. Here the rear wall was painted to represent a garden. The Villa of Diomede was situated outside the town, beyond the Herculaneum Gate. It was built on sloping ground, so that the entrance door in the centre of the main front, is 5 feet above the roadway, and the ground at the rear is at a lower level. The central axis of the villa lies at an angle of 45 degrees with the road, and the triangular plot on the left of the entrance door has been utilised for a complete set of baths. From the entrance porch (the only example projecting in front of a house) one

[1] Herms or Hermæ were in great demand by the wealthy Romans for the decoration of their gardens, and they were generally crowned with the busts of philosophers and poets. They were derived from the Greek custom of raising a heap of stones or sometimes a single block as a sign-post with distances inscribed upon it, etc., to mark a boundary of land or a cross road, and were dedicated to Hermes, the god of roads and boundaries.

entered direct into the peristyle. At first sight it resembles the Corinthian atrium, especially as the tablinum occupies the usual position ;
but the centre court was planted with shrubs and flowers, with a
fountain in the centre as in a peristyle. The rooms round also are of
larger size, and one of them (probably the principal bedroom) is of
elliptical shape, with three windows overlooking a garden, being
virtually a bow window. At the back of the tablinum a colonnade
with terrace in front overlooking the garden. Under the terrace, at
a lower level, was. a series of rooms, of which the vaults remained
intact. These were all lighted through a portico overlooking the
garden, which measured 85 feet by 73 feet, with a small fish-pond
in the centre, and beyond it an arbour with columns round carrying
trellis-work. The portico was carried on all four sides of the garden,
and consisted of square piers with moulded caps standing on a low
wall. Beneath the portico on three sides were cellars in a
cryptoporticus, vaulted and lighted through openings in the low
wall above.

HOUSES IN ROME.

Passing on to the two most important examples in Rome, we
find that the house of Livia[1] was on two levels. On the lower
level, reached from the cryptoporticus, was a court, the impluvium
of which was supported by two square pillars. Facing the entrance
are three rectangular rooms, with fine paintings. To the right is
the triclinium, by the side of which was a flight of steps leading to a
large number of rooms and a set of baths, all on the higher level
behind the tablinum. A staircase in the court round which the
.bedrooms were placed led to an upper storey, of which nothing
remains.

The House of the Vestals (Fig. 34) differed from any of the examples already described, in that it consisted[2] mainly of one immense
atrium (180 feet long by 48 feet wide), surrounded with a peristyle
of columns in two storeys giving access to a large number of rooms
on three sides. At the farther end of the peristyle was the so-called
tablinum, a hall 41 feet long by 29 feet wide, and 41 feet to the soffit
of the barrel vault with which it was covered. On each side of the

---

[1] It is really the house that Augustus bought from the Hortensii.

[2] The description given in the text applies to the building only in the form
which it assumed after its restoration by Septimius Severus. For its previous
architectural history see Van Deman, *Atrium Vestæ*.

PLATE LXXXVI.

AN APARTMENT IN THE HOUSE OF SIRICUS AT POMPEII.

PLATE LXXXVII.

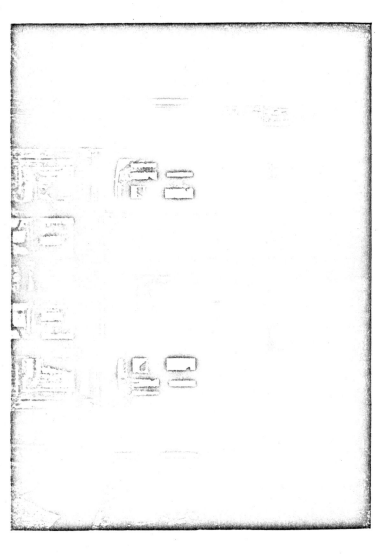

AN APARTMENT IN THE HOUSE OF THE VETTII AT POMPEII.

tablinum, with doorways opening into it, were three rooms assumed to have been the private rooms of the six Vestal Virgins. Baths, kitchen and bakeries, and stairs occupied the farther corner of the site. A great portion of the upper storey of the House of the Vestals still exists on the side of the Palatine Hill, and is of special interest as being the only instance in which hypocausts have been found above the ground floor. The rooms were small, but the walls were all at one time faced with marble slabs, and many of them contained baths sunk in the floor and lined with

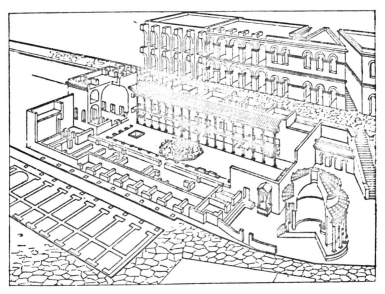

FIG. 34.—THE HOUSE OF THE VESTALS.

marble. With the exception of the several offices, all the rooms on the ground floor were also cased and paved with rich oriental marbles on both wall and floor, and the columns of the peristyle were monoliths of cipollino and " breccia corallina."

The earliest houses in Pompeii have façades of blocks of limestone ; in those of the next period tufa is used. Artistically they are still under Greek influence, and their architectural forms are pure and good.

After the foundation of the Roman colony in 80 B.C., marble and a finer limestone (wrongly called travertine) came into use. The internal walls were built of rubble masonry of tufa, at first laid in clay mortar only, with occasional bond stones, and these required therefore a stucco coating to preserve them. In the time of Augustus burnt brick was employed for quoins and bonding courses, and the rubble masonry was laid in mortar. The system of building in brickfaced concrete practised in Rome does not seem to have been extensively used in Pompeii, but the outside walls were faced with opus incertum and opus reticulatum, subsequently covered with stucco and painted. Externally the colours employed were very simple, and confined to yellow with a darker colour for the lower portion. Sometimes, as in the illustration shown (Plate LXXXV), there would be an architectural treatment, with pilasters and panels between, all moulded in stucco. In the main streets the fronts of the houses were occupied by shops, which were gaily decorated with colours. Architectural character was given to the house by the entrance doorway, which was flanked with pilasters and capitals in stone carrying an entablature, and the upper storey, as we have seen, generally had a balcony or colonnade.

In some cases, as we have seen, the internal roof was a flat plaster roof, with fresco decoration. The terra cotta decoration of the exterior was of considerable importance and beauty. The sima or gutter round the compluvium, of which there are some very rich examples, was the first feature which would attract the attention of any visitor to the atrium, and above this the antefixæ forming the termination of the covering tile roll would rise and break the skyline.

The wall paintings were executed in fresco by painting in with water-colour on the moist stucco of a freshly-prepared surface. Vitruvius gives descriptions of the methods employed in Rome, but those in Pompeii do not seem to have been so elaborately prepared. As a rule the design and composition of the figure subjects are so far superior to the execution that we may fairly assume they are replicas of well-known subjects. On the completion of the work it is thought that the colours were heightened and fixed by the application of wax under heat, and in consequence of this they are sometimes described under the head of encaustic painting.

There are three, if not four, distinct styles of decoration in Pompeii and Herculaneum. The first is the (wrongly) so-called " incrustation " style (better " structural "—for " incrustation " is marble inlay). This was derived, according to one view, from Asia Minor perhaps by way of Sicily, and direct from Greece,

according to another, which is probably the better.[1] Its use appears to have begun about the end of the second century B.C., and it consists in the division of the surface into panels in actual relief, in imitation of marble facing.

The early second style in Pompeii belongs to the end of the Republic (see the houses of the Labyrinth and of Gavius Rufus, the villa Item and the villa of Boscoreale[2]). Here marble facing is imitated only by painting on a flat surface ; and architecture is introduced. In it, Delbrück maintains, we see the late Hellenistic architecture of the end of the Republic ; and the style is, he thinks, taken from Greek painting, possibly by way of Syria. Rostowzew, on the other hand, thinks that the second style developed in Italy itself, owing to the fact that the negative evidence shows that no parallels to it can be found in the East in the first century B.C. It is, however, very likely as Fiechter thinks, that Pompeian painting, both of this and of the third style, was modelled on Hellenistic stage decoration, in which columns (with, later on, screens between them) were placed in front of the back wall of the stage, which was itself decorated with columns and openings. And this shows that the smaller scenes which are introduced into the architectural setting are, as a rule, intended to be seen through an opening in the wall, and are not to be considered as pictures fixed to it.

To the first style belongs the system of dividing the surface into panels and varying the colours.

To the second, the introduction of reproductions of well-known Greek paintings, enclosed with architectural features, such as columns, entablatures, and friezes.

In the third style (up to about 50 A.D.) we find a highly ornamental decoration strongly under Egyptian influence (whether developed there or not is uncertain) with considerable purity of form and delicacy of colour, but with no reference to reality. As Vitruvius, who condemns it unreservedly,[3] remarks, " we now have fresco paintings of monstrosities, rather than truthful representations of definite things. For instance, reeds are put in the place of columns, fluted appendages with curly leaves and volutes instead of pediments, candelabra supporting representations of shrines, and on top

---

[1] Rostowzew in *Journ. Hell. Stud.*, xxxix (1919), 159.

[2] There are some interesting examples of a transitional style in a Republican house under the " Lararium " of the Domitianic Domus Augustiana on the Palatine (as yet unpublished).

[3] VII, 5, 3, 4.

of these pediments numerous tender stalks and volutes growing up from the roots having human figures senselessly seated upon them . . . . . . such things do not exist and cannot exist and never have existed. Hence, it is the new taste that has caused bad judges of poor art to prevail over true artistic excellence."

In the fourth style the architectural accessories are of the wildest description (Plates LXXXVI and LXXXVII), and have led some authorities to recognise in the attenuated forms given to the columns a metallic origin. It is true that the use of iron and bronze, to which we have already drawn attention, shows that the Romans were well acquainted with these materials, and the bronze candelabra, tripods, and lampholders (Plate LXXXVIII) found in Pompeii have precisely that tenuity which is represented in the columns painted on the walls ; but on the other hand, the mutules in the overhanging eaves, the panelling of the ceilings, and the arched ribs in the vault (all constructional features in wood and concrete and brick), are rarely missed in these paintings, and never found in candelabra or lamp-holders. Whatever may have been the origin of the wire-drawn columns, the effect of the general composition of these wall paintings is of the most charming description, and one is often surprised by the effect of distance suggested by them.

There is still one other type of decoration, that which consists in the representation of natural objects, such as plants and flowers, etc., which seems to have arisen in Egypt; and from the descriptions given of the marvellous dexterity of celebrated Greek artists in this class of work we may assume that the Pompeian artists followed their example, and sometimes with exceptional ability.

The examples of mural painting in Rome are much superior. There are far finer examples than any in Pompeii (with the exception of the frescoes of the Villa Item)[1] of the second style in the House of Livia, and in the house found on the right bank of the Tiber near the Farnesina, the paintings of which are now in the Museo delle Terme, together with the beautiful stucco decorations of the vaults, but they require adequate publication and further study before their place in the history in art can be fixed.

Mosaic pavements are rare in Pompeii, and those of the Casa del Fauno (including the famous mosaic of Alexander at the battle

---

[1] For the villa Item see Mudie-Cooke in *Journal of Roman Studies*, iii (1913), 157; Rizzo in *Memorie Acad. di Napoli*, Nuova Serie, iii (1918), 39.

PLATE LXXXVIII.

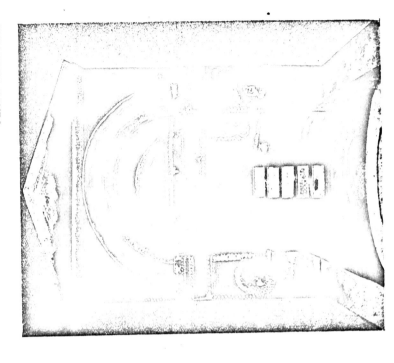

MOSAIC FOUNTAIN, POMPEII.

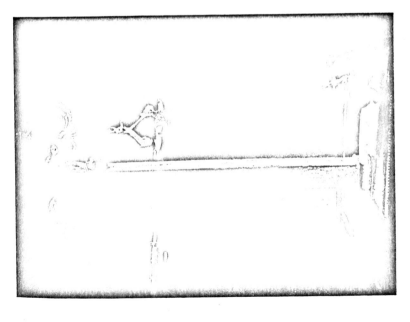

BRONZE LAMP STANDARD FROM THE VILLA

PLATE LXXXIX.

TIMGAD: MOSAIC FROM THE PISCINA.

MOSAIC AT WOODCHESTER, GLOUCESTERSHIRE.

of Issus, now in the museum of Naples) are quite exceptional.
Their origin has been traced not to the art of Alexandria, but to that
of the Greek mainland.[1] Better examples of decorative mosaics
will be found in Rome, Ostia and elsewhere in Italy ; but of the more
elaborate none are so fine as those at Timgad (Plate LXXXIX).
While that at Woodchester (*ib.*) is still more complicated in design,
though less skilfully executed. Some of the small fountains at
Pompeii are decorated in mosaic, and are quite attractive (Plate
LXXXVIII).

It remains to speak of Ostia, close to the mouth of the Tiber,
where excavations still in progress are bringing to light the remains
of a great commercial city, the port of Rome.[2] Its trade was almost
entirely connected with the importation of foodstuffs for the needs
of the city.

Of the harbour works at Ostia itself nothing has so far been
brought to light ; and, since it was the practice for ships to enter
the river, and there discharge the whole or some portion of their
cargoes, these works were probably confined to quay walls along the
river bank, the ancient line of which has so far not been explored.
Scanty traces of the harbour built by Claudius on the right bank of
the river may still be seen, but the hexagonal basin of Trajan's
harbour, the channels connecting it with the sea and with the river,
and the extensive buildings round it, which are situated on the
further (right) bank of the navigable arm of the river, though
hastily studied in 1867, still await thorough exploration. At
Ostia, on the other hand, the remains that have so far been laid
bare belong to the principal streets and buildings of the town.[3]
The main street, a prolongation of the road from Rome, is flanked
by tombs until it reaches the city gate, from which it has been laid
bare for a distance of about 800 yards in a perfectly straight line.
After this (outside the shoreward gate of the original rectangular
fort out of which Ostia grew) it turned to run at right angles to the
coast. The portion of the town on the right of this street is laid
out in rectangular blocks, having been rebuilt in the time of Hadrian,
while the remains of earlier buildings of several periods have been
found below, and even under some of the streets ; there are traces

---

[1] W. Leonhard in *Neapolis*, ii (1914), 42 ff., 135 ff.
[2] See Ashby in *Wonders of the Past*, pt. 17, p. 836 *sqq.*
[3] See T. Ashby in *Journal of Roman Studies*, II (1912), 153 *sqq.* The plan
there given is not repeated here, as it is no longer up to date. A new one is
now available in Calza's *Guide*, which should be consulted by all students and
visitors.

of a diverged orientation on the left, determined by the line of the coastroad.   The street was flanked by colonnades, and on it lie the most important buildings of the town.   First come the public baths, remarkable for their pavements in black and white mosaic, representing marine deities, Tritons, etc.   The courtyard in the centre was a *palæstra*, built over a huge water reservoir of an earlier period.   Behind them are the barracks of the *vigiles*, a police force which also served as fire-brigade, established in a large private house which had been altered for the purpose.

Next to the baths comes the theatre, behind the stage of which is a large open space known as the Foro delle Corporazioni (Plate XC).   In the centre is the temple of Ceres, and round three sides of the space is a portico, containing the offices of the various commercial corporations of Ostia and the shipping guilds of Sardinia, N. Africa, etc., which traded with Ostia, their names and emblems being shown in the mosaic pavements of the offices.   Some distance further on, on the right, is the most prominent ruin in Ostia—the lofty temple generally known as that of Vulcan, though it is certainly that of Jupiter, Juno, and Minerva,—the Capitolium, as restored in Imperial times.   Opposite to it is the Forum, the area of which has now been entirely cleared.   The most prominent building in it was the temple of Rome and Augustus, some interesting architectural remains of which have been found and set up.   On the north-east of the Forum was a colonnade, and on the south-east an arcade, behind which lies the much ruined basilica.   Its short side fronted on to the main street opposite the Curia, which was on the same side as the Capitolium.   The rest of the town is occupied by stores and private houses ; the latter are of especial interest, for in Ostia we find, almost for the first time, houses of quite a different type to the traditional Pompeian house, which occurs only twice in the whole town.   The atrium is lacking, light being obtained from numerous windows opening on to the streets or open areas ; and the houses are divided into a number of independent apartments or flats.   Calza [1] discusses the new type of house which has come to light in Ostia, which has very many characteristics of the modern house, while it differs from the *domus* as hitherto known in the following points :—

(1) the existence of three or four floors, each identical in plan, with a continuous roof.

---

[1] *Mon. Linc.*, xxiii (1915), 541 *sqq* ; xxvi (1920), 32 *sqq.* ; *Architettura ed Arti Decorative*, iii (1923), I, 49.

(2) the introduction of façades on streets or open areas.

(3) the formation of blocks composed of several independent apartments or flats (*cenacula*) furnished with one or more staircases opening on the street.

(4) the dependence of the plan of the apartment on the façade.

(5) an abundance of windows in a continuous line, opening into every room.

(6) the introduction of alleyways (*angiportus*) to facilitate communication with the street.

(7) the independence of the several floors and apartments.

(8) the introduction of porticos, loggias and balconies in the external façades.

(9) the introduction of courtyards or open spaces in the interior of the block, as subsidiary to the façade. The best example is the so-called Casa di Diana, which reminds one of a house of the seventeenth or eighteenth century in Rome (Plates XC, XCI).

(10) the equal importance of the rooms in each apartment and the consequent disappearance of the *atrium*.

(11) the use of unfaced brickwork, the arches being picked out in deeper red (Plate XC).

In this new type of house he finds the *insula*, or tenement house, of the ancient writers, and in it sees many of the characteristics of Italian domestic architecture of to-day. He lays special stress upon the plan of an important group of three houses occupying the greater part of a block (the rest of which was taken up by a row of thirteen shops)[1], and united by a common façade, probably four stories in height. The larger house at the corner was probably an inn, while the two smaller houses, which are identical in plan and size, contained (as did the upper floors of the inn) a series of flats one above the other, which could be let off separately. Light and air were provided by the garden in the centre, upon which a number of large windows opened, while in the large house most of the rooms faced on the street (Plate XCI). As at Pompeii, a number of the houses still have their external balconies preserved. The paintings with which these houses are decorated are of inferior quality, but the brick and *opus reticulatum* facing to the concrete walls is admirable, and the houses have an aspect of solidity and strength which is lacking at Pompeii.

---

[1] It is noticeable that these two constructions, in obedience to the building law of Nero, have not a party wall but two separate walls, with a space of 2 feet wide between them.

AA

CHAPTER IX.

PRIVATE LIFE AMONG THE ROMANS.

WE have already seen that the original Italic and Mediterranean house developed from the circular or oblong hut, which had a hearth in the centre. As a result it was simply a room with an opening to let out the smoke from the fire; and this is the origin and perhaps the actual derivation of the term *atrium* (*ater*, black, because the beams were blackened by soot). As the opening (*compluvium*) in the roof became larger, a basin (*impluvium*) was placed in the centre to receive the rain; then the *tablinum* was added; and later still, under Greek influence, the peristyle was built behind the *atrium*.

We must remember, however, that the only type of house that has been known until lately is the Pompeian, and that the apartment house, which has recently come to light at Ostia, gives us probably a far better picture of the average house in Rome. In both these cities space was far more valuable than at Pompeii, and only the wealthy could permit themselves the luxury of a large internal courtyard. The *insulæ*, or tenement houses, showed such a tendency to increase in height that they were limited by Augustus to 70 and by Nero to 60 feet.

The small size of the houses of the poor, and of the individual rooms, and especially of the bedrooms, was compensated for by the existence of large public buildings and numerous places of public resort. It is often said, with a certain amount of truth, that the modern Italian of the poorer classes (to whom both the word and the idea of comfort are unknown) lives in the piazza or in the street; and the ancient Romans (except the very rich) seem, under the Empire and in the cities, to have spent almost equally little time at home. They had a variety of places of public resort and

PLATE XC.

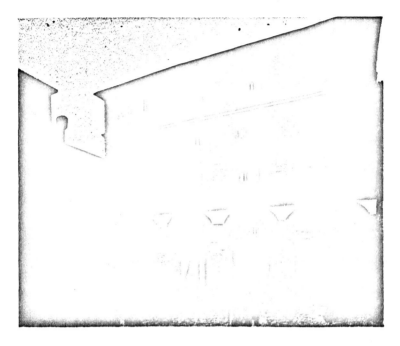

OSTIA : RESTORATION OF THE CASA DI DIANA.

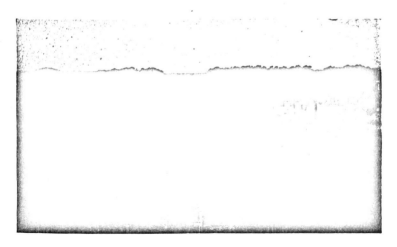

SO-CALLED "FORO DELLE CORPORAZIONI," OSTIA.

PLATE XCI.

THE "CASA DEI DIPINTI," OSTIA.

THE "CASA DI DIANA," OSTIA.
(NOTE THE BALCONY.)

while the streets of ancient Rome were proportionately far narrower than those of the modern city, we must remember that there was very little vehicular traffic, especially in the daytime. Driving through the streets of Rome was only permitted, until the fourth century after Christ, to those who were taking part in the service of the gods and in public festivals; and heavy carts could only circulate at night, except for the transport of materials for public buildings. The narrow streets, well suited to the climate, as they kept out the winter wind and the summer sun, were sufficiently wide for foot traffic.

A large proportion of the area of the city of Rome was well provided with parks and gardens, both private and public,[1] the former predominating; for though Cæsar bequeathed his gardens to the Roman people, and Augustus and Agrippa provided public gardens in the Campus Martius, their successors did nothing to increase them, devoting their attention rather to public buildings (porticos, thermæ, etc.) of which gardens formed an integral part; while the parks, in our sense of the word, of Ancient Rome, were almost entirely imperial or private property. The cupidity of Agrippina and Messalina had led to very large increases of the imperial domain at the expense of the lives of the rich owners of the gardens they coveted; and Nero's formation of the Golden House was only the culmination of a process which they had begun. Smaller gardens also arose round temples and tombs.

The houses of Pompeii and Ostia have so far not thrown much light on the dwellings of the very poor, and both the traditional type, and the newly discovered apartment house provide fairly comfortable accommodation. We may notice the almost complete absence of hypocausts, except for baths, even in the Imperial Palaces on the Palatine. Seneca, writing in the first century after Christ, regarded them as an enervating luxury, and even in a cold climate like Britain, only one or two rooms in each house were as a rule provided with them. Portable braziers were largely used, but cannot have produced sufficient heat. We may remember, however, that until the introduction of central heating, the majority of rooms in the houses of modern Rome were without proper means of warming, and many of the older houses in Italy still lack them;

---

[1] Lanciani, *Ruins and Excavations*, 396 *sqq*; Lugli, *Giardini e Ville di Roma Antica*, Rome, 1919 (a reprint from De Ruggiero, *Dizionario Epigrafico di Antichità Romane*, iii, 993 *sqq*.).

the modern Italians, like their ancestors, build mainly for the summer and not for the winter, though the latter is often colder than in England.

Lighting was effected by oil lamps of bronze or terra-cotta, sometimes supported by candelabra or stands, sometimes suspended by chains or hooks ; the larger lamps often have several nozzles (Plate LXXXVIII). The bronze lamps show great variety of form, while the terra-cotta lamps, which are made from moulds, are decorated with scenes in relief.

The water supply was invariably good and abundant where it was at all possible to obtain it.

Aqueducts and water cisterns are among the commonest of Roman ruins, and the arrangements for the distribution of water within the city and in the houses were extensive and good. Lead pipes, often stamped with the owner's name as a guide to the plumber, were used as a rule in Rome itself, though terracotta and wood pipes (the latter joined together by iron collars) are also found elsewhere. Special ingenuity was displayed in the construction of ornamental fountains, a variety of jets and spouts for which were used, if, as was often the case, a bronze or marble figure were not employed. Drainage and sanitation were also the object of considerable solicitude and were facilitated by the abundant water supply, which would have permitted of proper flushing of latrines, though in some cases this was undoubtedly left to be done by the rain and neglected in fine weather. The larger houses were provided with kitchens, the hearth being a simple rectangular structure of masonry. The fuel was wood or charcoal, the latter being still frequently used in Italy at the present day. The kitchen implements, as we learn from those found at Pompeii and elsewhere, differ but little from those in modern use, except that they are of bronze. Among the most striking of recent discoveries at Pompeii was that of a drinking bar, with the bronze utensils, etc., still in place. Similar bars have also come to light at Ostia.

The ordinary house furniture was of bronze, or of wood decorated with bronze, silver, ivory or bone. We have beds, couches, seats, small tables, etc., and a number of metal, ivory or bone objects, generally of tasteful artistic design, such as feet of tables or chairs, handles of cupboards or chests, etc., etc., but owing to the fact that, except at Pompeii and in Egypt, the wood has generally perished, it is not always easy to recover the forms of the pieces of furniture to which they belonged. It is obvious, however, that there was

comparatively little furniture in each room. The dining-room (*triclinium*) contained a square table round which were three couches with three places each, at which the guests reclined; but round tables, sometimes of citrus wood (which was imported from Africa, and very highly prized), were also used, and in this case the three couches were transformed into a simple semi-circular couch, with from five to eight places. The reclining position left only the right hand free, and, while we have evidence for the use of table knives and spoons, table forks were unknown until the Middle Ages, though used in the kitchen and for carving in Roman times, and the fingers came somewhat freely into play. The marble *trapezophori*, of which so many are preserved (pairs of marble supports generally decorated with two griffins in relief) carried a flat slab of marble, bronze or silver, which was used as a sideboard. The table furniture was of silver or bronze, but the finer kinds of pottery, such as Arretine ware (in which metal work was directly imitated, just as the glass workers reproduced in a cheaper form the work of the gem engraver) were also used in poorer households. Curtains and rugs were largely employed, the former on the walls and as portières and in the intercolumniations of porticos, the latter both as coverings to seats and on the floor. Pictures, reliefs, statues and busts were also used as decoration, apart from the usual wall facing of marble or painted plaster or stucco. The floors were of mosaic (of which there were three varieties: (1) *opus signinum*, made of broken tiles and lime, and decorated with a pattern in small white stones; (2) the ordinary tesselated pavement; and (3) *opus sectile*, or marble mosaic) or of marble slabs. Classical wall and ceiling mosaics are distinctly rare,[1] and we know little of the art except as applied to the small fountains and columns of some of the Pompeian houses, and to shrines of Mithras, etc.[2] The bulk of the mosaics we have belong to the pavements of private houses in town or country; the patterns are often very elaborate, especially in the provinces; whereas in Italy the figure subjects, where they occur at all, are the more important part; until, in the third century A.D., the geometrical border disappears, and gives place to large and

[1] Perhaps the only extant example of a classical building with almost the whole of its mosaic decoration preserved is a circular domed building of the second century after Christ, near the Via Tiburtina, to which I was the first to call attention (*Papers of the British School of Rome*, III, 104: cf. Cecchelli in *Architettura ed Arti Decorative*, II (1922-3), 3, 49, where the question of the origin of wall and ceiling mosaics, which were so much developed in the ecclesiastical architecture of Rome and Ravenna, is dealt with.).

[2] The name is derived from the original use of mosaic (*opus musivum*) for the decoration of *musæa* or artificial grottoes dedicated to the Muses.

rather coarsely executed figures in black and white. Plate XCII shows a villa at Utina, in North Africa, decorated with a number of pavements of this kind, and Plate LXXXIX, the well-known pavement at Woodchester, in which the geometrical element predominates.

The daily life of the people was thus very different to our own, and of course much affected by the institution of slavery. The distinctive features of earlier Roman life were the strength of the family tie, the importance of the home, with the daily religious rites which were celebrated there in the shrine of the household gods, and the power of the paterfamilias over his household, all of whom were legally subject to him. His power over his children and slaves (who often belonged to the family for generations) was theoretically absolute, and over his wife hardly less so ; though the latter came to occupy a position of dignity and authority within the household itself to which, while not secluded like the women of Greece and the Orient, she confined her activities. Slaves, too, were often granted their freedom after long and faithful service, while still remaining under the protection of their former master, who became their *patronus.* In the imperial period the position of women completely changed owing to the spread of luxury and of Greek and Oriental culture and worship, as is shown by the freedom with which they joined in the banquets of the men, and attended games and gladiatorial shows. Divorce, too, became easier, and the strength of the family tie was greatly relaxed owing to the reluctance of men to marry. Augustus' stern laws on the subject led unfortunately to evasion and blackmail, and to the activity of informers—one of the most sinister features of life in Rome in the Imperial period. No doubt our literary sources lay stress on the worst cases, and it is improbable that the vice and profligacy of which they speak was so widely spread as they would have us believe. The comparative peace, prosperity and well-being which the Roman Empire undoubtedly enjoyed during the first two centuries of the Christian era would have been possible without a thoroughly efficient central administration, of the details of which we know very little. The task of this administration was greatly facilitated by the imperial posting service, making use of the splendid network of roads which, built originally as military lines of communication, extended over the whole Roman Empire, and served for trade and intercourse among its component parts. Nor is it probable that society was nearly so corrupt in the provinces as in the capital. The middle and lower classes in Rome itself, however, must have shared to a

PLATE XCII.

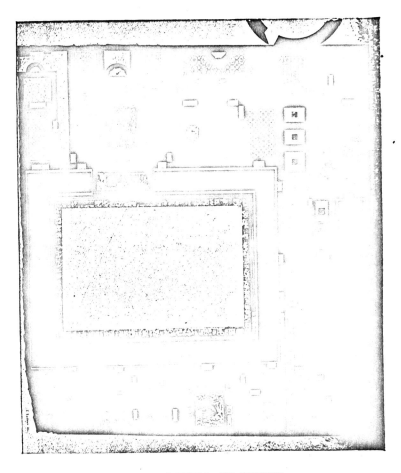

PLAN OF VILLA AT UTHINA.

large extent in the demoralization of the upper. They had, under the Empire, no part in even the government of the city (whereas in other towns certain municipal activities were at least open to them)[1] and in Juvenal's well known phrase, were kept quiet by doles and amusements (*panem et circenses*). Public shows or "games" in Rome had originated in religious observances, but numerous celebrations were established, especially under the Empire, for the glorification of its rulers; and a calendar of 354 A.D. gives 175 public holidays, *i.e.*, nearly half the year. These spectacles consisted either of dramatic performances in the theatre (*ludi scænici*) or of chariot races in the circus, gladiatorial shows and fights with wild beasts in the amphitheatre (*ludi circenses*). Dramatic performances were not confined to the regular tragedy and comedy, but included also the *mimus* or character sketch and the *pantomimus* in which the lyrical portions of the drama were illustrated by a dramatic dance; and these two latter forms appear to have robbed the legitimate drama of much of its popularity.

Racing brought even more excitement than at the present day, inasmuch as it was enhanced by party rivalry, the charioteers belonging to first two, then four different companies, distinguished by different colours. The careers of some of the principal drivers are known from the inscriptions on their tombstones, in which their victories are set forth in full detail. On the enthusiasm for gladiatorial shows we will not dilate here—the subject is now almost a common-place—except to note that it is a common error to suppose that *naumachiæ* or naval combats were regularly held in the amphitheatre. In Rome a special building was constructed for the purpose, and in these shows, as in others, trained gladiators, condemned criminals, or prisoners of war were the combatants.

Much more might be said on these subjects—as on the influence of the great thermæ on private life—but space will not permit of our enlarging further on such topics, and they have indeed already been briefly dealt with in our treatment of the various classes of buildings which we have described. They should, however, be constantly borne in mind, inasmuch as needs so different to our own were found to lead to the construction of buildings of quite a different character to those with which we are familiar from our earliest years.

---

[1] A good deal of light on this is thrown by the frequency with which we find inscriptions on the walls at Pompeii in which candidates in the municipal elections are recommended by the barmaids.

PLAN OF THE CENTRAL PORTION OF ANCIENT
AS RECONSTRUCTED

PLATE XCIII.

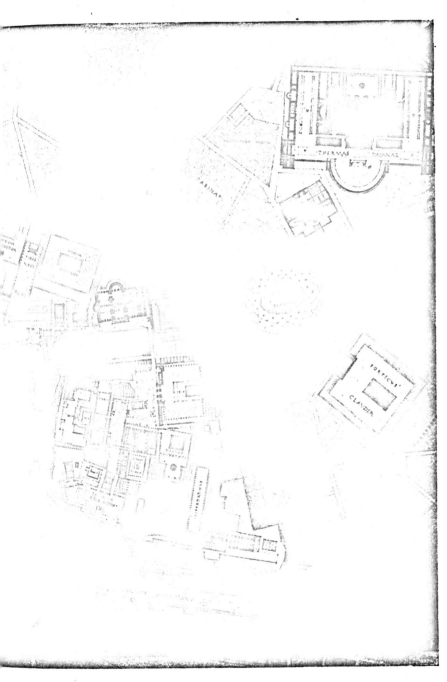

E IN THE TIME OF CONSTANTINE THE GREAT
CHALTON BRADSHAW.

CENTRAL PORTION OF THE M

PLATE X

OF ANCIENT ROME BY BIGOT.

From " The Builder,'

ITALY

GREECE
AND
ASIA MINO

GREECE
AND
ASIA MINOR

Byzantium

Macedonia

Samothrace

Lemnos

Epirus

Dodona

Thessalia

Troy
Neandria
ASSOS

Mysia

Kolumdado
MESSA
PERGAMUM

Lesbos

AIZANI

Actium

Aetolia

THERMON

Euboea

AEGEAN

Lydia
SARDIS

Locri Ozolae

DELPHI
ORCHOMENOS
Thebes

Chios

Philadelphia

Clazomenae
Teos
EPHESUS

Hierapolis

Achaia

Marathon
ELEUSIS
ATHENS
Megara

Tralles
MAGNESIA-
AD-MEANDRUM
APHRODISIAS

Elis
OLYMPIA

Arcadia

CORINTH
MYCENAE
AEGINA
EPIDAURUS

Samos
PRIENE

EUROMUS (YAKLI)

Argos
Tegea
TIRYNS

Mylasa

PHIGALEIA

Laconia

Megalopolis

Halicarnassus

Caria

Messene
Messenia

PELOPONNESOS

Sparta

Paros

Naxos

Telmissus
Pinara

Lycia

XANTHOS

Melos

Cnidus

Patara

Thera

Rhodes

Crete

CNOSSUS

PHAESTUS

SELECTED BIBLIOGRAPHY.

I.—GENERAL WORKS ON ROMAN ARCHITECTURE.

BENOIT (F.).—L'Architecture : I., Antiquité. Paris, 1911.

BROWN (F. C.), and others.—A Study of the Orders. 8vo. Chicago. 1906.

CHAMBERS (Sir W.).—The Decorative Part of Civil Architecture. 1759, &c.

CHOISY (A.).—Histoire de l'Architecture. 2 vols. 8vo. Paris, 1899.
Ditto.—Vitruve. 3 parts, 4to. Paris, 1909.

D'ESPOUY (H.).—Fragments d'Architecture Antique. Folio. Paris, 1896.

Ditto.—2nd Series. Folio. Paris, 1905.

Ditto. — Monuments Antiques relevés et restaurés par les architectes pensionnaires de l'Académie de France à Rome. 3 vols. Paris, 1906. Supplement, 1923.

Donaldson (T. L.).—Architectura Numismatica. 8vo. 1859.

Ducati (P.).—L'Arte Classica. 8vo. Turin, 1920.

Durand (J. N. L.).—Parallèle des Édifices de tout genre. Folio. Paris, 1800.

FERGUSSON (J.).—A History of Architecture in all Countries. Vols. 1 and 2.

Ditto.—Ancient and Mediæval Architecture. 2 vols. 8vo. 1893.

FIECHTER (E. R.).—Baugeschichtliche Entwickelung des Antiken Theaters. Munich, 1924.

FLETCHER (Sir B.).—A History of Architecture on the Comparative Method. 8vo. London, 1924.

HAMLIN (A. D. F.).—Text-book of the History of Architecture. London.

KIMBALL (F.) and EDGELL (G.).—A History of Architecture. New York and London. 1917.

LEROUX (G.).—Les Origines de l'Edifice hypostile en Grèce, en Orient, et chez les Romains. Paris, 1913.

LEVEIL (J. A.) and HIBON.—Vignole : Traité élémentaire practique d'Architecture, ou Etude des Cinq Ordres. 4to. Paris.

MITCHELL (C. F.).—Classic Architecture. Folio. London, 1926.

MORGAN (M. H.).—Vitruvius' Ten Books on Architecture. 8vo. Cambridge, Mass., 1914.

NOACK (F.).—Der Baukunst des Altertums. 1910.

NORMAND.—Parallèle des Ordres d'Architecture des Grecs et des Romains. Folio. Paris, 1819.

PLINY.—Historiæ Naturalis XXXIV.—XXXVII., translated by K. Jex Blake, with commentary and introduction by Eugenie Sellers and notes by Dr. H. L. Urlichs. London, 1896.

RIVOIRA (G. T.).—Roman Architecture, translated by G. McN. Rushforth. Oxford, 1925.

Ditto.—Lombardic Architecture, translated by G. McN. Rushforth. London, 1910.

SIMPSON (F. M.).—A History of Architectural Development. Vol. I. 8vo. 1905.

SMITH (Sir WM.).—Greek and Roman Antiquities. 2 vols. 8vo. 1895.

SPIERS (R. PHENÉ).—The Orders of Architecture. 4to. London, 1926.

STATHAM (H. H.).—A Short Critical History of Architecture. London, 1927.

STURGIS (RUSSELL).—European Architecture. 8vo. New York, 1896.

Ditto.—A Dictionary of Architecture and Building. Imp. 8vo. 3 vols. New York, 1901.

Ditto.—A History of Architecture. Vol. I. Antiquity. 8vo. New York, 1906.

TEXIER (C.).—Description de l'Asie Mineure. Folio. Paris, 1839–49.

TEXIER (C.) and PULLAN (R. P.).—The Principal Ruins of Asia Minor. Folio. 1865.

VIOLLET-LE-DUC (E. E.).—Lectures on Architecture. Translated by B. Bucknall. 2 vols. 1877–81.

VULLIAMY (LEWIS).—Examples of Ornamental Sculpture in Architecture. Folio. 1825.
Ditto.—New edition of 20 plates, with description by R. Phené Spiers. Folio. 1907.

WARREN (H. L.).—The Foundations of Classic Architecture.

II. WORKS ON SPECIAL SUBJECTS AND PERIODS,

MONOGRAPHS, &c.

ADAM (R.).—Ruins of the Palace of the Emperor Diocletian at Spalato. Folio. 1764.

BAALBEK. 2 vols. 4to. Berlin and Leipzig, 1921–3.

BLOUET (G. A.).—Restauration des Thermes d'Antonin Caracalla à Rome. Folio. Paris, 1828.

BOISSIER (G.).—Rome and Pompeii. Translated by D. H. Fisher. 8vo. 1896.

BROWN (Prof. G. BALDWIN).—Origin of Roman Imperial Architecture. Sessional Paper, R.I.B.A. 1889.

BUTLER (H. C.).—Architecture and other Arts in Syria. 4to. New York, 1904.

CAMERON (C.).—Baths of the Romans, with the Restorations of Palladio. Folio. 1775.

CANINA (L.).—L'antica Etruria Marittima. 2 vols. Folio. Rome, 1846–49.

Ditto.—Gli Edifizj di Roma Antica. 6 vols. Folio. Roma. 1848–56.

CARISTIE (A. N.).—Monuments Antiques à Orange, France. Folio, Paris, 1856–57.

CASSAS (L. F.).—Voyage pittoresque de la Syrie, de la Phœnicie, de la Palestine, et de la Basse Egypte. 3 vols. Folio. Paris, 1799.

CHOISY (A.).—L'art de batir chez les Romains. Folio. Paris, 1873.

D'Amelio (P.).—Dipinti Murali Scelte di Pompei. Folio.

DELBRÜCK (R.).—Die Drei Tempel in Forum Holitorium. Rome, 1903.

Ditto.—Capitolium zu Signia. Apollotempel in Marsfelde. Rome, 1903.

Ditto.—Hellenistische Bauten in Latium. 2 vols. Strassburg, Berlin, 1907–12.

DÉSGODETZ (A.).—Les Édifices Antiques de Rome. 1 vol. Folio. Paris, 1682; reprinted and enlarged to 4 vols. Folio. Rome, 1822, 1843.

DENNIS (G.).—Cities and Cemeteries of Etruria. 2 vols. 8vo. London, 1883.

DUCATI (P.).—Etruria Antica. 2 vols. Turin, 1925.

DURM (JOSEF).—Die Baukunst der Etrusker und der Römer. 4to. Stuttgart, 1905.

DUTERT (F.).—Le Forum Romain et les Forums de Julius César (&c.). Folio. Paris, 1876.

GELL (Sir W.) and GANDY (J. P.).—Pompeiana : Topography, Edifices and Ornaments of Pompeii. First and Second Series. 3 vols. 8vo. 1819–32.

GEYMÜLLER (Baron H. VON).—Documents inédits sur les Thermes d'Agrippa, le Panthéon, et les Thermes de Dioclétian. 4to. Lausanne, 1883.

GSELL (S.).—Les Monuments Antiques de l'Algérie. Paris, 1901.

GURLITT (C.).—Denkmäler der Kunst in Dalmatien. 1910.

GUSMAN (P.).—La Villa Imperiale de Tibur (Villa Hadriana). Preface by Gaston Boissier. 4to. Paris, 1904.

Ditto.—L'Art Décoratif de Rome. 2 vols. 1908.

HAVERFIELD (F.).—Ancient Town Planning. Oxford. 1913.

HÉBRARD (E.) and ZEILLER (J.).—Spalato : le Palais de Dioclétian relevés et restaurations. Folio. 1912.

HOMO (LÉON).—Lexique de Topographie Romaine. 12mo. 1900.

HULSEN (C.).—The Roman Forum. Rome, 1909.

ISABELLE (C. E.).—Les Edifices Circulaires et les Domes. Folio. 1855.

JACKSON (T. G.).—Dalmatia, the Quarnero and Istria. 8vo. 1887.

JORDAN (H.) and HÜLSEN (C.).—Topographie der Stadt Rom. 2 vols., in four parts. 1878–1907.

KIEPERT (H.) and HÜLSEN (C.).—Formae Urbis Romæ Antiquæ. 2nd edition. Berlin, 1911.

LABORDE (Marquis L. DE).—Voyage de l'Arabie Pétrée. Folio. Paris, 1830.

LANCIANI (Prof. R.).—Pagan and Christian Rome. 8vo. 1893.

Ditto.—Ruins and Excavations of Ancient Rome. 8vo. 1897.

Ditto.—Ancient Rome in the Light of Recent Discoveries. 8vo. 1889. And other works.

Ditto.—Plan of Ancient Rome. Folio. Rome, 1893–1901.

Latin Studies, Companion to. 8vo. Cambridge, 1921.

LUGLI (G.).—Zona Monumentale. 8vo. Rome, 1924.

MARTHA (J.).—L'art Etrusque. Small 4to. Paris, 1889.

MAU (A.).—Pompeii: Its Life and Art. Translated by F. W. Kelsey. New York, 1899.

MAZOIS (F.).—Le Palais de Scaurus, ou description d'une Maison Romaine. 8vo. Paris, 1822.

MIDDLETON (Dr. J. H.).—The Remains of Ancient Rome. 2 vols. 8vo. London, 1892.

NICCOLINI (F. è F.).—Le Case e i Monumenti di Pompeii. Several volumes large folio. Naples, 1854–96.

NICCOLINI (F.).—Arte Pompeiana. Small Folio. Naples, 1887.

PALLADIO.—Ed. Banister Fletcher. London, 1902.

PARKER (J. H.).—Archæology of Rome. 8 vols. 8vo. 1874–77.

PAULIN (E.).—Restauration des Thermes de Diocletian. Folio. Paris.

PIRANESI (G. B. and F.).—Various works on the Antiquities of Rome. 1743–1792.

PLATNER (S. B.).—Ancient Rome. Boston, U.S.A., 1911.

PLATNER (S. B.). and ASHBY (T.).—A Topographical Dictionary of Ancient Rome. Oxford, 1927.

PONCE (N.).—Description des Bains de Titus. Paris, 1786.

PORTER (H. K.).—What Rome was built with. London, 1907.

PULLEN (H. W.).—Handbook of Ancient Marbles. London, 1894.

STRONG (Mrs. ARTHUR).—Roman Sculpture. 8vo. **1907.**

STUART JONES (H.).—Companion to Roman History. Oxford, **1912.**

TANZER (H.).—Villas of Pliny the Younger. New York, **1924.**

TATHAM (C. H.).—Etchings of Grecian and Roman Architectural Ornament. Folio. 1826.

TAYLOR (G. L.) and Cresy (E.).—The Architectural Antiquities of Rome. 2 vols. Folio. 1821–22.

THÉDENAT (H.).—Le Forum Romain. Paris, 1908.

VAN BUREN (E. DOUGLAS).—Figurative Terra Cotta Revetments in Etruria and Latium. London, 1921. *id* Archaic Fictile Revetments in Sicily and Magna Græcia. London, 1923.

VOGÜÉ (Comte de).—Syrie Centrale : Architecture Civile et Réligieuse. 2 vols. 4to. Paris, 1867.

VULLIAMY (H.).—Examples of Ornamental Sculpture in Architecture. Folio. 1818.

WAGNER (H.).—Das alte Rom (panorama). 1892.

WATT (J. CROMAR).—Greek and Pompeian Decorative Work. Folio. 1897.

WINNEFELD (H.).—Tusci und Laurentium des jungeren Plinius. Jahrb. d. Inst. vi (1891). 4to.

WOOD (R.).—Ruins of Balbec. Folio. 1757.

Ditto.—Ruins of Palmyra. Folio. 1758.

The following works contain interesting sketches of Private Life among the Romans :—

CHURCH (A. J.).—Roman Life in the Days of Cicero. London.

QUENNELL (C. H. B. and M.).—Everyday Life in Roman Britain. London, 1924.

N.B.—A selection of smaller and less important works, articles in Periodicals, &c., will be found in the footnotes to the particular sections to which they refer.

GLOSSARY

ABACUS.—The uppermost member of a capital, plain in the Doric order, moulded in the Ionic and Corinthian orders. The sides are concave in the Corinthian capital, and curved over the canted volute of the Ionic capital.

ABUTMENT.—The masonry or brickwork which counteracts the thrust of an arch.

ACROTERIUM (*pl.* ACROTERIA).—The plinths at the angles or apex of a pediment provided to carry figures or ornaments.

AGORA.—A public square or market-place in Greek cities corresponding to the Forum in Roman cities.

AISLE (Lat., *ala*, a wing).—Term given to the side passages in a basilica, separated from one another and from the central area by columns or piers.

AMPHIPROSTYLE.—Term applied to a temple with portico of columns in front and rear only.

ANATHYROSIS—The projection of the outer edges of two blocks of stone towards one another, so as to effect a close joint.

ANCONES.—(1) Projecting bosses left on masonry blocks; (2) the vertical corbels on either side of a Roman doorway supporting the cornice over the same.

ANTA (*pl.* ANTÆ).—Pilaster (or corner post) of slight projection terminating the end of the lateral walls of a cella, or serving as respond to a column. In the latter case the columns are said to be in antis.

ANTEFIX.—The decorative termination of the covering tile-rolls of a roof at the eaves.

ANTHEMION (Gr. ἄνθος, a flower).—Term given to the sheathing leaves of the flower of the acanthus, sometimes, but erroneously, called honeysuckle (Fr. *palmette*), employed in various ways to decorate acroteria, antefixes, friezes, and the necking of some Ionic capitals.

APODYTERIUM.—The dressing room of the Roman bath.

APOPHYGE (ἀπό, from, and φεύγω, I flee).—A. the inverted cavetto or concave sweep taken by the lower part of the shaft in the Ionic and Corinthian Orders in its junction with the base.   B. The hollow or scotia beneath the Doric echinus, forming the junction between the capital and the shaft.

APSE.—A recess in the wall of a building, generally semi-circular and vaulted over.

APTEROS.—Without wings. Applied sometimes to a prostyle or amphiprostyle temple.

ARABESQUE.—Term given to the moulded and painted stucco decoration of walls, vaults, and ceilings in ancient Roman buildings where scroll work, intertwining leaves, etc., are employed.

ARÆOSTYLE.—Wide-spaced. The term given by Vitruvius to the wide intercolumniation of the Tuscan portico, carrying an architrave in timber. *See* INTERCOLUMNIATION.

ARCADE.—A range of columns supporting arches.

ARCHITRAVE.—A lintel in stone or beam of timber carried from the top of one column or pier to another. The lowest member of the entablature (*q.v.*). Applied also to the mouldings round side posts or jambs and the lintel of a door or window.

ARCHIVOLT.—A moulded architrave carried round an arch.

ARENA.—The central space in a Roman amphitheatre wherein the gladiators fought, or where contests with wild beasts took place.

ARRIS.—A sharp edge formed by two surfaces meeting at an external angle, as in the flutings of the Doric column.

ATLANTES.—The Greek term for the male figures employed in architecture in place of columns. *See* TELAMONES.

ATRIUM.—The entrance court of a Roman house, roofed over at the sides, but open to the sky in the centre. In an atrium of large size four or more columns would be introduced to carry the roof. *See* CAVÆDIUM.

ATTIC.—Term applied to a story above the main cornice, sometimes decorated with bas-reliefs, or utilised for an inscription.

ATTIC BASE.—The favourite base of the Romans, consisting of an upper and lower torus and a scotia between, with fillets over.

BALNEÆ.—The Latin term for the public baths.

BASILICA.—The Roman exchange and court of law. A rectangular building with aisles, sometimes terminated at one or both ends with a recess or hemicycle (large apse).

BIBLIOTHECA (Library).—A chamber provided with cases (often fitted in rectangular niches) to hold manuscript rolls.

BOULEUTERION.—The Greek Senate House.

CABLING.—*See* FLUTING.

CALIDARIUM.—The hot chamber of the Roman bath.

CANALIS (Channel).—Term given to the space between the fillets of an Ionic volute ; in early work, convex ; in the fully-developed types, concave.

CARCERES.—A row of stalls or horse-boxes at one end of a circus enclosed by double doors, within which the chariots waited till the signal was given for starting, when the doors were simultaneously thrown open.

CARYATIDES.—Figures of maidens which take the place of columns in supporting an entablature, as in the Erechtheum, Athens.

CAULICOLUS.—The stalk of the acanthus plant as found in the Greek stele and in Roman Corinthian capitals.

CAVÆDIUM (the Roman Atrium).—According to Vitruvius (VI. 3) there were five kinds—Tuscan, Tetrastylar, Corinthian, Displuviatum and Testudinatium. In the Tuscan, cross-beams carried the roof, in the centre of which was an opening called the compluvium ; the Tetrastylar had columns at each angle of the compluvium, which carried the beams round the opening ; whilst

in the Corinthian there were also intermediate columns; in the Displuviatum the roof sloped down outwards on all four sides; and in the Testudinatum there was no opening in the roof.

CAVEA.—The auditorium of a theatre, so called because originally it was excavated in the rocky side of a hill.

CELLA.—The enclosed chamber or sanctuary of a Roman temple, corresponding with the naos of a Greek temple.

CHRYSELEPHANTINE.—The term applied to a statue in which gold and ivory overlay a wooden core, the drapery and ornaments being of the former and the flesh of the latter material.

CLOACA.—The name given to the sewers which drained the low marshy grounds between the hills of Rome. The *cloaca maxima* drained the Forum Romanum.

COFFER.—A sunk panel in a vault or ceiling.

COLONNADE.—A range of columns supporting a lintel. *See* ARCADE.

COLUMBARIUM.—A pigeon-house. The name is used to designate the apertures formed in the walls of a tomb to hold the cinerary urns, and hence the sepulchral chambers themselves.

COMPLUVIUM.—The uncovered portion of a Roman atrium.

CORNICE.—The upper member of the entablature (*q.v.*) subdivided into bed-mould, corona, and cymatium; a term also employed for any projection on a wall, provided to throw the rain-water off from the face of the building.

CORONA.—The lower portion of the projecting member of the cornice having a vertical face.

CRYPTOPORTICUS (literally a secret passage).—Term given to an underground vaulted corridor, lighted through openings in centre or side of vault.

CUBICULUM.—A bed-chamber.

CUNEI.—The wedge-shaped groups into which the seats of a theatre or amphitheatre are divided by radiating passages.

CYCLOPEAN MASONRY.—The term applied to rude polygonal masonry used both in Greece and Italy, especially in the form of city walls. It is as a rule used in embankment walls, and only rarely in walls standing free.

CYMA.—A moulding of double curvature. When the concave portion is uppermost it is called a cyma recta; when the convex part is at the top it is called cyma reversa.

CYMATIUM.—Another term given to the crowning moulding of an entablature when it takes the cyma recta form.

DADO.—The lower portion of a wall when treated as a separate architectural feature.

DELPHINÆ (Dolphins).—Ornaments on the spina of a Roman circus; in allusion to Neptune, the patron deity of horses and racing.

DENTIL.—Rectangular blocks in the bed-mould of a Doric cornice, originally representing the ends of joists.

DIASTYLE.—*See* INTERCOLUMNIATION.

DIAULOS.—The peristyle round the great court of the Palæstra described by Vitruvius (V. 11).

DIAZOMA.—The Greek term for the passage which separated the several ranges of seats in a theatre or amphitheatre.

DIE.—The square base of a column. Applied also to the vertical face of a pedestal or podium.

ECHINUS.—The convex moulding which supports the abacus of a Doric capital. Also the circular moulding carved with egg and tongue between the volutes and sometimes carried under the cushion of the Ionic capital.

ENTABLATURE.—The trabeation carried by columns. It is divided into three parts: viz., the architrave (the supporting member, carried from column to column); the frieze (the decorative

portion) ; and the cornice (the crowning and projecting member). It is occasionally used to complete, architecturally, the upper portion of a wall, even when there are no columns, and in the case of pilasters or detached or engaged columns is sometimes profiled round them.

ENTASIS.—The increment or slight convex curve given to the column, in order to correct an optical illusion. If the shaft tapers as it rises and is formed with absolutely straight lines, it appears hollow or concave.*

EPISTULION (EPISTYLE).—The Greek term for the architrave (*q.v.*).

EUSTYLE.—*See* INTERCOLUMNIATION.

EXEDRA.—A semi-circular stone or marble seat, or a rectangular or semi-circular recess.

FASCIA.—The term given to the planes into which the architrave of the Ionic and Corinthian Orders is subdivided.

FAUCES.—Side passages between the atrium and peristyle in a Roman house, or from the peristyle to the xystus or garden.

FLUTES.—The vertical channels (segmental, elliptical, or semi-circular in horizontal section) employed in the shafts of columns in the classic styles. The flutes are separated one from the other by an arris in the Greek Doric Order, and by a fillet in the Ionic, and Corinthian Orders. In early and late Doric columns the flute was usually segmental, but at the best period, in order to emphasize the arris, it was formed of three arcs constituting what is known as a false ellipse ; a similar curve was given to the flutes in Greek Doric, Ionic, and Corinthian columns and in early Roman examples ; in later work the flute was semi-circular. In the Roman Ionic and Corinthian Orders, the lower portion of the flute up to about

---

* For Entasis in Roman Columns *see* Stevens in *Mem. Amer. Acad. Rome,* IV (1924) 121.

one-third of the height of the column was sometimes filled in with a convex moulding, to which the term cabling is applied. In one or two late Roman examples the flutes were carried spirally round the columns as in the Portico of the Agora at Aphrodisias in Asia Minor. Similar spiral fluting is found on the sides of Roman sarcophagi.

FRIEZE.—The middle member of the entablature. Applied also to any horizontal band enriched with sculpture. *See* ZOPHOROS.

FRIGIDARIUM.—The room or court in the Roman baths containing the cold water bath.

GEISON.—A Terra Cotta slab bearing decoration which runs round both the upper and lower edges of the pediment.

GROIN.—The arris formed by the intersection of two vaults.

GUILLOCHE.—A continuous flat band or convex moulding carved with interwoven fillets, leaving circular centres, sometimes filled with rosettes.

GUTTÆ (drops).—Small pendant cones under the triglyphs and mutules of a Doric entablature.

GYMNASIUM.—A school for physical education and training.

HELIX.—The spiral tendril which is carried up to support the abacus of a Corinthian capital. There are four helices on each face.

HEMICYCLE.—Term given to semi-circular recesses of great size, sometimes vaulted.

HIPPODROME.—The course provided by the Greeks for horse and chariot racing.

HYPÆTHRAL.—Term given to a temple the naos of which was wholly or partly open to the sky.

HYPOCAUST.—A space contrived under the floor of a hall or room generally by raising it on pillars : these spaces were connected

with furnaces, by means of which they were warmed. Employed in Rome to heat the calidarium and other halls of the Thermæ and Balneæ, and, in colder climates, the principal rooms of a house.

HYPOTRACHELIUM (Gk., under the neck).—One or more grooves under the necking or gorge of the Greek Doric capital which mask the junction of capital and shaft.

IMPLUVIUM.—A shallow tank in the atrium of a Roman house, provided to receive the rain falling through the compluvium.

INTERCOLUMNIATION.—The distance between the columns of a peristyle, always defined in terms of the lower diameter of the columns. They are thus set forth by Vitruvius (III. 3)—Pycnostyle, where the columns are $1\frac{1}{2}$ diameters apart; Systyle, 2 diameters; Eustyle, $2\frac{1}{4}$ diameters; Diastyle, 3 diameters; and Aræostyle, $3\frac{1}{2}$ diameters; the latter carrying architraves in wood only.

LABRUM.—A stone bath, circular or oblong. The large vessel of the warm bath, sometimes of marble, granite, or porphyry.

LACONICUM.—The sweating room of a Roman bath.

LARARIUM.—The room in which the Lares, or household gods, were placed. Sometimes represented by a niche only.

LESENE.—Flat pilasters supporting blind arches, and serving as the external decoration of a building.

META.—The goal or turning-point for the chariots in a Roman circus.

METOPE.—Originally the open space between the beam-ends of the Doric ceiling, and applied afterwards to the slabs filling up these openings between the triglyphs.

MODILLION.—The horizontal corbels, or brackets, carrying the corona of a Roman cornice.

MODULE.—The half diameter of the lower part of the shaft of a column.

MUTULE.—A projecting slab, or bracket, on the soffit of the Doric cornice.

NYMPHÆUM.—A chamber (sometimes subterranean) in which were plants and flowers and a fountain or running water.

NAOS.—The term given to the cella of the Greek temple.

ODEON.—A circular building in which rehersals and musical contests took place.

ŒCUS.—In Greek houses (according to Vitruvius, VI. 10) the room in which the mistress of the house sits with the spinners. It was used also as a banqueting room. There were four kinds of œci, viz., the Tetrastyle, the Corinthian, the Egyptian, and the Cyzicene.

OPAION.—The Greek word for the lacunaria or ceiling panels of a peristyle. Applied also to an hypæthral opening in a roof.

OPISTHODOMUS.—The treasury of a Greek temple (the term is sometimes given to the epinaos when used for a similar purpose).

ORTHOSTATÆ.—The bottom course of the walls of the naos of a Greek temple, generally twice or three times the height of the upper courses.

OVA.—Seven marble eggs placed at each end on the spina, one being removed after each lap of the race.

PALÆSTRA.—A training school in physical exercises.

PARASCENIUM.—The side walls of the stage.

PENDENTIVES.—The triangular surfaces (called spherical, if curved) which serve as the transition from vertical walls to a domed roof.

PERIPTERAL.—Term applied to a building surrounded by a row of columns.

PERISTASIS.—The lines of columns standing round the cella of a temple.

PERISTYLE.—Term given (A) to a covered colonnade which surrounds a building or court. (B) The inner court of a Pompeian house.

PINACOTHECA.—A picture gallery.

PODIUM.—The Greek term for a low wall or continuous pedestal on which columns are carried. It consisted of a cornice, a dado and a plinth, and the Etruscan and usually the Roman temples were raised on it. The term was also applied to the enclosure wall of the arena of an amphitheatre upon which were placed the seats of the principal dignitaries.

PORTICO.—A porch or entrance to a building. The term, when applied to a Greek or Roman temple, is classed as (Distyle inantis), two columns between antæ ; (Tetrastyle Prostyle), four columns in front ; (Hexastyle), six columns ; (Heptastyle), seven columns ; (Octostyle), eight columns ; (Enneastyle), nine columns ; (Decastyle), ten columns ; and (Dodecastyle), twelve columns.

PORTICUS.—A building with its roof supported by one or more rows of columns, either in one straight line or enclosing a court. The same as the Greek stoa.

POSTICUM.—The Latin term for the recessed porch in the rear of a Roman temple.

POZZOLANA.—The Italian form of the Latin *pulvis Puteolanus,* the volcanic earth formed near, or shipped from, Puteoli (Mod. Pozznoli, near Naples). This volcanic earth is also found in the environs of Rome and elsewhere, and is especially valuable for making mortar.

PRONAOS.—The porch in front of the naos.

PROPYLÆUM.—The entrance gate to the Temenos or sacred enclosure of a temple, when there is one doorway only ; when there is more than one doorway, as at Athens and Eleusis, the term *propylæa* is given.

PROSCENIUM.—The stage in ancient theatres—a term sometimes given to the scæna (*q.v.*).

PROSTYLE.—Term applied to a temple with portico of columns in the front.

PROTHYRUM.—The vestibule or entrance passage to the atrium of a Roman house.

PRYTANEUM.—The state dining-room or guest-house in a Greek city.

PSEUDODIPTERAL.—Term applied to a dipteral temple with the inner row of columns omitted.

PSEUDOPERIPTERAL.—Term applied to a peripteral temple where some of the columns are engaged in the wall of the cella.

PYCNOSTYLE.—*See* INTERCOLUMNIATION.

PULVIN.—The " cushion," or inverted truncated pyramid surmounting the capital, which is a characteristic of the Ravennate and Byzantine styles.

PULVINAR.—A cushioned couch. Applied sometimes to the hemicycle or enclosed space in the stadium where the Emperor sat.

QUADRIGA.—The ancient four-horsed chariot.

REGULA.—A narrow strip under the tænia of a Doric architrave, beneath which the guttæ are curved.

RESPOND.—(1) The wall pilaster behind a column. (2) The wall pier carrying either the end of an architrave or beam or the springing of an arch.

SCÆNA.—The back wall of the stage ; a term sometimes given to the retiring room behind the stage, hence the word proscenium.

SIMA.—The term sometimes given to the marble, stone or terracotta gutter of Archaic temples to distinguish it from the cyma or cymatium of later examples. The sima of the Archaic Temple of Diana was 2 feet 10 inches high ; it lent slightly forward in one plane, was decorated with figures in low relief, and was provided with outlets for rain-water at intervals in the form of lion's heads. The cymatium, on the other hand, was ogee in section.

SPINA.—The podium wall down the centre of the Roman circus on which the delphinæ, ova, statues, obelisks, &c., were raised.

SQUINCH.—An arch placed diagonally in the internal angle of a square chamber, so as to bring it to an octagon or other polygonal figure.

STADIUM.—(Gr. Stadion).—A racecourse.

STEREOBATE.—The substructure of a temple.

STOA.—In Greek architecture a term corresponding with the Latin porticus (*q.v.*).

STYLOBATE.—The upper step of a peripteral temple which formed a platform for the columns. The term is often applied to the three steps of a Greek Doric temple.

SUDATORIUM.—The sweating room of a Roman bath. Same as laconicum.

SYSTYLE.—*See* INTERCOLUMNIATION.

TABERNA.—A small rectangular chamber behind an arcade or colonnade (*e.g.*, in a basilica) used as a shop or office.

TÆNIA.—The projecting fillet which crowns the architrave of the Doric entablature.

TELAMONES.—The Roman term for male figures forming supports. *See* ATLANTES.

TEMENOS.—The sacred enclosure in which a Greek temple stands.

THOLOS.—Term given to a Greek circular building with or without a peristyle, and having a domed roof.

TRACHELIUM (Gk.).—The necking or gorge of the Greek Doric shaft between the annulets on the echinus and the grooves or Hypotrachelia.

TRICLINIUM.—The dining-room of a Greek or Roman house, so called from κλινη, a couch, as it contained three couches upon which the ancients reclined at meals.

TRIGLYPH.—A projecting band dividing the metopes, emphasised with vertical channels and chamfers.

TYMPANUM.—Term given to the triangular recess enclosed by the cornice of the pediment and the entablature.

VELARIUM.—An awning of great size stretched above an amphitheatre to protect the spectators from the sun and rain, used sometimes also in the atrium of a Roman house.

VILLA.—In Roman architecture the term given to a country mansion or palace.

VOLUTE.—The spiral scroll of the Ionic capital.

VOUSSOIR.—A wedge-shaped stone which forms one of the units of an arch.

XOANON.—A rude and primitive image, generally of a deity, carved in wood.

XYSTUS.—A Roman garden planted with groves of plane trees, and laid out with flower-beds. In Greece the xystus was a covered promenade.

ZOPHOROS or ZOOPHOROS.—Term given to a continuous frieze sculptured in relief with the forms of human beings and animals.

INDEX TO TEXT.

INDEX TO ILLUSTRATIONS.

References in Roman numerals refer to the PLATE Numbers of Illustrations, those in Arabic to the PAGE Numbers.